HIDDEN TERRORS

ALSO BY A. J. LANGGUTH

Macumba: White and Black Magic in Brazil

Marksman

Wedlock

Jesus Christs

HIDDEN TERRORS

BY
A.J. LANGGUTH

PANTHEON BOOKS, NEW YORK

Library of Congress Cataloging in Publication Data

Langguth, A. J., 1933–
Hidden terrors

' 1. Mitrione, Dan.   2. Intelligence agents–
United States–Biography.   3. Police–United
States–Biography.   4. Kidnapping–Uruguay–
Case studies.   5. Murder–Uruguay–Case Studies.
I. Title.
JK468.I6L35 1978 327'.12'0924 [B] 77-88769
ISBN 0-394-73802-0

Design by Kenneth Miyamoto

FIRST PANTHEON PAPERBACK EDITION

For Arthur Langguth
(1906–1976)

HIDDEN TERRORS

CHAPTER

1

ON THE DAY that Dan Mitrione's body was brought back to lie in state in his hometown, President and Mrs. Richard M. Nixon sent a commemorative wreath both large and patriotic—red carnations, white chrysanthemums, and blue cornflowers. The city's officials agreed that a tribute from the Chief Executive took precedence over all others, and they put it at the head of Mitrione's coffin. A wreath of white carnations from the Secretary of State was set to one side.

Around Richmond, Indiana, people were still stunned by the calamity in Uruguay. Only three days had passed since the news of Dan's murder first reached them; and now, as though by miracle, his body was back from South America and on display in the lobby of the new Municipal Building. Hundreds, thousands, of the men and women who had known Dan were lining up, many with their children, to pay their last respects.

On reaching the head of the line, however, the mourners found that they could not see the body. The Uruguayan government had tried to demonstrate its profound regret by returning Dan's body sealed in a beautifully carved antique coffin.

But Henrietta, the widow, asked for another casket,

something made at home. Dan's brother Ray, who wanted very much to oblige her, went to the funeral directors and spoke to them about his sister-in-law's wishes. While the morticians agreed to make the change, they requested that someone from the family be present when the old coffin was unsealed. Ray asked his older brother, Dominic, to be the witness, but Dom refused.

So it was Ray who stood by, dreading the ordeal, as they pried open the lid. Inside was yet another coffin, this one of heavy metal. The funeral directors had already sent over to a neighborhood casket maker for a coffin—Richmond had once been a center of the coffin industry—and now they asked also for the loan of a hacksaw.

All the while, they were warning Ray that because his brother's body had not been embalmed in Montevideo, the opening of this inner box was apt to be extremely disagreeable. Reluctantly, Ray took that information back to Henrietta; everyone had always called her Hank. Today, though she looked tense and drawn, she was bearing up remarkably well after ten days of waiting and then the long flight from Montevideo. She listened to Ray's explanation and said that they should just forget the whole thing.

Meanwhile, late word had come from Geneva, Switzerland, that Father Robert Minton was on his way home and would arrive in time to conduct the funeral. The family had never doubted that, if they could only reach him, the priest would cut short his vacation to say a final mass for Dan.

Dan's murder had also brought Ray back early from a vacation, and his isolation upstate at Lake Chapman explained why he had been just about the last one in the family to hear the news about his favorite brother. Like many bachelors, Ray turned on his radio each morning as soon as he woke up. But on that particular morning, he had glanced out the window of his cabin and seen his Chrysler listing in the yard.

That flat tire distracted him for the next hour. Afterward, he wondered why no one around the gas station at the crossroads had told him the news. Either they had not heard it themselves or they did not connect it with Ray. That would be understandable. He had bought his cabin only a few months earlier, and had been urging his brothers to make the cabin their retreat too. Dom could come up for his days off from his work as a greenskeeper, and Dan would relax there when he came back on leave from his government job down in South America.

Around Richmond, men who did not know the brothers very well said that both in temperament and looks, Ray, who was forty-two years old that summer of 1970, was a lot like Dan, who was eight years older. To Ray, such a claim would have verged on sacrilege, and he never made it for himself. He was just pleased that when Dan came back home and looked over Ray's wardrobe, he would think enough of a sports jacket or a necktie to wink and walk off with it.

The flat tire fixed at last, Ray headed back to his cabin. He was sorry to think that this was the last day of July and his vacation was already half gone. Possibly he did not guess that there were people in Richmond who asked one another why Ray Mitrione needed a vacation. What Ray deemed a job struck them as little more than a paid hobby.

Every Monday morning, Ray loaded up a station wagon with sports equipment and set off cruising around Wayne County to call on his friends who coached at different high schools. Between the joshing and the speculation over the coming games, Ray took orders for footballs and baseball gloves. Nights and weekends, he relaxed by refereeing at basketball games around the county, a form of moonlighting that had made him a minor celebrity.

If his two jobs meant that nearly everybody knew Ray, his manner insured that they would like him. The worst anyone could say was that he was just an overgrown kid, and why should anyone take offense at that?

In the last year, his thatch of black hair might have gone

a bit gray, and his body was decidedly thickening. But his
smile was nearly as broad as his beam, and from behind
black-rimmed glasses, Ray's ruddy round face shone on his
corner of Indiana like a Wabash moon.

Ray did not have a telephone at the cabin, but as he
pulled into his yard, he found his neighbors waiting to flag
him down. His sister Rosemary had called, they said. Long
distance from Richmond.

Ray first thought of his mother. Maria Mitrione was
seventy-seven. In the years following her husband's death,
she and Ray had lived together. When she started needing
more care, she moved in with Rosemary and her husband,
Dick Parker. Then, last March, Maria's condition had
worsened, and the family had no choice but to put her in
a nursing home. The doctors diagnosed Parkinson's disease.
Ray had his own opinion: after a lifetime of hard work, his
mother's body had just worn out.

Ray said something to the neighbors about his mother,
but they reassured him on that score. The message had
specified that there was no emergency, that Ray was not
to worry; but he should call Richmond right away.

When Ray got through to Rosemary, she asked him,
"You haven't heard about Dan?"

As she spoke, Rosemary was dazed. She had first received a call from Dom's wife, passing along what a man
from the State Department had said. Rosemary could not
believe it, and she called Washington herself for confirmation.

For the moment, Ray was still more curious than
alarmed. "No," he said, "I haven't heard a thing. What
about Dan?"

"Dan's been kidnapped."

Usually the drive south to Richmond took Ray three
hours. Today, pushing hard, he bent the speeding law and
burst into Kessler's Sporting Goods store sooner, desperate
for details.

Before Ray got there, a clerk had taken a call from a radio station in one of the big cities near Richmond—Indianapolis to the west or Dayton over the Ohio line. The newsman had reported that Dan had been murdered, but he had already retracted the story by the time Ray got home. Not that Ray would have believed it. Dan did not have an enemy on earth.

But then Ray knew very little about his brother's life since Dan had resigned as Richmond's chief of police. He knew that Dan had been in Uruguay these past thirteen months, advising the country's police force. Now it appeared that a band of thugs or Communists in the capital city of Montevideo had kidnapped Dan that morning on his way to work.

Ray began trading information with the newsmen who called for background material on his brother. Until today, Ray had never realized how many reporters there were in the world; and between taking calls from New York and Chicago, he was trying to help the local boys put together their story, around the corner at Richmond's own daily, the *Palladium-Item*.

As the radio bombardment went on through the afternoon, Ray got accustomed to hearing the family name mispronounced. Every announcer sounded the final *e*—Mit-tree-own-nee—instead of leaving it silent, as his parents had done. The radio's way sounded more Italian, more foreign. Ray learned, too, that his brother's abductors called themselves Tupamaros, another name strange to his ear. Thinking over their last talk together when Dan was home in the spring, Ray was sure his brother had never mentioned the group.

In his entire life, Ray could remember meeting only one Uruguayan, and that was just about a year ago. A clean-cut, well-dressed fellow—suit and tie in the middle of Indian summer—had come into Kessler's and introduced himself as Billy Rial. He was visiting his sister, Rial explained. She had married a teacher from Centerville, down the road. He had heard that Ray's brother was working in

Montevideo, and Rial wanted to leave his address. The next time Ray wrote, he should tell his brother that he would be welcome any time he stopped by. In all, a pleasant and mannerly young man.

Ray thought again about their mother at the Heritage Nursing Home. Frail as she was, the shock of hearing the news could carry her off. But he checked and found that the nurses had anticipated this possibility; they were turning off the radio at the start of each news bulletin.

A newsboy delivered the *Pal-Item* to the nursing home but that mattered less, since Maria Mitrione could neither read nor write. In times past, her family had regretted that she had never learned. Today Ray took it as one more sign that the Good Lord looked after his own. Overnight, their mother's handicap had become a blessing.

Their father, Joseph Mitrione, had been born in the village of Bisaccia, sixty miles southeast of Naples. He had gone through the fifth grade before being sent out to work in the vineyards of Avelino province. When his bride, Maria Arincello, joined him in the fields, she had never been to school.

Because Joseph Mitrione had been working in the vineyards, when he decided to gamble on a trip to the United States, he thought first of California. With the Napa Valley as his goal, he set forth not long after the birth, on August 4, 1920, of his third surviving child and second son. The family would follow afterward. Once in the United States, Joseph changed his plans. From a relative in Indiana, he heard that the Pennsylvania Railroad was hiring men in Richmond, and he decided that picking grapes in central California held little more promise than picking grapes in the south of Italy. The railroad meant industry, development, the future.

Summoned to join her husband, Maria arrived in New York, a twenty-eight-year-old immigrant, with a little daughter, Anna, a younger son, Dominic, and a baby. In their first concession to the new culture, the Mitriones

Anglicized the baby's name to Daniel Anthony Mitrione.

Over her child-bearing years, Maria was pregnant fourteen times. Eight children either were miscarried or died in infancy. The other six lived, and sometimes they inherited a name: before Ray, there had been another baby Raymond, and another baby Josephine before the Josie who survived.

Although she had left a twin sister behind in Italy, Maria never showed an interest in going home. To go back, she said, to see the poverty again, knowing that she would soon be escaping for a second time to America, would be too cruel, for herself as well as for her relatives.

Economic considerations had dictated where Joseph Mitrione's family would settle, and their new life in Indiana was far removed from anything Italy had prepared them for. The community of Richmond, Indiana, had been settled in 1805 by soldiers of George Rogers Clark, the Revolutionary general and brother of the Northwest explorer. But it was a band of Quakers who gave the town its distinctive character by establishing in Richmond the Friends Boarding School—later Earlham College—an institution pledged to oppose all war and oppression.

After the Quakers, it was the German migration of the mid-nineteenth century that came to the midwestern tundra. Eighty years later, when the Italians began to arrive in force, they found the banks and department stores in competent, if not notably cordial, Teutonic hands.

But the land itself was marvelously hospitable. From New York to the Rocky Mountains, the United States had annexed a vast plain capable of feeding a nation, a hemisphere; if necessary, a world. Indiana was one of the states marked out across that rich soil. Yet the same sweeping horizon that made life fruitful for the farmers could prove less nourishing to the spirit. The broad, empty spaces that yielded corn and wheat in such abundance rarely seemed to liberate the people who settled there. Instead, the very unbroken low edge to the sky could cramp the better part

of them. Abraham Lincoln spent his rail-splitting years in
Indiana, and he called it "as unpoetical as any spot on
earth." Lincoln tried all the same to fashion a poem out of
his feelings about returning there:

> I range the field with pensive tread
> And pace the hollow rooms;
> And feel (companion of the dead)
> I'm living in the tombs.

More than a hundred years later, Father Robert Minton
was sent to found a Catholic parish in Richmond. In his
younger years, he had traveled the world; as he surveyed
Indiana's limitless vista, he asked himself whether any man
who had seen a mountain or the sea could ever be happy
there.

Not only could this ocean of solid land leave a man
feeling both strangled and stripped bare, but if the newcomer had grown up in a gentler climate, he learned
quickly that the weather would be an enemy for the rest
of his life. Against the raw winter wind and summer sun,
the farmer raised thick roofs and stayed beneath them.
Every planting and harvest, every journey out and trip
home, was at the mercy of the wet snow or searing heat,
and so a midwesterner learned to calculate his life, to avoid
whim or sudden change. Nature had reserved for herself
the right to be capricious. It was only prudent for man to
be steady and long-headed.

Endured long enough, that necessity came to seem a
virtue. Booth Tarkington was already beloved for his stories of the impish Penrod when he stood up in the Indiana
State Legislature to oppose Franklin Roosevelt's New
Deal. Tarkington offered a testimony to the rigorous life:
"Hardship, it seems to me, is a part of life, a test and a
builder of character."

Other native daughters and sons rejected that lifelong
challenge. Leaving Indiana behind, they emerged from
their protective cocoons in a dazzling new guise. Irene

Dunne, from Madison, Indiana; Carol Lombard, from Fort Wayne; Clifton Webb, from Indianapolis; Cole Porter, from the town of Peru.

For those who stayed behind, the physical isolation, the distances between the farm and a meager cluster of shops, sometimes bred suspicion of any new arrivals, or fear and then intolerance. Writing about the time the Mitriones arrived in Richmond, Irving Cobb poked fun at the enthusiasm with which Hoosiers were embracing the Ku Klux Klan. Cobb claimed that the Klan had swept the state like a hurricane, that the situation had become so bad in some Indiana towns that there was hardly an extra sheet in case company came.

Richmond called itself the City of Roses; a botanist, E. Gurney Hill, had built thirty acres of hothouses that sent fresh roses across the entire country. But even half a million rose bushes near the city limits could not brighten Richmond itself. When one mayor printed on his official paper the slogan "Richmond the beautiful," residents took it for the wistful gesture it was.

Given the wariness and rancor of their new neighbors, Italian immigrants tended to group together near the railroad tracks on the north side of Richmond. Joseph Mitrione's children grew up in a section called Goosetown. Sixty years ago, a settlement's name could be both fond and derisive. Besides Goosetown, poor Hoosiers lived in communities called Needmore and Lickskillet.

Richmond's blacks also lived in Goosetown but south of Hibbard Street. There were more of them than there were Italians, and they were quiet and polite. Each Sunday on their way to 5 A.M. mass, Ray Mitrione and his mother passed groups of black men, Saturday-night revelers lingering on the street, sorry to see the dawn. They gave Ray no cause to be nervous as they cleared a path and greeted his mother respectfully. "Hello, there, Mrs. Mitrione! How are you today?"

The Mitriones' first house on North Twelfth Street was

in a neighborhood of clapboard sidings and tar-paper roofs, with every wall either gray or faded green. The house stood scarcely two blocks from the railroad loading platform; and even though more trash cans than trees lined the street, scrap still piled up in the gutters, and all that sparkled in the dusty front yards was the tin foil from gum wrappers.

But the elder Mitriones' feeling for nature and warm colors survived the drabness. Maria loved flowers and surrounded her house with them. During the time Ray was growing up, his father rented a vacant lot a mile away, and in the evenings the whole family would walk out to work in the vegetable garden.

If Ray's had been a temperament inclined to bitterness, it might have soured him that his father never once came out to watch his sons play ball. Joseph Mitrione preferred to spend the time in his garden. Part of that dedication may have been homesickness; more of it was the economic good sense of raising vegetables for a family of eight. He raised corn, hot mangoes and lettuce, potatoes and cabbage, tomatoes for canning, and always one row of garlic for Maria's cooking.

Ray's father also had a winter refuge. Down the street on North Twelfth was the Italian Club, and there Joseph Mitrione retired every Saturday and immediately after Sunday mass. The members were fellow immigrants; the language and practices, exclusively Italian. The Mitrione boys hung around the club and, when they were old enough, became members. With the club and the family talk at home, they all grew up speaking Italian before they learned English.

The clubhouse was one unpretentious room with a small bar at the rear. In the basement a shower was available to members who did not have a bathroom at home.

Italian Club members worked late. They all had big families. If they saw each other on a week night, it was liable to be at a funeral home, paying respects to someone's infant daughter or aged parent. But each weekend, they gathered faithfully to drink beer and play cards. The winner became the club's padrone, the man to decide who got a bottle of beer.

The men worked with their hands. At Dille-McGuire they made lawn mowers. At International Harvester, they ran lathes and key punches and turned out cream separators and tractors. Joseph Mitrione worked a punch for I-H.

One day he came home early. He had lost a finger in his machine. Whatever the doctor had been able to do for him had not eased his suffering. Ray and the other children listened, horrified at the groans, and never forgot his misery.

The life of his children would be better. To fulfill that promise the young Mitriones were sent to a school to be Americanized in classes where English was the language and British law and custom were the rule. If some Italian children came out still talking a bit louder than Richmond thought appropriate or gesturing too expansively with their hands, the schools were not to blame.

With Dan Mitrione, the transformation seemed efficient and painless. He spent his first eight years at St. Mary's Elementary School, under the charge of a band of nuns who could wield a knitting needle until the knuckles stung. It was a Catholic education, and a good one. Teachers at Test Junior High School said the students from St. Mary's arrived better prepared than pupils from the public schools.

But it was not an Italian education. At Morton High, Dan was playing football, not soccer, and he was preening himself in a way no village boy in Bisaccia could afford. Lamenting more than complaining, their mother told Ray how Dan demanded a shirt freshly washed and pressed for every school day. He wanted to look just right, and with his stocky body and dark good looks, he usually did.

Morton's football team was made up of strong, willing, and mediocre players, boys like Dan, who played guard.

For them, it had to be a game for its own sake. There were no scouts watching, no athletic scholarships to crown a winning season. Dan's one tangible reward was his photograph in the high school yearbook, with the caption: "Our tall, dark and handsome football hero."

Since the patterns of American life were strange to his parents, Dan tended to take over for his father with Ray. Parents of the elder Mitriones' generation respected authority; they were aghast to hear that any child of theirs talked back to a teacher. If a neighborhood boy pocketed a candy bar, he was headed for a life of crime. So while Ray heard his mother threaten, "Wait till your father gets home," it was Dan who usually dispensed justice. Ray, idolizing his brother and modeling himself on Dan as best he could, accepted those spankings, thrilled that if he had to be spanked, it was Dan who was doing it.

When his high school days came to an end, Dan may have given a thought to college. He had been only an average student, but conscientious and disciplined. Some of his classmates were heading for Indiana University with no better qualifications except that their fathers could afford to send them. Instead, Dan went to work at International Harvester.

A year passed. Anyone might have predicted that Dan Mitrione was firmly launched on the path his father had laid down for him in the new country. Dan would marry an Italian girl from the neighborhood; he would work at a machine until the day he retired. If he profited from his father's misfortune and stayed alert, he would not lose a finger. Otherwise, that was the die that Dan seemed cast to fit.

But his future proved very different. The new year brought the Second World War and, in Richmond as throughout the country, young men flocked to enlist in the armed services, impelled by patriotism, joblessness, or a sense that this could be their deliverance.

A Hoosier named Ross Lockridge, Jr., spoke for generations of those men in a novel set in a mythical section of Indiana—Raintree County. One of his male characters, Lockridge wrote, "was bounded by a box, the country, inside a box, the state, inside a box inside a box inside a box...." To trapped men, the worst that war could do was to send them home in one last pine box. Catching the national mood, Dan Mitrione joined the navy.

Indiana's recruits did their duty. Typical was Tommy Clayton, whose actions were written by a neighbor, Ernie Pyle, of Dana, Indiana. Clayton, the mildest of men, had killed four of the enemy for sure and probably dozens more that he could not account for. And through the carnage, Pyle said, Tommy remained just a plain old Hoosier.

Reading every day of such heroism, the men not called upon to fight could feel, depending on their characters, lucky, guilty, or cheated. Dan apparently felt cheated. Years later, when he was sent to Latin America, he said that his belated duty overseas might make up for missing action during the war.

He served out his time at a naval base in Grosse Ile, Michigan, tame duty compared to the adventures of other young men from Richmond, but significant enough to consolidate the change in his fate.

He had worked his way to the verge of promotion to chief when peace was declared, and along the way he had been assigned as sergeant of the guards. It was his first taste of patrolling, and he took to the duty naturally. Growing up in a stern Italian home had prepared him for discipline. Now government directives, not simply a personal need, demanded that he follow the rules and devote minute attention to his dress and grooming. It would be another year or two before he knew it, but Dan had found his career.

And in the nearby Michigan town of Wyandotte, he also found his wife. He asked Henrietta Lind to marry him, and she accepted. The marriage was held in Richmond. To the elder Mitriones, nothing was said about Hank Lind having just converted to Catholicism. There were concessions to life in the United States that a dutiful son could spare an Old World family.

In Goosetown, opinion divided over Hank Mitrione, and hometown girls who had fancied Dan could be excused a touch of malice. But she was a serious girl, and Dan, for all his surface pleasantry, was a sober man. Hank worshipped her new husband: the Protestant gentry around town granted that much, even when later they scorned her obedience to her new church and complained that Hank Mitrione had kids like a cat had kittens.

A cruel observation with some truth to it. Eleven months after the wedding, Hank produced one daughter. By the time the war ended eighteen months later, she was pregnant with another. The pattern held over much of the next twenty years, until Hank had given her husband nine children.

When he was discharged from the navy, Dan had for the moment no better thought than to return to International Harvester. He moved his new family into his parents' frame house on East Twenty-first Street. By now they had escaped the railroad tracks and were living near a large park.

On the first day of December 1945, Dan went to police headquarters and filled out an application to join the force. One of the top lines asked for the candidate's political affiliation. Boldly or ignorantly, Dan wrote Democrat.

Later, like most patrolmen, he changed his registration to Republican. But just as he had shielded his parents from learning that Hank had been born outside their faith, he also kept this news from his father. Seeing his son don a police uniform had brought Joseph Mitrione great pride, and there was no point in clouding his pleasure.

In the style of the day, the form asked other bald questions: "White or Colored?" Dan checked white. "Read?" Dan wrote yes. "Write?" He wrote yes again. On the ap-

propriate lines, he listed his past employment, the names of
his two children, his Italian birthplace, and his one ailment
—the repair, five years earlier, of a left internal hernia.

He was hired, accepted as one of Richmond's finest.
Police forces in Indiana might be notoriously underpaid
and boneyards for inept political appointees. Those draw-
backs could not stop Patrolman Mitrione from going out
on the street each day to give the job his professional best.
He would treat the police as an extension of the navy and
do his duty. To be his partner, Dan drew an easy-going cop
named Orville Conyers.

Given his coloring, his dark-red hair and flushed red
cheeks, Conyers was destined never to be called by his
Christian name. Red was five years older than his new
partner. Assigned to ride in the same squad car in 1946, Red
and Dan were partners for thirty months and friends long
afterward.

By big-city standards, their duty was undemanding—
drunk drivers to book, breaking and entering cases to investigate. Richmond did not have a dog warden in those days,
and a patrolman sometimes had to shoot a stray dog. It was
the one use the average cop had for his Colt .38 special.

For Red, their most dangerous calls were those times
they would be sent out to quiet a family squabble. It was
worse when the trouble came from the north side of town.
They would enter the house, Red glad to have such a
solidly built partner, and whatever the couple's complaints
they could usually resolve them and get out by repeating,
"Just settle down now, just settle down."

Sometimes a man or his wife might say, "You're here
only because I'm Negro." That was Red's cue to say, "I
don't care what color you are. Just calm down."

It was the era of easy G. I. mortgages for $6500 bunga-
lows and hamburger at three pounds for a dollar; yet Red
and Dan found it hard to raise their families on something
less than $180 per month and felt compelled to moonlight.

Off hours, they went down to Dille-McGuire and loaded lawn mowers onto the railroad siding. They also cultivated such private patrons as the manager at Sears, who would let them wash his car during the day so that it would be dry and ready for simonizing at night. For a three-hour waxing chore, Dan and Red picked up nine dollars apiece.

Throughout the time Dan was washing other people's cars, he could not afford one of his own. When he pulled the night shift, and there were no buses and not enough traffic so he could hitch a ride, he would set out from the south end of town hunched down in his leather coat, the temperature at zero, and walk the two miles to headquarters.

The days following the kidnapping kept Ray feverishly excited. In deference to the throng of television cameras and photographers, Ray wore a suit every day, and that was strange for him. The family had expected Dan to dress up but not Ray. Years ago, Ray had come home wearing a Stetson, and his mother had mistaken him for Dan. Now he was temporarily out of his sports clothes and possibly the change touched a chord in his mother's memory, for when he visited her at the nursing home, she asked, "Have you heard from Dan?"

Ray said, "Oh, yeah, Mom. Just the other day."

"Well, say hello for me when you answer him."

It pained Ray to lie to his mother, and he may not have been good at it, for two days later, with the biggest *Pal-Item* headlines still about Dan's abduction, Maria Mitrione asked again, "Have you answered Dan yet?" And then, "Is something wrong with Dan?"

For Ray and the rest of his family, it was a time of helplessness. The Tupamaros had announced that they would free their kidnap victims, Dan and the Brazilian vice-consul in Montevideo, only after the Uruguayan government had released its 150 political prisoners.

From the news accounts, Washington and Brasília were each pressing Uruguay to make the trade. But the president down there, a man named Jorge Pacheco Areco, seemed to be stubborn. He was quoted as saying he would never negotiate with criminals.

Yet there were hopeful signs. Representatives of the Vatican in Uruguay were trying to start negotiations to free Dan. Ray also received a call from a man who identified himself as Cesar Bernal. Bernal said he had been an associate of Dan's in Uruguay, and he spoke lightly about the Tupamaros. From spending four years in Montevideo, he knew them like a book, he said, and they were not bad people. That was the phrase Ray remembered, "not bad people."

In addition, the newspapers sometimes recounted the fate of other kidnap victims, particularly in Brazil, where the U. S. ambassador had been seized and sequestered until the Brazilian government agreed to exactly the sort of swap the Tupamaros were demanding. That ambassador—his name was Charles Burke Elbrick—had been released with nothing worse than a bruised skull.

The family knew that Dan's condition had to be more serious than that. Wire services reported that he had been shot during his capture; a communiqué from the Tupamaros said the bullet had entered his upper right chest and gone out through his right armpit. At the State Department, a spokesman protested that by not getting Dan to a hospital, the Tupamaros had "magnified the inhumanity of the act."

But the Tupamaro bulletin had been couched in medical language and specified that no vital organ had been damaged. It sounded as though Dan might be suffering some discomfort but would survive.

When the *Pal-Item* commented that Dan's kidnapping was unbelievable, it was one of the rare times Andrew

Cecere could agree with an editorial. Unlike the Mitrione boys, Cecere had chosen to live in Richmond; he had not been raised in Goosetown. Perhaps that was why he, among the Italian-American community, had been the one to challenge Richmond's old-line politics.

Stocky and frizzy-haired, outgoing and amiable enough to star in productions at the local little theater, Cecere graduated from law school at the University of Michigan, served in the marines, and settled in Richmond in 1949. The Italians accepted him readily. He was invited to the clubhouse on the north end, where he played cards and met a lot of Italians his own age. One was a young cop, Dan Mitrione.

But the powerful men, the wealthy and conservative leadership of the town, were not interested in one more ambitious young Italian who had forsaken his native Pittsburgh to dwell among them. After two years of practicing law and another tour of duty in the Marine Corps, Cecere came back to Richmond in 1953, in a fighting mood.

By then he knew who ran the town. It was a short list. Hill of Hill Floral Products; McGuire of Dille-McGuire; Lontz, who had sold the local telephone company to General Telephone; Rudolph Leeds, the publisher of the *Palladium-Item*. Those men shopped for a public official as they might hire a caretaker for their estates. Of the qualities they esteemed in a public servant, an independent mind ranked at the bottom. When Andy Cecere made his assault, the occupant of the mayor's office was Lester Meadows, a barber.

In 1955, Mayor Meadows announced that he would be laying down the burdens of public office, and the downtown businessmen chose a florist as their candidate. Cecere, who had become city chairman for the Democratic party, saw his chance and encouraged the Democrats to pick, for the second time, Roland Cutter, an insurance man from a family sufficiently old and respectable to have made a strong showing against Meadows four years earlier.

Cecere knew the Democrats had to overcome years of lethargy and outright intimidation. Around Rudy Leeds's *Pal-Item*, very few employees had the courage on election day to ask for a Democratic ballot. They voted Republican or they stayed home. The hearts of policemen like Dan Mitrione might be with the new Democratic coalition, but when Cecere thought about it at all he assumed that in the last presidential election Dan had voted for Eisenhower over Stevenson.

This year, Cecere's coalition took hold. The schoolteachers joined. Labor was showing an unexpected militancy. At the International Harvester plant, organizers for the United Auto Workers were ready to challenge the city's anti-labor policies, which had guaranteed for years that during any strike the pickets would clash with a line of truculent cops.

Three days before the election, the sitting mayor made labor the central issue. He endorsed the entire Republican slate on the grounds that "none of the Republican candidates are obligated in such a way as to prevent them from preserving 'law and order' when and if in labor disputes the need arises." That candor, together with Cecere's organizing efforts, led the Democrats to a victory that even the *Pal-Item* called smashing. Cutter beat the Republican candidate by nearly two to one and became the first Democratic mayor in twenty years. To reward Cecere, the new mayor appointed him city attorney.

Sometime later, an old-timer cornered Cecere and asked him plaintively how it could happen that foreigners came in and took over the town. By that time, Andy Cecere was not offended. He laughed and said, "There's been such a void in Richmond that even somebody like me looked good."

Other times, speaking before a civic group, the new city attorney tried to explain what he felt about being part of a minority. The United States was a colossus, Cecere would say. It had great biceps and bulging thighs.

But, he would add, it was we Italians who gave that giant a heart.

A week had passed with no yielding on either side. For Dan's brothers and sisters, it was becoming harder to believe that this horror could end with his being restored to them. News accounts made it sound as though the Uruguayan government was putting hundreds of suspects in jail. But President Pacheco went on refusing to free the original 150 Tupamaro prisoners, and only their release could save Dan.

In Richmond, they had proof that Dan himself wanted the United States to act on his behalf. The editors from the *Pal-Item* called Ray, and he went to the newsroom to inspect a facsimile that had come over the wire, a note from Dan to Hank. Ray looked it over and said there was no doubt that the handwriting was his brother's.

The note had been found after a Tupamaro called a newspaper reporter in Montevideo and told him to look around the toilet of a bar in the center of the city. There, taped to the tank, he found this message:

> Dearest Henrietta,
>   I am recovering from the wound I received when I was taken. Please tell the ambassador to do everything possible to liberate me as soon as possible.
>   I have been and am still being interrogated deeply about the AID program and the police.
>   I send all my love to you and the children.
>   Love ya,
>   Dan

In view of that appeal, the wire stories speculated that President Pacheco would now declare a general amnesty for the political prisoners. But another day passed, and still the Uruguayan government did nothing. In Richmond, Ray and his family knew that their nerves were raw. There was, however, a worse effect to the delay: the kidnappers were giving signs that their patience had run out. In a note delivered to a Montevideo radio station, the Tupamaros said they would wait until midnight Friday, August 7, for the authorities to announce the release of their comrades. "If there is no official announcement by then, we shall terminate this affair and do justice."

The Associated Press reported that it was not clear whether the last sentence constituted a threat; but in Richmond they understood plain talk, and they could not read it any other way.

By the weekend, there was a feeling throughout Richmond that events in Uruguay were now out of control. A new note from the Tupamaros accused Dan of being a spy for the United States. If the family had not been so apprehensive, that far-fetched charge might have left them indignant. The message continued: "He is representative of a power that has massacred entire populations in Vietnam, Santo Domingo and other places." Then came the explicit threat the family had been dreading. Unless the Uruguayan government agreed to release its prisoners, Dan would be killed at noon on Sunday.

The deadline came and went. No prisoners were released. The Tupamaros issued no further communiqué.

At about 4:30 A.M. Monday, Ray's telephone rang in his apartment above Kessler's. It was a UPI reporter from Indianapolis. He had spoken with Ray on Sunday, and Ray had asked him to call back the minute the bureau got any news.

"We just heard," the reporter said. "They found his body in the north part of Montevideo."

"Is it confirmed?" Over the past week, Ray had had his fill of rumor and speculation.

"Not yet. Do you want to make a statement?"

Maybe it wasn't true. Maybe it was propaganda. Maybe they had killed someone else. "I have nothing to say at this time."

Ten minutes later, a call came through from David Dennis, the congressman from Ray's district, who had been solicitous throughout the ordeal. "Have you heard about Dan?"

"Well," said Ray, "it wasn't confirmed."

"I'm confirming it, Ray."

With good reason, Roland Cutter believed that he had launched Dan Mitrione on the career that would end at St. Mary's Catholic Cemetery. Until this past week, the part he had played was a matter of pride to him—and some puzzlement—as he watched Dan use the helping hand Cutter had extended to him to pull himself nearly to Cutter's level and then out of Richmond altogether.

Cutter's grandfather had come to Richmond from Germany in the last century. Henry Cutter had spoken no English, but he learned the names for different foods and opened a grocery. Roland Cutter had inherited a burgher's face, to which he added a dapper mustache. After Indiana State, he returned to Richmond to settle into the insurance business.

Cutter was one of those men—the parish priest, Father Minton, was another—who admired the way the Italians over on the north end raised their children. For years, Cutter had seen Dan around town, always neat and well-behaved, and he knew that the young man had come out of the tradition that what Poppa says, goes.

In recent years, two Italians had won seats on the city council, and they had proved to be so patriotic that their oratory could be shaming to the third- and fourth-generation Americans. Cutter and his friends used to agree that some of those Italians appreciated their country more than they did.

In 1955, when Andy Cecere's coalition put Cutter in office, the new mayor prided himself on being politically naïve, and he would say that he did not know a precinct from a bale of hay. A week or two after the election, Cutter was down on the Indiana University campus, visiting a son at the Delta Epsilon house, and it was weighing on him that he would soon have to name a fire chief and a chief of police.

Although it was Sunday, the new mayor went to the university's School of Police Administration. He found the director in his office and appealed to him: How do you go about picking a police chief, anyway? The director thought Cutter was joking. In Indiana, chief of police was a prime patronage job. Until wealthy men ran out of indolent nephews, there would be no need to ask for the university's help in filling the post.

When he was convinced that Cutter was serious, the director dispatched a team of researchers to Richmond. The mayor rented a hotel room, and the university staff called every member of the force to the room for aptitude tests. Some men grumbled that many of the tests seemed far afield from police work, and in his heart, the mayor agreed. But he continued to support the mysterious method, counting on it to produce the very model of a modern police chief.

The team first gave Cutter advice about the kind of chief he did not want. You're not looking for a so-called brave cop, they kept repeating. You don't want to name a great hero. Remember that the chief's job is administrative.

Then, after all the suspense, and to a reaction from the other cops that ranged from surprise to outrage, the team nominated a young juvenile officer with barely ten years' experience on the force. Mayor Cutter appointed him.

The new chief was no hero, nor did he pretend to be. He was, however, the first scientifically selected professional chief of police Richmond had ever had, and he would amply vindicate the mayor's faith in the process that chose him. Yet Roland Cutter could never help but think of his chief, fondly, as little Danny Mitrione, the Italian boy from Goosetown.

. . .

After the strange official silence while Dan was alive, his murder seemed to have triggered a thousand mimeograph machines in Washington, D. C. Public officials were queuing up to denounce the Tupamaros. Some of them even remembered to send condolences to the Mitrione family.

The two highest-ranking responses did not come from men but from buildings. "The White House said Monday," began an Associated Press account, "the kidnap-murder of U. S. official Daniel A. Mitrione in Uruguay is 'a despicable act that will be condemned by men of decency and honor everywhere.' " The Vatican, in an unsigned article on the front page of *L'Osservatore Romano,* condemned crimes committed in the name of fanatical ideologies. Pope Paul VI a day earlier had called all political kidnappings "vile."

The political figure to speak at greatest length on the killing was House Minority Leader Gerald Ford, of Michigan. Although the murder had led some voices to suggest that the United States should not be engaged in the activities that had taken Dan to Uruguay, Ford took the murder as proof of how important it was for the United States to persevere. Ford also expressed confidence that the Uruguayan government had done all in its power to obtain Dan's release. On the U. S. side, Ford singled out for special commendation Dan's boss, Byron Engle, the director of the Office of Public Safety.

Louis Gibbs owed his job to Dan Mitrione and, he realized on a day like this, much more. Gibbs had applied to the police force six times, and each time when he had come to the line at the upper right corner of the form that asked his political affiliation he had left it blank. Someone in the department was not appeased by his reticence. Six times Gibbs was rejected.

In April 1956, on Gibbs' seventh application, the new chief summoned him to his office. Mitrione's doubts about the young applicant were not political, only economic. Working as a meat cutter, Gibbs made $9,000 a year. A patrolman's salary was little better than half of that.

Mitrione asked him, "Are you sure you want to join the force? You know you're making more than I am."

After seven applications, Gibbs was sure. His application was approved.

Until Mitrione took office, experienced officers in Richmond had trained their new colleagues with a casual apprenticeship. The rookie got in the back seat of a patrol car, and the two veterans in front told him: Keep your ears open and your eyes open and your mouth shut. But the chief had benefited from a modern approach to police science, and he wanted to extend that advantage to his department. Mitrione himself had overcome some resistance on the city council to go off to the FBI training program in Washington. Back home, he arranged for Indiana University to offer recruits a six-week training course on its campus.

After his training, Gibbs found that life for patrolmen under the new chief was rigorous. From the start, the older men had not liked Mitrione, but then they had been passed over for his job. Gibbs granted that the chief was tough. There was only one way to do things: his way. But in a showdown, Gibbs and the other new recruits decided that the chief was usually right.

Mitrione told his troops frankly, "That door swings in and it swings out. You either play the game or you don't play at all." Sometimes an older cop got drunk on duty or would be caught out carousing. The chief was hard-nosed. "Sign this resignation and get out."

Later, the policemen started to negotiate their contracts through the Fraternal Order of Police, and an offending officer was guaranteed a formal hearing. Although in his day, Mitrione held absolute power over his men, he

strained to use that power fairly. Once Gibbs was patrolling with a partner who outranked him, a sergeant, when
they captured a man who had held up a gas station. The
tip said the robber was carrying two guns, and the sergeant
kept slapping the man, trying to find out where he had
hidden them. When Gibbs could take no more, he said,
"You hit that man once more and you'll have to hit me."

Humane motive or not, Gibbs knew that he was being
insubordinate, and he was not surprised to be summoned to
the chief's office.

"You were right," Mitrione told him, "and you were
wrong. You were right about the slapping. But never talk
that way again to a piece of brass."

Another reprimand even less equivocal came after a Sunday night call: a complaint from a black neighborhood
about a drunken girl. Trying to subdue her, Gibbs slapped
her hands, her head. He had not yet returned from the
women's jail when the complaint reached the chief. Mitrione decided from the sound of it that Gibbs had used too
much force. Take care of him, the chief told the captain
on duty. Get him cooled down.

Although in those days most Richmond cops carried a
blackjack, Mitrione dissuaded young Gibbs from taking
one out on his beat. "You don't need it," the chief said.
"You're young. You don't know your own strength."

Most of the time the patrolmen, especially those the
chief had hired, did not worry about displeasing him. They
had come to understand his quirks and aversions. Trim and
neat himself, he expected his officers to look equally pre-
sentable. Around headquarters, appearance was important.

One experience Gibbs would never forget occurred at
2 A.M. on a rainy night. Calling in from his beat, Gibbs was
told to hurry over to a certain room at the hotel. He got
to the corner, saw the chief's blue car at the curb, and
thought, It's a raid! What else could it be on a night like
this?

Gibbs charged upstairs, his wet shoes squishing, and

found Mitrione conducting a surprise inspection for the third shift. Citizens who see patrolmen on the midnight trick, the chief was saying, pay the same taxes as everybody else. They deserve to see neat, clean officers.

Below their raincoats, every cop was soaked—trousers, socks, shoes. But when they unbuttoned those coats, the chief expected them to be sharp from the knees up. Gibbs passed the test. But Mitrione caught one man with a faulty weapon and sent him home.

The rules could be bent but only in a good cause. One year Richmond experienced what it regarded as a juvenile crime wave. It was during the late fifties—the advent of the curled lip, duck-tail haircuts, and rock 'n' roll—and the elder citizens did not like the way teenagers were scoffing at the law by staying out after curfew. Some minors were drinking beer, others stood on corners and yelled offensive remarks after the cars of older drivers. A couple of stores were broken into, and a few dollars taken from the cash drawers.

Mitrione knew the respectable people of town were looking to him for action. He went to Mayor Cutter. "I may make some people mad, but I can clean this thing up."

"Go ahead," said the mayor.

Over the next weeks, the police rousted groups of teenagers wherever they congregated. When the curfew sounded, they ran stragglers into headquarters and called their parents. The teenage nuisance abated. Stern but fair, the chief himself was a model parent. If other fathers shirked their obligations, then it was up to the police to demonstrate how children should be handled.

Ray's first impulse after Dan's murder had been to fly to Montevideo and help bring Hank and the youngest children home; however, the State Department reassured him that all was being taken care of. Dan's four oldest daughters and sons, who were living around Washington,

D. C., were flown to Uruguay to accompany their father's body and the rest of the family back to the United States.

The air-force jet carrying the family landed a little past 8 A.M. Wednesday morning, August 12, at the nearest jet strip to Richmond, Cox Municipal Airport in Dayton. City officials had planned to have Dan's body lie in state all day Thursday; but Hank, who had endured this tension for nearly two weeks, wanted the speediest possible end to it, and a day was cut off the period of mourning.

An honor guard, forty airmen from Wright-Patterson Air Force Base, used a hydraulic lift to bring the body down from the cargo hatch. Traveling at a solemn 45 miles per hour, they provided an escort for the ride back on I-70 to the interchange and along U. S. 27 into Richmond. State troopers from Indiana and Ohio joined the entourage, and police blocked the intersections, allowing the caravan to pass.

The procession pulled into the Stegall-Berheide-Orr Funeral Home, where, for two hours, Hank received Dan's family and friends. Part of the time John, her youngest, sat on her lap.

Hank had boarded the plane in Uruguay wearing a tweed coat as a shield against the August winter wind. In the humid heat of Richmond, she slipped it off, but the sunglasses remained, barely disguising the redness of her eyes.

By 1 P.M., Dan's body was lying in state at the new Municipal Building. Red Conyers was outside the building with a police guard that lowered the flag to half mast while thirty-three Boy Scouts stood at attention.

For six hours and fifteen minutes, Dan's coffin lay on display. According to the *Pal-Item*, nine thousand persons came to pay tribute, an expression of grief unmatched in Richmond's history. The pastor of Reid Memorial Presbyterian Church was among those who stopped by, and he told of the day Dan had come to address an ecumenical youth service. "At that time, Roman Catholic and Protestant relations were not very cordial," the clergyman recalled, "but I told him he was welcome to sit in on our service. Dan said, 'Give me a hymn book.' And he sang as lustily as anybody."

On Thursday morning, the homage and the public mourning reached their climax. Shortly before 10 A.M., Secretary of State William Rogers and his wife arrived at the Holy Family Parish together with the Uruguayan ambassador. President Nixon had also sent his son-in-law, David Eisenhower, who, uncharacteristically glum, tagged at the end of the official party.

A few minutes later the family arrived at the church, and the five hundred other worshipers took note of the dignitaries in their midst, gratified by the honor to Dan. Promptly at ten o'clock Father Minton appeared in vestments of red and gold, and the mass was under way.

That Father Robert Minton stood two inches over six feet tall may have contributed to his theory about the Italians in his parish. The priest had decided that with their round faces and their diminutive size, Italians—indeed, all small people—had a childlike way of looking at life. It was easier for them than for bigger people to believe that they were the children of God.

Father Minton did not mean to be patronizing, and he exempted men like Dan Mitrione who were only three or four inches shorter than he was. But along with many others in Richmond, he regarded the Italian community as a people apart. The Mitriones were definitely what Father Minton considered "good Italians." They went to church, paid their bills, and disciplined their children. The good Italians from the generation that produced Dan's father had a method that Father Minton thought American men envied: they taught their wives to love them and their children to obey them. Some of the rest—ah, they seemed to think that no matter what they did, God would understand.

Father Minton had founded the Holy Family Parish

seventeen years earlier. When he arrived in Richmond, the town had felt strange to him. He had been a chaplain in China during the war, an exciting time in his life, and he found himself falling back on his memories. Tame or not, the years passed. At parochial school, he began to get students whose fathers he had taught, and that gave his life a stability, a continuity, that a professional bachelor like himself found warming. He was getting spoiled by the greetings on the street. Everyone, even Protestants, knew him and called out at the sight of him.

The people of his parish were much like Ray Mitrione, simple and unspoiled. Among the five hundred families at Holy Family there was only one professional man, a dentist. Dan, however, had been different. In any community, Italian or not, he would have been considered promising.

Dan had his faults, including that quick anger he had to learn to control. But when he spoke before a service club or the chamber of commerce, he left behind an impression of competence without being in any way spellbinding or giving his audience the feeling he was leagues ahead of them.

Once—it was before Dan became chief, when he was still a juvenile officer—he told a church group that the United States was like a jigsaw puzzle: put all the pieces in place, turn the puzzle over, and there on the back was a boy, symbol of American youth. The imagery was not Father Minton's style, but over the years he had remembered it.

Then Dan left Richmond for Belo Horizonte, beautiful horizon. On his trips back, first from Brazil, then from Uruguay, he seemed to be taking on with his years a new urbanity. He came home fatter and grayer; in that he was no different from other men. At the end of the visit, Dan would bring to the rectory a box of the half-empty bottles he had bought for entertaining his friends. The priest accepted the bottles gladly and took their exotic labels—

Cherry Heering and that coffee drink, Kahlúa—as further proof that travel was indeed doing Dan good.

It struck Father Minton that Dan might even have been developing a touch of charisma, one of those modish qualities that had emerged during the Kennedy years. Not, he thought, that Dan could compete with the Kennedys. Father Minton knew; he had met both Jack and Bobby when they came to town for a Jefferson-Jackson Day dinner in April of 1960. Those were the days before big motels had circled Richmond with their easy anonymity and lascivious billboards: TRY US ON FOR SIGHS. The Leland Hotel downtown was still the select gathering place, and Senator Kennedy met at the Leland with a band of local Democrats. Since Holy Family had the largest open space, the dinner was held there.

This was three months before Dan left for Brazil, and he was still police chief and charged with traffic control and the local security arrangements. Hank came to the church with the other parish women who had volunteered to serve the gala dinner. John F. Kennedy may have been no more than a senator, but he was marching resolutely toward his party's presidential nomination, and a thousand curious Democrats bought tickets.

While stumping Indiana, Jack had lost his voice. In the town of Seymour, he compensated by handing out cards on which was written: "Sorry, I have a sore throat and cannot talk, but please vote for me anyway." The senator's administrative assistant, Theodore C. Sorensen, read Kennedy's prepared address, an attack on the Soviet Union tailored to the conservatism of the farming community.

"For the first time in history," Sorensen read, as Kennedy stood mute at his side, "Russia has its long-sought political foothold in Latin America." He meant Cuba.

Later, at Earlham College, the senator's voice had come back sufficiently for him to read the prepared text himself. "We have been complacent, self-contented, easy-going. I think we can close the gaps and pull ahead. But we must not minimize the Red threat. We know from experience that we cannot rely on their word."

Ten years later, on the day of Dan's funeral, Father Minton could not remember the exact words Jack Kennedy had spoken at Holy Family, but their effect still lingered. As he had listened, he thought, If that man asked this audience to go up on the roof and jump off, they would do it. That was charisma.

The time had come for Father Minton to open the mass. He believed in funerals. They were occasions for the Catholic church to speak out, to affirm that the world is not everything, to say that Dan should not have been afraid to die, and wasn't.

Those were the thoughts Father Minton had been putting together since he received word in Geneva of the murder. He managed to say most of them, though three times he was so overcome that his parishoners wondered whether he would be able to go on.

The week after Dan had been buried in the shade of a silver maple in St. Mary's Cemetery, Ray was out of his business suit and back on the road in shirt sleeves. Returning to Kessler's late one afternoon, he got a message: "You're supposed to call the chamber of commerce office. Frank Sinatra wants to talk with you."

"Yeah," said Ray, "I'm sure of that."

But people were not yet back to joking much with the Mitriones. Ray went ahead and checked with the chamber. Be here tonight at 7:30 P.M., he was told. Ray followed instructions and took the call when it came from Frank Sinatra's agent.

Sinatra had read of the double tragedy—the murder, and the plight of a widow with five of her nine children left to raise on a government pension. The singer proposed flying to Richmond and sponsoring a benefit for the children's education. He had invited Jerry Lewis to join the show;

and along with his own nineteen-member stage band, he would bring a seven-piece rock group, Orange Colored Sky.

(Hank Mitrione got a similar call. Her temperament had always been less ingenuous than Ray's; she had been exposed for ten years to the machinations of federal bureaucracy and had lost her husband to a conspiracy. At 11 P.M., Hank called Dan's old boss, Byron Engle, to check out any hooks to Sinatra's offer.)

Sinatra's one free night was August 29, so despite the muggy summer heat and the people away on vacation, the concert was set for 9 P.M. that evening.

Tickets went on sale at the major banks, Kessler's, and Phillips Drug Store. Since the Civic Hall seated 4,200, tickets were also made available in Dayton, Cincinnati, and Indianapolis. Richmond High School's football jamboree had already been scheduled for the same night. Its time was moved forward an hour so that everyone could be at Civic Hall by nine o'clock.

Dan's kidnapping and murder had been crowding other news off the front page of the *Pal-Item* for nearly a month; the aftermath was covered on the *Pal-Item*'s inside pages, where the newspaper ran a series on the background of the Uruguayans who had murdered Dan. One headline ran, "Tupamaros, Financed by Russia, Are Trigger Men for Castro." On the same inside page, George Smathers, a former senator from Florida, revealed that the late President Kennedy had frequently discussed ridding the hemisphere of Fidel Castro through assassination.

In Washington, the director of the Catholic Conference held a press conference to demand an international investigation of charges that U. S. officials from the Agency for International Development (AID) were instructing police in Brazil and Uruguay in the techniques of torture; he mentioned Dan by name. The *Pal-Item* printed the article on a page with news of Sir Laurence Olivier's recovery from a thrombosis.

More prominently placed was a story from Montevideo: a death squad of vigilante Brazilian policemen was vowing to avenge Dan's murder by killing twenty relatives of the Tupamaro guerrillas. With Dan back and buried, however, Richmond's interest in Latin America and its problems had dwindled considerably.

And on the day of the concert, nothing could compete with the imminent arrival of Frank Sinatra. The basketball floor of the hall had been covered with folding chairs; and in the upper reaches of the bleachers, two immense spotlights were already in place.

Sinatra himself was the liveliest topic. Around Wayne County, some people were vocal in condemning him for the way he lived, for his women, for the hints of dubious associations. To his critics, Sinatra represented the antithesis of Hoosier values, and although they lowered their voices around Dan's family, they were sardonic about this one *paisano* coming to town to help out the family of another, as though they felt the American-Italian Club was overreaching itself.

Most of the county felt differently. Only a few advertisements had run in the *Pal-Item*, but the concert was heading toward a sellout, helped along when Sinatra himself paid for 450 tickets to be passed out among servicemen in the area and another batch for Richmond's policemen and firemen. With no fanfare, his corporation also absorbed the $27,000 in operating costs. All proceeds would go to Dan's family.

Shortly before 8 P.M., the stars arrived on the flagship of Cal-Jet Airways, a charter service owned by Sinatra Enterprises, and they faced the five hundred fans who crowded the runway apron. Interviews had been denied to the press, but one Dayton television announcer drew from Sinatra that he felt "we owe a debt of gratitude for men like these who work for our country."

Lewis clowned for the crowds, but when the newsmen caught him, he turned taciturn. "Just play back what Frank said and you know how I feel."

One reporter persisted, "Are you glad to be in Richmond tonight?"

Lewis stared straight ahead. "Of course I'm glad to be here. If I wasn't, I'd be back in Los Angeles."

But then a photographer yelled, "Hey, Jerry! Look this way!" The comic walked directly into his camera, treating viewers at home to a screen filled with nose. At that, everyone laughed and wrote off any touch of sulkiness to an understandable fatigue.

That night, Sinatra's performance was as generous as the impulse that brought him to Richmond. By the time he took the stage at 11 P.M., the temperature inside Civic Hall was 110°. Sinatra wiped away the sweat and did a dozen of his standards, ending with "My Way."

The audience responded with a standing ovation. The houselights came up, and Sinatra stepped forward to deliver a statement prepared for the occasion: "I never met Richmond's son, Dan Mitrione," Sinatra began. "Yet he was my brother. Just as you and I and Jerry are brothers. As all of us in America are brothers."

Sinatra checked off the problems that currently beset the United States: smog, campus revolt, muggings in the street, polluted water. But then he said, "You sit back and think of Dan Mitrione, and you know that things ain't all that bad."

Sinatra exhorted his audience to put its trust in love and "a genuine belief in the Man Upstairs," and he ended, "I've got this hunch that there's a lot of the Dan Mitrione quality in you folks. And believe me, in my book of human beings worth knowing and remembering, Dan Mitrione is really something else."

CHAPTER

2

DAN MITRIONE WENT OFF to Belo Horizonte as part of the team that Dwight Eisenhower was fielding against the nation's newest and most potent villain. In the Soviet Union, Joseph Stalin had been dead for seven years, and Nikita Khrushchev was proving too earthy, too much the rustic uncle, to frighten the American public for long. The China of Mao Tsetung, though a sworn enemy, remained separated from the United States by its extreme poverty and the Pacific Ocean. But since 1959, Fidel Castro had been ruling over an island so close to the U. S. that John Quincy Adams had considered it an apple that gravity would ultimately bring into our hands.

In fact, at the height of the 1960 presidential campaign, the one sure fact most U.S. voters knew about Latin America was the distance of Cuba from Florida's coast. Taking note of the nation's obsession, Castro commented, "You Americans keep saying that Cuba is ninety miles from the United States. I say that the United States is ninety miles from Cuba, and for us that is worse."

Castro had barely routed the dictator Fulgencio Batista when conservatives within the U. S. government launched a propaganda campaign against him. In April 1959, Vice-president Richard Nixon met with Castro in Washington

and afterward wrote a confidential memorandum to the
CIA, the State Department, and the White House, stating
flatly that Castro was either a Communist dupe or a disci-
ple and should be treated accordingly. At the FBI, J. Edgar
Hoover told Nixon he agreed with his view. Eleven
months later, President Eisenhower ordered the CIA secretly to prepare an invasion of Cuba that would depose
Castro and his band of bearded reformers.

The Democratic presidential campaign of 1960 reflected
the confusion in the electorate's mind over Castro's revolution. John Kennedy began the year by referring to Castro
as a fiery young rebel in the tradition of Simón Bolívar.
That was before those U. S. investors who controlled 40
percent of Cuba's sugar land expressed outrage over Castro's reforms.

When Castro expropriated the larger cane fields, including those of his own family, he offered in payment twenty-
year bonds yielding 4.5 percent annual interest. Slyly, he
proposed to pay for the land at the value the U. S. owners
had placed on it when they paid their Cuban taxes. To the
companies involved, the offer was not a fair one; and in
protest, Washington cut off a sugar quota that had been
advantageous to Cuba.

As mistrust of Castro spread, Senator Kennedy, now the
Democratic nominee, changed tactics. He suggested that
the Eisenhower administration should have avoided Castro's revolution altogether by using its influence on Batista
to cause him to relax his dictatorship and permit free elections.

Between the time Kennedy was elected and his swearing
in as president, Eisenhower broke diplomatic relations with
Cuba. As a result, the new president entered office with a
bipartisan foreign policy. Even such domestic liberals as
Arthur Schlesinger, Jr., now perceived Castro's policies as
a perversion of the Cuban revolution, and Democrats and
Republicans were united in their resolve that Castro's success not contaminate the rest of the continent.

. . .

Before the decade had ended, Dan Mitrione, along with hundreds of other Public Safety advisers, had been sent into combat against communism in Brazil and elsewhere in Latin America. Yet the battle they entered, unlike Vietnam, was no shooting war. Since U. S. policy makers saw communism on the continent as a hidden enemy that would subvert a society from within, they prepared what they felt to be an appropriately secret counterattack.

In Vietnam, the Green Berets often defined war as months of boredom illuminated by moments of sheer terror. That characterization was truer still of the hidden war for which Mitrione had volunteered. Even when the shooting in Brazil began, Mitrione's routine remained comparatively calm, filled as it was with inspection tours and conversations in outlying police stations, requisitions for weapons and supplies, speech making, and daily paper work. He left for his office early in the morning and usually returned home before dusk to be with his family. His most difficult ethical dilemmas, at least in public, came when he served as umpire in local baseball games and had to decide whether or not to call his oldest son out at home plate.

Police advisers like Mitrione were the foot soldiers in Latin America; the CIA officials were the officer corps; the ambassadors, the ranking military attachés, and the CIA station chiefs from the upper echelons of each U.S. embassy were the field commanders. Until Mitrione was given his own unit to command in Uruguay, the CIA officials and the ambassadors overshadowed and ignored him. These were the men, with no need to know Mitrione's name, who were laying down the strategies and pursuing the courses of action that would later take his life.

Had Mitrione chosen to stay in Indiana, today he would still be years away from his retirement, and his youthful days would interest no one but his own devoted family. His upbringing, the degree to which he was typical of his generation, became important only when he took the atypical step of shipping off to a foreign land. His service in Brazil and Uruguay happened to coincide with a critical period in both countries. In a way no one could have predicted, his modest biography became intertwined with Latin American political history. Yet, throughout many significant chapters of that history, Mitrione deserves no more than a footnote.

Then, in death, Dan Mitrione became a symbol. Internationally, he was treated as the embodiment of United States policy in Latin America, even though it was a policy he never had the slightest voice in formulating. As a result, to understand the significance of his life, the message behind his killing, requires turning away from his everyday routine, from his many months of boredom, to examine instead those men and policies that brought him to his moment of terror.

It was not considered usual behavior for a Midwesterner on the threshold of forty who had never traveled abroad to quit his job, crate his belongings, uproot his wife and children, and set off to live on a new continent; and because it was not usual, the citizens of Richmond speculated on Dan Mitrione's abrupt departure. Some said that after four years as chief of police, he had run out of challenges. They detected in Dan a desire to serve that was too compelling to be satisfied in one small Indiana town.

Hank knew the truth was more practical: Dan wanted more money. He had asked the city for a pay raise; and when it was turned down, he felt he had to look elsewhere. Even as chief he had been driven to accept such odd jobs as painting offices at midnight, his car parked around the block so no one would know that the dignity of the chief's office was being compromised.

Contacts he had made during his term at the FBI school

informed him that through the foreign-aid program, the State Department had begun to recruit advisers to train police forces overseas. Quietly, in case he was rejected, Dan sent in an application.

The head of the program was Byron Engle, a former personnel director from the police department in Kansas City, Missouri. Engle tried to keep the federal salaries between $8,000 and $10,000, roughly 10 percent higher than what an officer was being paid at home. But for recruits from a few states, especially Mississippi and Indiana, that was not a fair ratio, their salaries being so much lower than the national average.

By enlisting with Engle, Dan received more money than he had been refused by the council, plus housing and other allowances, and at the end of his working years, the prospect of a better pension. Here at last was a chance for a man with seven children—and no guarantee there would not be more—to draw a living wage. Almost as important, he would be recognized by his government nationally, even internationally, as a professional in his field.

In May 1960, a month after John Kennedy came campaigning through Richmond, the International Cooperation Administration interviewed Dan in Washington and indicated that the job was his.

Back in Richmond, Dan went in to speak with Mayor Cutter about a leave of absence. It would have to be long: two years and four months was the length of the temporary post that was being offered him. Such a leave would be unprecedented. Was it legal?

Andy Cecere reported back that Dan could not be granted leave as chief of police, and that the loosest reading of Indiana law indicated that if Dan ever hoped to be chief again, he would first have to serve five years as a patrolman. There was no alternative. With trepidation but with encouragement from Andy and his other friends at City Hall, Dan resigned the post that had come his way so unexpectedly.

Standard training called for five weeks in Washington and three months studying Portuguese in Rio de Janeiro before Dan would take up his duties in Belo Horizonte, an industrial city northwest of Rio. The authorities recognized the limitations to any cram course, particularly in Portuguese, a language which, more appealing sung than spoken, could sound, if badly rendered, at once mushy and guttural, like drunken German. So Dan, along with most other U. S. Public Safety advisers, would come to depend heavily upon an interpreter. Still, though not exactly boasting, Dan later let friends in Richmond know that those years of speaking Italian at home had proved a boon after all, and that he had passed with remarkable speed through the language training.

July found Hank packing for the long sea voyage. The children's attitude toward Brazil ranged with their ages. When Dan had called them together for the sort of family conference rare to their household, the novelty had aroused everyone's interest.

"I want to talk to you about moving to South America," Mitrione began. The children knew he had already decided on the change. They had been brought up equating respect with love, and they attempted no serious mutiny. In fact, the older girls found that their father could make their future home sound highly romantic. Dan had been strict with his daughters, not allowing them to date until they were sixteen; and for them, the snobberies of a small town cut closer than for their parents. Dan, Jr., was dismayed to hear that the Brazilians favored soccer over baseball, but he confined his carping to neighbors along his newspaper route.

Joseph Mitrione had lived long enough to rejoice when his son put on the police chief's hat. Now his widow watched with misgivings as Dan prepared to leave the United States. Maria Mitrione, too, had once left her homeland and had never seen her family again.

Hank and the children landed in Brazil in September of

1960, and the girls, at the right age for it, succumbed to the country unconditionally. South of the equator it was winter, but they did not mind the rain. Brazil was so alive, so vivid; and after the dusty plains, it was like seeing life through a freshly washed window.

Possibly no new home their father might have chosen could have contrasted more sharply with Richmond. From the time of the first Portuguese explorers, foreigners had found Brazil rich in more than spice and precious stones. Missionaries and adventurers alike told the world that the temperament of the handsome natives was unlike anything to be found in Europe.

That difference persisted through the centuries of colonization. Stefan Zweig, an Austrian novelist, was one of many who tried to describe it. "A certain softness, a mild melancholy," he wrote, contrasted strongly with the dynamism of the North American. The violent, the dangerous, qualities of man had seemed to dissolve in the racial mixing of native Indians, slave blacks, and immigrants from southern Europe.

Some Portuguese explorers—Padre Fernão Cardim, for example, in 1585—had taken that passivity for nothing more than *remissa*, laziness. The Brazilians themselves did not entirely disagree. They told of the explorer Pedro Alvares Cabral first stepping onto the Brazilian coast in 1500 and hearing a voice from the depths of the jungle call, "Tomorrow!" to which the echo answered, "Patience!"

Zweig argued, though, that the quality he described was a virtue. "Anything brutal, cruel or even slightly sadistic is foreign to the Brazilian character." Brazil's history supported his observation: the country had separated itself from Portugal without a war of independence, and it ended slavery tardily but also with no bloodshed. Brazilians themselves pondered this peaceable strain in their national character. One student of Brazilian art from the colonial days noted, "In Brazil, even Christ hangs comfortably from the cross."

Portuguese Brazil was not the same as Spanish America, but north of the equator, the nations of Latin America melded in the popular mind, and the combined stereotype was seldom favorable.

Latin Americans were voluble. ("Oh, my God," cries an Englishman in a Rebecca West novel when his wife tells him whom she has invited to dinner. "South Americans. They will never go home.") Latin Americans were volatile. Seven years before Russia's revolution, Mexico staged a social revolution, and the example proved addictive to its neighbors. Political reports from south of the Rio Grande were always chaotic. (James Thurber, at his fussiest and blindest, described himself as being "more troublesome than Argentina.")

Latin America was dirty. Here the popular conception had some foundation. Until the 1920s, Rio de Janeiro was the most unhealthy of the world's large cities, with raging yellow fever, a high incidence of tuberculosis, and syphilis a badge of honor among the city's young men.

Even after those epidemics were brought under control, Latin America remained intellectually contaminating. For reporters at *The New York Times,* the continent was a notorious graveyard. At Harvard University the dean of the faculty was understood to have been referring to Latin America when he remarked, "Second-rate subjects attract second-rate minds." Six months after Dan Mitrione arrived in Brazil, that dean, McGeorge Bundy, went to the White House as John Kennedy's foreign-policy adviser.

Perhaps the continent's Luso-Hispanic background was to blame. Another Harvard professor, Henry Kissinger, confessed later in his career that his interest in world politics stopped at the Pyrenees. Even Edmund Wilson, insatiable in his erudition, admitted to one blind spot: "I have been bored by everything about Spain except Spanish painting. I have made a point of learning no Spanish, and I have never been able to get through *Don Quixote.*"

When South America did arouse fleeting interest, it was

usually proprietary. In 1899, the *Literary Digest* reported a strong sentiment in the United States for annexing Cuba. Campaigning in 1920, Franklin Roosevelt told crowds that as assistant secretary of the navy he had helped to run a couple of the continent's smaller republics. "The facts are that I wrote Haiti's constitution myself, and if I do say it, I think it's a pretty good constitution."

Lanier Winslow, once a first secretary at the United States embassy in Mexico City, told friends that Mexico had the makings of a great country, "if it could be dipped in the sea for half an hour and all the Mexicans drowned."

Latin Americans bore this neglect and contempt with a mixture of anger, resentment, and, especially in Brazil, self-deprecating humor. Brazilians mocked not only themselves but their colonial inheritance: "Brazil is the country of the future and always will be"; "The Portuguese language is the tomb of thought."

Brazilians acknowledged their aversion to labor with the slogan, "Work is sacred, don't touch it." While other Latins valued that trait called machismo, Brazilians told a joke about the man who had been grievously insulted but refused to fight for his honor: "You're a man, aren't you?" his friends demanded. "Yes," he replied, "but not fanatically so."

With their sweetness of disposition and genial humor went the melancholy that Zweig observed, and that may have finally reached him: Zweig killed himself in Petropolis, the mountain town that had once been Brazil's royal capital.

Despite a penchant for poetry, the classic sounding of the Latin American soul was done in prose. At the turn of the century, a young schoolteacher in Uruguay, José Enrique Rodó, wrote an essay called *Ariel.* The book swept through Spanish-speaking America, producing a mild defiance of those values that had shaped the Protestant Colossus to the north.

Invoking the spirit of Ariel from Shakespeare's *The Tem-*

pest, Rodó cautioned his readers against false and vulgar ideas of education, those aimed solely at utilitarian ends. Such materialism, he said, mutilates the mind's natural fullness, and young people should hold instead to a single principle: to maintain the integrity of their humanity.

Rodó then expanded his attack: the enemy was a United States democracy preoccupied with its own materialism. Untempered by other values, such democracy extinguished respect for any superiority that cannot be turned to self-interest. Rodó saw his continent, seduced by the greatness and strength of the United States, voluntarily making over its society in the northern mold.

Do not, he pleaded, yield to that temptation. Hold to the sense of beauty you were born with, for it is more powerful than a steam-driven engine. Hold to your own virtues, to your capacity for heroism, because the other way, the northern way, produces monsters. Let the United States, if it must, be Caliban. It is your duty to save the hemisphere, to save the world. Be Ariel.

In Argentina, Mexico, and the Dominican Republic, poets and politicians—very often the same young men—took up the challenge, proclaiming themselves Arielists. Yet in New York and Washington, Rodó went untranslated for many years and unread.

By the early 1960s, the United States was more convinced than ever before that its technicians—engineers, agronomists, and now policemen—had vital knowledge to import to the less progressive nations of the world. In Washington, Byron Engle had been charged with putting together a task force that could train police in Asia, Africa, and particularly in Latin America. He had been chosen because of his experience both in training Japanese police after the Second World War and in setting up a police advisory board in Turkey. His was also a genial yet foxy manner that disarmed even those people conditioned to distrust cops. He had an avuncular way about him, a bland reasonableness, that served him well at staff conferences and at those times when the press could not be avoided.

It was President Eisenhower who first proposed adapting the training of German and Japanese police to meet the needs of the Cold War. Eisenhower told a meeting of the National Security Council: "We're building up military forces that we all know wouldn't last a week or ten days in a hot war. But what are we doing about the constabulary forces?"

The meeting adjourned in confusion. What, the council members asked each other, does he mean? The urban police? Or is he speaking literally of the rural force, the constabulary? Like other oracles, Eisenhower had to be interpreted, and one adviser divined that the President had just returned from the Philippines, where policemen were called constabulary. Ike merely meant police.

With the decision ratified, the project had to be brought under the aegis of an advisory agency. Police advisers in Okinawa and Japan were under army control, along with those in Korea and the Philippines; Berlin's police advisers reported to the State Department; and the four-man group in Iran came under the Foreign Operations Administration.

Officially, the new advisory unit was given to the State Department to be administered as part of the foreign-aid program, but Engle had other allegiances. He had been recruited by the CIA after it was established in 1947. If council members had misgivings about selecting a CIA man to head the program, Engle disarmed any criticism. In 1955, he was given a title and a secretary, and Washington launched itself on its efforts to improve the Free World's police.

From the start, some officials within the foreign-aid program disliked Engle's operation. Economists were the most outspoken, complaining that they were trying to shape a new social structure, and here was this other group, repressive by definition, doing its work under the same banner.

Engle believed that the executive arm of a government —its police and military—were the last to change. But change itself—at least orderly change—depended on stability, and Washington was not prepared to underwrite any other kind of change. Since order required policemen to enforce the law, it served the interests of the United States that those officers be efficient.

If Engle was not finding much support at the State Department, neither was the FBI proving cooperative. J. Edgar Hoover told associates that the police program was simply one more CIA cover—Engle's appointment proved as much—and that he did not intend to pump his life's blood into a competing bureaucracy.

At the CIA, the advantages to putting U. S. operatives in close contact with the local police were obvious, but as late as 1960, with the CIA immersed in training men in Guatemala for an invasion of Cuba, Engle's operation was still allowed to struggle along under the unfriendly cover of the State Department.

When Dan Mitrione applied to the program in the spring of that year, he was put through a rigorous security check. Since Engle was only fielding eighty advisers world-wide, he could draw on his intelligence sources to be sure that each recruit was stable, competent, and loyal to his country.

It was easier in those days to define positive loyalty than to determine precisely who the enemy was. Until 1959, Engle's outline had called for "combatting communism and subversion." But then the King of Iraq was assassinated by an armored unit said to owe its fealty to Nasser of Egypt. More alarming, two hundred bearded men sent by Fidel Castro landed in a mangrove swamp for a botched invasion of Panama; yet, in 1959, it was still a moot question whether Castro was a Communist. As a consequence, the words of the police mission were changed to read "combatting interests inimical to the United States."

When the Kennedy-Johnson team moved into the White

House, Engle's program, rather than being dismantled by the liberals taking over Washington, acquired its premier patron. Investigating his duties at the Justice Department, Robert F. Kennedy was impressed with the way the FBI trained policemen from around the country and thought the time was right to expand that ecumenical approach to foreign lands.

At the same time, his brother, as president, was confronted by stirrings in Southeast Asia and throughout Latin America. To seek solutions to the unrest, he convened a number of high-ranking officials and called them the Counter-Intelligence Group. The members agreed that it was not an inspired name. Too negative. Given the time, they would have worked "nation building" into their title, but for now C-I would have to do.

The first chairman, Maxwell Taylor, was an army general who had dropped from favor during the Eisenhower years for warning the country against the Pentagon's reliance on nuclear weapons. He had written a book setting forth his views, and on the New Frontier he was regarded as that most elusive hybrid, an intellectual general, and as a useful counterweight to bombardiers like Curtis LeMay. Later Taylor was named ambassador to South Vietnam.

With his ability to convert passion into energy, Robert Kennedy actively prodded the C-I Group. Its key mission was to develop methods for promoting internal order around the globe. Cabinet departments were represented, and a delegate from the CIA sat in. At no time did any of its members question the C-I Group's goals. As one participant recalled, "We knew we were acting from damn good motives."

Out of the C-I Group's deliberations came Jack Kennedy's Special Forces; new training in counter-insurgency at military schools from the National War College down; and new courses at the Foreign Service Institute to make officers from the State Department, the CIA, and military branches more alert to insurgency problems in the field.

Furthermore, the C-I Group saw early on how important the police would be in a country's battle against its rebels. So it set up a Committee on Police and Police Training, and as chairman appointed a career diplomat, U. Alexis Johnson.

Johnson resembled the British politician Edward Heath, having one of those long faces that are bland but not always reassuring. When Lyndon Johnson became president, he sent Johnson to South Vietnam as deputy ambassador. His job would be to steer Taylor through the complexities of Vietnamese politics, while Taylor would guide General William Westmoreland to victory on the battlefield.

Alexis Johnson's committee recognized immediately that there had to be a new central and more powerful police office, and that decision led to the committee's thorniest discussions. The Pentagon argued that any expanded police effort should come to them. A State Department veteran, Johnson found it easy to insist that the training of police was a civil function. After all, he said, we aren't training MPs.

Having won that battle, Johnson was not concerned that the officials of the police program had been turning to the CIA for the help they could not get through the aid bureaucracy or from the FBI. Perfectly natural, Johnson thought. In an ideal world, he might have preferred a program director without Byron Engle's involvement with the CIA. But Engle's credentials seemed so superior to those of his rivals—hadn't he once trained 100,000 Japanese policemen in only two months?—that Johnson talked with the CIA director and got permission for Engle to assume the expanded job.

Next came the setting of standards for recruits to this newly prestigious program. Engle had been sitting in on the Johnson committee meetings, and he moved adroitly to hold the committee's interference to a minimum. A senior member brought up the subject: "What kind of person do we need?"

That was Engle's cue. He produced a tablet and tore off sheets he passed around the table. "Gentlemen, here are some blank pieces of paper. I'd like to see what you think we should require. So please write down the minimum attributes for a chief police adviser."

On the papers Engle collected, one member had written that the man must be young and, since the work would be arduous, physically fit. Another demanded a college degree, preferably in the social sciences. Another stipulated at least one foreign language; another, a military background. Engle then elaborately calculated the various requirements. "Gentlemen, your minimum standards add up to some ninety years of experience. And yet you don't want our recruits to be over thirty-five."

The committee members, all expert bureaucratic infighters, recognized a master. All right, they told Engle, you know more about it than we do. And he went on exercising sole authority over hiring.

A police academy was another of Engle's deferred ideas whose time had come. Until then, the State Department had been importing promising young officers to the United States. But once on hand, they were often shipped off to Kansas City to sit around a station house.

The first alternative, for Latin American officers, had been the Inter-American Police Academy. Theodore Brown, a former police chief from Eugene, Oregon, and then the director of a Public Safety program on Guam, ran that school at Fort Davis on the Isthmus of Panama. Captains and majors from around the continent, but particularly from Central America, spent eight to twelve weeks learning how to be more effective officers. They then spent another week or two at nearby Fort Gulick, learning counter-insurgency. But police officers from the larger and more sophisticated cities, particularly in Brazil, found the courses in Panama simple to the point of being insulting. Although a few could be placated with invitations to stay on at the academy as guest instructors, most of them shunned the school entirely.

Then, too, with the issue of the pronounced CIA role in past police training already raised within the C-I Group, it was now agreed that the school should be moved to the continental United States. There the civilians could keep a better eye on it. Already reports were filtering up to the mainland that the training in Panama was rougher than the United States would tolerate on its own shores.

To these accusations, the CIA formulated an answer that it employed later, with modifications, when those stories began to appear in print. From 1955 until today, ran Byron Engle's denial, we have been teaching nonlethal riot control in Panama. Before that, Latin American police were equipped with submachine guns. Every year there would be deaths in the streets. We disapproved, and we introduced instead the use of tear gas and stressed its advantages. Tear gas may not be pleasant, but it isn't fatal. You can scrub it off.

In August 1962, Jack Kennedy approved the C-I Group's report; however, a year later, the police academy was still functioning in Panama, turning out seven hundred graduates, and pressure was building to move the school to the United States. Engle tried to explain that finding an appropriate building was no overnight job. In Japan, he had put his academies in bombed-out buildings, but in Washington Engle had personally checked eighty buildings before, on the edge of Georgetown, he discovered the Car Barn.

The barn, more than two hundred years old, had been first a tobacco warehouse and than a turnaround point for streetcars in the District of Columbia. O. Roy Chalk, the owner of the transit system, planned to reserve a part of the ground floor for his law offices. Otherwise, the cellar would do for a firing range, and the remaining three floors of the solid red brick building seemed a natural spot to train police.

But to protect his flank, Engle called Michael V. Forrestal in McGeorge Bundy's office in the White House basement. Forrestal had served on Johnson's committee. With his proximity to the president, if he approved the location none of the committee's nay-sayers could prevail.

The two men toured the premises. The elevators designed to take the streetcars upstairs were still there. A lot of work would be needed before it would look like an academy. But Forrestal, playing the graybeard at thirty-six, said "You guys are young and full of piss and vinegar. You can get it in shape." Then he paused. "It brings back a lot of memories. I used to get my butt spanked for sliding down that hill."

Only then did Engle realize that the site he had chosen was next door to the James Forrestal estate, where Harry Truman's secretary of defense once lived, in the days before the menace of the Cold War helped to unbalance his mind and lead to his suicide.

Drawing on the Inter-American Police Academy, Engle imported the twenty instructors as the nucleus for his new school. They all spoke Spanish, and that was an asset, since Washington's chief concern remained Latin America. Grudgingly, J. Edgar Hoover donated one man to the staff.

Although the move out of the Canal Zone had been set for nearly a year, when it finally took place, it coincided with the Panama rioting of 1964. The U. S. adviser to Panama's police called Engle on the night a Panamanian was killed to say, "Well, they got their first martyr."

Among CIA propagandists, it was widely held that the Marxists—and everyone else with interests inimical to the United States—followed a standard technique for agitation, which they taught around the world: first, get one of your own supporters killed in the rioting. That's why Engle advised the police of other countries against using bayonets: in a crowd, it was too easy for the Communists to push a demonstrator onto the point of one. Next, get physical possession of the body. Carry your dead martyr through the streets. Stage a public funeral. Lastly, hold a public commemoration.

. . .

About the time Dan Mitrione went to Washington for his cursory training, a younger man, also headed for Latin America, was completing a far more rigorous regimen. The disparity in their preparation reflected the difference in value that Washington placed upon a middle-aged cop from Indiana and a young college graduate recruited by the CIA.

The recruit in this instance had been four years in arriving at the agency. In the spring of 1956, a CIA official first went to South Bend, Indiana, to look over a senior at Notre Dame, a philosophy major named Philip Burnett Franklin Agee. Agee would bring obvious assets to the CIA. He came from a comfortable middle-class Catholic family in Tampa, Florida; a family friend already held a post within the CIA; Agee was diligent, a little sour, and more than a little arrogant. But those last traits did not disqualify him for an agency with the CIA's background and bloodlines.

Agee's intellectual approach to Catholicism presented more challenges to him than religion did to a man like Dan Mitrione, who had taken his faith as an inheritance from immigrant parents. Phil Agee, for example, was tormented by the prospect of an eternity in Hell. He did, however, find comfort in lessons mastered at Notre Dame, and he agreed with his professors that a prime virtue in any decent citizen was his respect for authority.

President Eisenhower, though he kept the nation out of war, was not keeping its young men out of the army. The CIA recruiter offered Agee a means of escape from two years of potato peeling. If he volunteered for an extra year in the air force, Agee could become an officer inside a unit that was a CIA cover. With the air force's connivance, he would be wearing the uniform while he was beginning his career within the agency. Except, as Agee was learning, no insider called it the agency. It was "the Company."

His years in the air force ended, and Agee was transferred to Washington for studies in Spanish, communism, and Soviet foreign policy. The CIA's Office of Training did not waste time on political theory. Instead, the students learned about the expansionist aims of the Soviet Union and practical ways to foil them. Almost all of Agee's young colleagues wanted to go into Secret Operations, the field work that would pit them against agents of the Soviet conspiracy.

At this same time, Agee was called on to master the convolutions of scores of subagencies reduced to their initials: Office of Current Intelligence (OCI), Office of Basic Intelligence (OBI), Office of Operations (OO), and most interesting to the aspiring activists, Clandestine Services (CS) and its operations branch, Psychological Warfare and Paramilitary (PP).

On graduation, almost everyone was chosen to work in the field. For further instruction, they drove out to a mysterious training ground called the farm. It turned out to be at Camp Peary, fifteen miles from Williamsburg, Virginia.

The briefing officer informed them that the trainees included foreigners who were not even supposed to know that they were in the United States. They were called black trainees and kept away from those like Agee.

Training was physically taxing—calisthenics, self-defense, and to add piquancy, lessons in maiming and killing with the bare hands. But mainly the recruits learned how to gather information by the discreet use of foreign agents, often the intelligence officers of the host country.

By July 1960, Agee's course at Camp Peary had been broadened to include technical operations: telephone tapping, safe-cracking, lock-picking. He was introduced to such advanced bugging devices as an infrared beam that could transmit the vibrations of a voice as they bounced off a window pane. Agee also learned that some foreign police and intelligence services were so hapless that the U. S. government had to help them out. The International Cooperation Administration was sending Public Safety missions to work with the local police departments. That program provided cover for some CIA officers. The other police advisers, the ones without Company ties, were to be kept ignorant of the clandestine work of their associates.

After Agee had completed his term at the farm, his chief CIA contact suggested strongly that he volunteer for duty in Latin America, where Castro's revolution was causing the CIA to expand its operations. Agee had dreamt of Vienna or Hong Kong. Among the various CIA divisions, the Western Hemisphere (WH) enjoyed the lowest prestige. A number of former FBI men, veterans of the anti-Nazi years in Argentina and Brazil, had moved over to the CIA upon its creation in 1947, and Agee was embarrassed to find himself allied with them in something called the gumshoe division.

Coming to know the WH Division better, Agee's doubts were confirmed. He found a prevailing disinterest in either Latin American history or culture. Fluent Spanish was valued; it was a tool for a man to do his job. Otherwise, Agee was conspicuous for the way he dug into his new assignment and read widely about Latin America. His older co-workers assured him that to operate anywhere a man needed only a few well-placed contacts.

In August 1960, Agee heard exciting news: the branch chief of his division had approved him for an assignment in Ecuador. The CIA was arranging a full-time tutor in Spanish and wanted to get Agee to Quito as soon as possible. His cover would be assistant attaché in the U. S. embassy's political section. The job was a tribute to Agee's potential. Only one other member of his training class had been assigned earlier to the field, and that man was going no farther than New York. Under State Department cover, Christopher Thoron was appointed to the U. S. mission to the United Nations.

At last, in December 1960, Phil Agee and his wife, Janet, were flown first-class from Washington to Quito and arrived in the midst of Ecuador's Independence Day fiesta.

Agee's first working day was a heady one. <u>He saw</u> a <u>bullfight and deplored the butchery.</u> In the evening, he and Janet, along with Jim Noland, the CIA station chief, attended a party at the home of the Ecuadorian family that controlled the country's movie theaters. Every guest that night seemed to be rich and related by blood and marriage. Agee had the chance to meet an important contact, a nephew of the country's president and an undercover agent for the CIA.

That man, Jorge Acosta Velasco, had lately proved his worth by passing along information to the station about a CIA man, Robert Weatherwax, who had been operating in Quito under the cover of a Public Safety adviser. Weatherwax had recruited the chief of Ecuador's intelligence department, who was later exposed as the leader of an illegal secret society of young police officers. Weatherwax dropped from sight to avoid being tarred by his protégé's actions. Now Acosta was advising the CIA that Weatherwax could return safely.

Phil Agee had come to the end of a stimulating day. In a room of sleek men and expensively groomed women, he was not the least important person. And these were people who wanted to get along with him. To cope with the others, the working-class Ecuadorians, he had a drawerful of money for bribes and payoffs. There were also the Indians, but no one troubled about them.

Agee might not have the world in his pocket, but he had Ecuador, and at twenty-six, it was world enough.

During the time that Dan Mitrione was making a mild political gesture by permitting Hank to serve at Jack Kennedy's dinner in Richmond, a fellow alumnus of Kennedy's was holding himself aloof from all forms of politicking—a strategy that eventually secured for him the ambassadorship to Brazil.

Since 1955, Lincoln Gordon had been serving as profes-

sor of international economics at the Harvard Graduate
School of Business Administration. He particularly prided
himself on remaining untainted by Massachusetts' gamy
local politics: throughout 1960, he neither met John F.
Kennedy nor involved himself in his presidential campaign.

The most significant fact in Gordon's life may have been
that he began it acclaimed as a boy genius. He had enrolled
early at Harvard and graduated in three years, at the age
of nineteen. Along the way, he had developed a phenome-
nal memory for detail and a reputation as a man who could
devote an hour to answering a single question. By the time
he went off as a Rhodes Scholar to Balliol College, Oxford,
he might have outgrown that precocious need to shine, but
he remained a compulsive talker, a tireless explicator—a
chatterbox.

Gordon's career after Oxford was respectable. He
taught at Harvard and served in government, always on
important missions but seldom as the top man. He assisted
Paul Hoffman in the agency that administered the Marshall
Plan; he was a part of a delegation to the United Nations
Atomic Energy Commission; and during the Eisenhower
years, he served as a consultant to NATO, but on the
alliance's nonmilitary aspects.

Then John Kennedy was elected. The academic ranks
around Cambridge began to thin. Although Gordon was
not immediately tapped, he tried to remain optimistic.
Waiting for the president's men to call, he began by setting
the proper value on his worth. There were only three jobs
he would take. But Paul Henry Nitze was appointed assistant secretary of defense for international security affairs,
and George Ball was named undersecretary of state for
economic affairs. That left only national security adviser,
and McGeorge Bundy received that post. Bundy was not
only six years younger than Gordon, but he might fairly
be considered a Gordon protégé, since Gordon had hired
him after the war to work on the task force for the Marshall Plan.

For a while, it looked as though Gordon might be left behind at the business school in Cambridge, grinding out a two-volume study on Brazilian investment. But salvation appeared in the autocratic person of Adolf Berle. Before his inauguration, Kennedy had set up a Latin American task force to establish broad lines of policy, and he named Berle as its chief. Gordon thought that Berle suffered from the small man's Bonaparte complex, but he was used to his ways. When Berle called and asked, "Heard from Sorensen yet?" Gordon understood that it was not a question.

He hedged, however. "About what?"

"You know, you know. Lots of names are floating around, but there's only one task force and I'm it." With that, Berle invited Gordon to join his committee as an economist. Gordon protested, as sincerely as he knew how, that despite his Brazil project at the business school, he was a newcomer to Latin America; others had devoted their lives to its study. Berle convinced him that the committee would not take much time, and Lincoln Gordon at last was aboard the New Frontier.

During the campaign, Jack Kennedy's aides had suggested that he take an initiative in Latin America as substantial as Franklin Roosevelt's, and, if possible, with a title as winning as The Good Neighbor Policy. Richard N. Goodwin, who had a talent for capturing Kennedy's cadences, had been assigned the job of concocting that program. Riding a campaign bus through Texas, Goodwin picked up a discarded copy of a magazine published in Tucson called *Alianza*. He took the name to Kennedy, who agreed that it was a start.

A Cuban who had broken with Castro and gone to work in Washington came up with two possibilities: Alliance for Development was instantly discarded because Goodwin was sure his chief could never cope with the Spanish word *desarrollo*. That left Alianza para el Progresso. Goodwin tried shortening the title to the more euphonius Alianza para Progresso, but objections from the U. S. Information

Agency convinced him that even south of the border there were purists who cared about grammar. Rhetoric was Goodwin's specialty, and he set to work on a speech that would match his fine title.

Gordon was asked to look over the speech for substance. He read through the first draft and protested the phrase in which Goodwin promised, within ten years, to close the economic gap between the United States and the nations of Latin America.

Gordon said, "Dick, this is ridiculous. If the United States worked at full speed to impoverish itself, we could probably meet that goal. Otherwise—"

But through eight drafts that unrealistic pledge kept appearing, and it was still in the final draft that Goodwin and Gordon took in to the new president. Trained in speed reading, Kennedy whisked through the draft at a pace that dazzled Gordon. Then he asked, "Any comments?"

Gordon said, "There's one phrase that I've been trying to get Richard to take out."

"What is it?"

After Gordon had explained, Kennedy turned to Goodwin.

"Sure, Linc is right," Goodwin said. "It's just rhetoric. But in ten years, we'll be out of office anyway."

When the president read the speech to an assembly of Latin American ambassadors, Gordon was relieved to hear him omit the offending phrase.

During those early months of the New Frontier, Gordon was given to understand that he would be the next ambassador to Brazil; and to prepare himself, he broadened his reading on the country. From U. S. intelligence estimates, it was clear that Communist infiltration in Brazil was now Washington's overriding concern.

It had once been different. During the Second World War, Brazil's president had been a dictator, Getúlio Dornelles Vargas, who had proved his allegiance to the United States by sending a regiment to fight the Axis in Italy and by allowing the United States to build huge aircraft staging bases on Brazil's northeast coast.

Vargas had first come to power in 1930, the beneficiary of a popular rebellion led by coffee growers protesting a drop in world coffee prices. Forming a military coalition that could challenge the industrial power of Minas Gerais and São Paulo, he ousted the president and became dictator.

Franklin Roosevelt, who came to office three years later, found Vargas an easy colleague who had also embarked on a program of deficit spending to rouse his country from the Depression. There were other parallels between the personal life of Vargas and that of his new friend in Washington. The dictator's legs had been crushed when a falling rock destroyed his car. Marrying late in life, Vargas produced five children; his wife, Dona Darcy, was admired for her good works. But it was known that the two led separate lives, and his partisans insisted that at seventy Vargas was still visiting a mistress once a week.

The two men seemed to enjoy gossiping together. One indiscreet joke to Vargas during the war about Charles de Gaulle helped to earn Roosevelt the French leader's lasting enmity. In the course of another candid meeting, Roosevelt told Vargas that he would not accept for the United States the degree of control that foreign companies exercised over utilities in Brazil.

It seemed a broad hint. In 1938, the Mexican government had nationalized the U. S. oil companies, and the oil executives had appealed to Washington for armed assistance. Theodore Dreiser once explained their thinking: "The whole principle behind intervention by the United States is that when one of her citizens buys property in a foreign land, that property is no longer subject to the law of that foreign land."

The response of the Roosevelt administration had been legalistic, only assisting in negotiating a long-term settlement. Given that background, Vargas might have expro-

priated the Brazilian utilities owned by U. S. corporations.
He did not; however, he was determined that no other
sector of Brazil's economy get itself so indebted to foreigners.

During his fifteen-year reign, Vargas faced a number of
armed challenges. The middle class of São Paulo revolted
in 1932; the Communists rose up in 1935. Vargas responded
by banning the Communist party and sending its leader,
Luís Carlos Prestes, to jail. In 1938, the Integralists, Brazil's
fascists, tried unsuccessfully to storm the presidential
palace.

For Brazil's industrial workers, the Vargas years were
marked by hope. The dictator instituted a social security
program and sponsored a labor movement. The unions
were subservient to Vargas's Labor Ministry; but with his
support, men and women who had worked from twelve to
twenty hours won an eight-hour day with two-week vaca-
tions, children under fourteen were banned from industry,
and women went from half pay to full pay. Yet Vargas did
little for laborers on the farms and great fazendas. They
were disorganized and still considered by the landowner to
be his personal property.

Nor were the Vargas years at all democratic. The dictator, in fact, had even forbidden the newspapers to print the
inflammatory word "democracy." However, the end of the
Second World War witnessed an outcry for the return of
parliamentary democracy. The officers' corps that had installed Vargas now put him out and called an election for
the presidency.

Democracy had returned to Brazil but only by the grace
of the army. Once again the generals showed that they
took seriously their right, inherited from the Portuguese
emperor, to serve the national interest as the *poder modera-
tor*, the moderating power.

Though literacy laws prevented Brazil's majority from
voting, three major political parties quickly sprang into
being. The most popular was a conservative alliance.

Formed, for the most part, by industrialists and landowners, it called itself the Social Democrats. Next in strength
was the National Democratic Union, Vargas's right-wing
and middle-class enemies. Finally there was a workers'
party, Partido Trabalhista Brasileiro. The Brazilian Communist party was then legalized as the fourth party, a legiti-
macy that proved temporary. In 1947, it was outlawed
again when Brazil broke diplomatic relations with the
Soviet Union.

The landowners of the Social Democrats and the workers' party each owed debts to Vargas, and they entered into
a coalition that gained in strength until, by 1950, the old
dictator could assume the presidency again, this time
through elections.

Vargas soon found it was the harder way to govern.
Without restrictions on the press, he had to bear a daily
onslaught from his opponents; and in a young journalist
named Carlos Lacerda, Vargas met his fate.

Gifted in elegant vilification, Lacerda increased his at-
tacks until it became impossible for Vargas and his loyal
friends to bear them. One night in August of 1954, an army
friend of Lacerda's was murdered in front of Lacerda's
apartment building. The evidence implicated one of Vargas's security men, called the black angel of death.

The resulting uproar left Lacerda in the enviable position of being not only a martyr but a living one. Vargas
saw that he could not continue as president, and he retired
from the scene in a way that none of his North American
counterparts had chosen. On August 24, 1954, he took his
own life.

Behind he left a remarkable document, bold and plead-
ing, in which he blamed outside forces for helping to create
the circumstances that killed him: "The foreign companies
made profits of up to five hundred percent. They demon-
strably deprived the state of more than a hundred million
dollars by false evaluations of import goods."

Vargas, a son of the pampas of Rio Grande do Sul, was

acting from a *gaúcho* code of honor. He ended his message: "Serenely, I take the first step on the road to eternity and I leave life to enter history."

After a caretaking period, a politician named Juscelino Kubitschek took over the presidency in 1955 and was confronted by another period of rising inflation and falling coffee prices. Every penny drop in the world price of coffee cost the Brazilian treasury $25 million. Kubitschek sought to convince foreign capital to invest in Brazil by offering concessions that neither Vargas nor Franklin Roosevelt might have approved. The new president canceled the ceilings on profits and allowed foreign investors to take their profits home. Factory equipment could come untaxed to Brazil. When a foreign investor launched a company, no percentage of Brazilian participation was required. By 1959, the U. S. Department of Commerce was reporting that the investment climate in Brazil was one of the most favorable in the world.

Brazil paid heavily for that expression of confidence. One local economist, Eugenio Gudin, calculated that Kubitschek's regime had given away $1 billion to foreign firms through tax credits and assistance in locating in Brazil. Yet, Gudin was no propagandist for the Left, and in a newspaper article he wrote that "to say that every man has a right to a decent life is a proposition worthy of a donkey."

In another study, the privileges extended to the new automobile industry—Volkswagen, Mercedes-Benz, General Motors, Ford—were shown to equal Brazil's national budget. In those same years of the late 1950s, Kubitschek's ministers cut off support to the National Motor Company, one of the state enterprises created by Vargas.

To some Brazilians, the foreign-aid program of the Eisenhower years, and even the Alliance for Progress, was a sham so long as five times more dollars were leaving Brazil in the form of earnings, dividends, and royalties than were entering the country as new direct investment. Those men, nationalists, joked that it was Brazil that was giving foreign aid to the United States.

But undeniably the infusion of capital had the nation booming, and Kubitschek celebrated the growth by creating a symbol, a city he called Brasília.

For generations, popular wisdom had held that Brazil would never be a great nation so long as it remained a collection of coastal cities with a jungle at their backs. In North America, the plains had been reward enough to draw settlers west. But Brazilians needed an incentive and a proof of the country's commitment to development, a capital city far away from the distractions of Rio de Janeiro.

No one questioned that Rio was a hindrance to hard work. It was said that municipal buses were never routed within a block of Copacabana Beach because the expanse of white sand caused office workers on their way downtown to jump from their seats and defect to the sun.

As Kubitschek built Brasília, the Gross National Product for five years kept going up a healthy 7 percent annually. In this harmonious union of Brazilian politics and foreign business there were only a few discords. Inflation was also on the rise and threatened the value of foreign investments. Then, too, Kubitschek, like Vargas, was assisting the large landowners through coffee subsidies while ignoring the peasants outside the industrial cities. His neglect led to several reformist movements in the arid and poverty-ridden northeast. From Washington these movements came to look dangerously radical.

As the elections approached, there was another difficulty. Brazil's electoral laws did not permit a president to succeed himself, nor were presidential candidates empowered to pick their running mates as Eisenhower had chosen Richard Nixon. In Brazil, the people's second choice became vice-president, and when Kubitschek won, the runner-up had been João Goulart.

A rancher from the south of Brazil, Goulart had been so cherished by Vargas that rumors spread that he was the

dictator's illegitimate son. Even in the largest nominally
Catholic land on earth, suicide had only enhanced Vargas's
standing. In Washington, it was clear, and displeasing, that
Goulart might win the next election.

The problem was ideological. As Vargas's minister of
labor, Goulart had been credited with the regime's reforms. Some U. S. intelligence reports found him peril-
ously open to Communist influence. But the alternative
was little better. Washington rated the other major con-
tender, Jãnio Quadros, nearly as susceptible. Between those
two imperfect options, a choice was made, and Brazilian
journalists had no trouble discerning from briefings with
the U. S. embassy staff that Quadros was Washington's
choice.

Throughout his term as governor of São Paulo, Quadros
had won the affection of the workingman. Now campaigning for president, Quadros repeatedly assured crowds that
he was no plutocrat.

Forty-eight percent of the Brazilian voters believed him,
the largest majority vote in Brazil's history. Once again,
João Goulart was elected vice-president on the labor
ticket.

On taking office, Quadros swung his rigid broom errati-
cally. He sharply devalued the cruzeiro, Brazil's unit of
currency. That pleased foreign investors more than it did
the Brazilians living on fixed incomes. In a campaign to
restore morality to Brazil, he banned the bikini from Rio's
seashore, a decree honored only in the breach.

A recent trip around the world had convinced Quadros
that Third World countries should move to a middle
ground between the capitalists and the Communists, and he
tried to retire Brazil to the sidelines of the Cold War. In
that intuition, public-opinion polls seemed to support him;
one survey found that 63 percent of the Brazilians preferred neutrality. The polls also showed that the higher a
person's income, the more friendly he felt toward the
United States.

Quadros met complaints about his shift to the political

center by saying his foreign policy was "grown-up, vaccinated and old enough to vote." But it was not inoculated against Washington's disapproval or against the venom of Carlos Lacerda.

As criticism from the conservative press grew strident, Quadros sequestered himself in the presidential palace, isolated from his natural allies and lacking a way to build bridges to the Vargas coalition. In line with his opening to the Left, Quadros proposed legislation that would have raised taxes on foreign firms to 50 percent. When Ernesto (Ché) Guevara went to Uruguay for a conference of the Organization of American States, Quadros invited him to stop in Brazil on his way back to Cuba.

At that conference in the sea resort of Punta del Este, Richard Goodwin, who had promised to end the economic disparity between the Americas, met the man sworn to hold Goodwin to that promise. By the time of the conference, relations between the United States and Cuba had reached their nadir; four months earlier, Washington had tried to overthrow Castro's government.

Consequently, Goodwin was not expecting to receive in his hotel room a polished mahogany box inlaid with the Cuban seal and filled with a commodity increasingly prized in the United States. The note accompanying the Cuban cigars read: "Since I have no greeting card, I have to write. Since to write to an enemy is difficult, I limit myself to extending my hand."

Goodwin brought the cigars back to the White House and offered them to the president, who took one and lit it. After he had puffed awhile, he said to Goodwin, "You should have smoked the first one."

Goodwin recorded the episode seven years later, after John Kennedy and Ché Guevara had both been assassinated, Guevara tracked down in Bolivia with the help of the U. S. Special Forces. Another seven years after his memoir, it was clear that Castro would have had more reason than Kennedy to be wary of a gift, what with the many attempts on the Cuban's dignity and life by the CIA, including a plan to cause his beard to fall out.

Goodwin and Guevara met discreetly at Punta del Este for a long midnight talk. According to Goodwin, Guevara warned him that "there would be either leftist revolutions or rightist coups leading to leftist takeovers, and that there was a strong chance that in some countries the Communists would come to power through popular elections." Writing two years before the election of Salvador Allende in Chile, Goodwin added, "None of this has come to pass."

Guevara put forth a number of suggestions to ease relations between the two countries, including a promise to pay for the U. S. property that Cuba had expropriated. Thus, it was not an intractable foe of the United States who left the Uruguay conference and stopped in Brazil to meet with Quadros.

During Ché's visit, Quadros confirmed his "grown-up" and independent policy by presenting Ché with Brazil's highest award for foreigners, the Cruzeiro do Sul. In Guevara's life, it may have been a minor honor, but to Carlos Lacerda, the presentation was an affront to Brazil and a splendid opportunity for a fiery rant. He went on the air to accuse Quadros's minister of justice of preparing a coup d'état that would give Quadros greatly expanded powers. "The man we elected doesn't want to be president," Lacerda told a television audience seven years after he drove Vargas to suicide. "He wants to be dictator."

Lacerda spoke on a Thursday. When Quadros made his move at three o'clock the next afternoon, he might have expected that the weekend would give the nation time to rally behind him. Whatever his thinking, Quadros resigned the presidency. His message had echoes of Vargas's suicide note: "I feel crushed. Terrible forces have risen against me. I wanted Brazil for Brazilians and I confronted in that battle corruption, lies and cowardice which subordinated general interests to the appetites and the ambitions of groups of individuals, including ones from abroad."

Quadros was to learn that committing political suicide did not engender the guilt and regret that Vargas stirred by putting a bullet through his head. Both men denounced the interests arrayed against them, but in Quadros's case, rival politicians joked that while they could not identify the domestic interests, the foreign ones were Haig and Haig, Teacher's, and Johnnie Walker.

Signs of support for Quadros were few and desultory. Several labor leaders urged him to return to office. A crowd understood his references to foreign influence well enough to stone the United States embassy. But the military moved to place Quadros under guard, which stopped him from making any rallying speeches. As public attention swung to his successor, the former president was heard to ask, "Where are the six million who voted for me?"

Whether cunningly or not, before resigning Quadros had dispatched his leftist vice-president on a good-will tour of the People's Republic of China. Now it fell once again to the military, who considered themselves the supreme political arbiters, to decide whether João Goulart, freshly contaminated by his exposure to Mao Tsetung, should be permitted to return and assume the presidency. The minister of war, Odilío Denys, said Goulart should not take office. The ministers of the various military services agreed with him.

At this point, the provisional president, Pascoal Ranieri Mazzilli, told Congress of the military decision and proposed legislation to keep Goulart from office. There was a precedent for such a law, but Goulart, half a world away, had a potent ally in his brother-in-law, Leonel Brizola, the governor of Rio Grande do Sul.

No one, least of all Brizola, would deny that he was a man of the Left. At the Punta del Este conference, he had urged Brazil to side with Ché against the Alliance for Progress; but as a governor, he could bring pressure on the commander of the Third Army, stationed in the state capital of Pôrto Alegre, and the heads of the country's three other armies were wavering.

There could easily have been a civil war. Goulart's enemies claimed that he had put Communists into sensitive
labor jobs. But the real threat—to the army, to the industrialists, and to the foreign investors—was the likelihood that
under Goulart organized labor would become the domi-
nant force in Brazilian politics. In neighboring Argentina,
Juan Perón had shown even better than Vargas how sturdy
a base the shirtless ones could provide for an ambitious
politician.

After ten days of uncertainty, Congress passed an
amendment that reformed itself on a parliamentary model.
Goulart, waiting in Paris to hear his fate, would be allowed
to come back as president, but his powers would be more
those of a prime minister. When the military indicated that
the compromise satisfied them, Goulart flew on to Brasília.

Given the Brazilian fondness of the *jeito*, the face-saving
fix that circumvents every difficulty, the agreement
brought an unearned luster to all participants. The army
was credited with restraint and devotion to democratic
principles, when all the episode proved was that the plotters against Goulart were not yet strong enough to resist
him.

Goulart, accepting the compromise but chafing under it,
seemed to demonstrate a defter political touch than later
events would bear out. Meantime, he was burdened with
an agreement that, among other curtailments of presidential perogative, allowed Congress to remove his ministers
without consulting him.

Not surprisingly, the uproar clouded Lincoln Gordon's
pleasure in his appointment as ambassador. President Kennedy had sent his name to the U. S. Senate one day before
Quadros resigned.

Lauren J. Goin, usually called Jack, appreciated
early in his tour of Latin America how crucial it was for
a police adviser to be simpatico. Very likely, it was a quality of the heart, and no one could set out to learn it. But

if a foreigner made an effort to be kindly and soft-edged, Latin Americans broadened their definition of simpatico enough that he could qualify—even when, as in Goin's case, the harder outlines of his native character sometimes showed through.

Before coming to Brazil early in 1960, Goin had set up the first police advisory team in Indonesia, and served on the advisory team in Turkey. Before that, he had directed the crime laboratory in Pittsburgh. It was this varied background that led Byron Engle to send him to Rio as an adviser in scientific investigations.

Goin's work took him up to the state of Minas Gerais, where he could evaluate the neophyte adviser in Belo Horizonte. They had long discussions about the job, and Goin was able to caution Mitrione against several pitfalls. Goin had seen men isolate themselves within the U. S. embassy compound, spending their off-duty hours exclusively with their countrymen. Such advisers did not last long in Engle's program.

Mitrione would heed that message. He was eager to make good—nine lives depended upon it—but even if he had not been ambitious, he would have found little reason to seek out his compatriots. Those from the State Department often shared their superior's opinion that the police program did not belong under the aegis of foreign aid, and probably did not belong in Brazil at all. Others, from the Central Intelligence Agency, whom the police adviser might have expected to be his natural allies, often let the policeman know that if a partnership existed, the ex-cops were very junior partners.

Sometimes the distinction between the CIA and the police adviser was made even more peremptory. Arriving in São Paulo in 1960, Maurice E. Calfee, a retired officer from the Los Angeles Police Department, was immediately set straight about the limits on his duties. He was told to stay away from the military police: the CIA was working with them. He should deal exclusively with the civil police. But in Brazil the Policia Militar, despite its name, was the main law-enforcement body in the civilian sector. Calfee understood that he was being shut out from any useful work, and after two frustrating years he resigned.

The attitude of the natives, the *brasileiros*, was entirely different. Not only was their tradition hospitable, but they could profit materially from a hearty friendship with their advisers. The Yankees brought a cornucopia of equipment to lavish upon them. Just reading through the catalogues about radios and radars and fingerprinting kits could make a police lieutenant see himself, if not a master detective, at least equal to apprehending a devious and resourceful criminal.

A strain of inferiority ran through the Latin American police departments, and it was particularly so in Brazil. Pay was low, nepotism was taken for granted, prestige was nonexistent. The young Brazilians around Belo had a saying: If you're too clumsy to be a soccer player and too stupid to get into the university and too ugly to play in a rock band, you can always join the police.

Brazilian officials acknowledged that their patrolmen were not of top quality, yet they could not help teasing these powerful North Americans who came to improve their performance. Sometimes it even seemed that the U. S. advisers were the pupils, that they were being measured continually against the ethic of the host country. Were they tough? Gentle? Intelligent? Humble? A few years later, thousands of young U. S. lieutenants and captains faced that same judging process in South Vietnam.

Jack Goin had warned Mitrione of the polite hazing he would receive. To minimize his gaffes, Mitrione conducted official business through an interpreter, a nineteen-year-old student, Ricard Pedro Neubert. To Ricard, everything about the Mitrione family was attractive, particularly the two teenaged daughters. But he knew his station and never approached either girl.

Other young people were also drawn to the bustling

household. At first they could not see past Mitrione's imposing bulk and his big cigars, and they called him the
Mafia Chief. Once he ceased to scare them, they hung
about the house every day.

Ricard had found that house, clean and pretty, in Belo's
Anchieta district. The yard was surrounded by a low wall
with an iron railing, which was for decoration, not security. Very few Brazilians knew that the United States had
sent a police chief to Belo, and those aware of Mitrione's
presence were entirely friendly.

Set near the top of a hill, the house had been faced with
blue-and-cream-colored tiles and built around an inner
patio. There were four bedrooms, which required some
doubling up, and two more rooms were set aside for the
maids. Outside, the road was made of cobblestones, and
there were three lime trees and a mango. The flowers
bloomed purple and pink.

Yet Hank Mitrione was not always happy. Buying meat
at an outdoor stall did not meet a Midwestern mother's
standard for hygiene, and running the drinking water
through a charcoal filter was a daily nuisance. She was not
always silent about the discomforts. To Brazilians, who
believed that the price for peace was never too high, her
complaints were sad to hear, and they felt that Mitrione
was very patient with her. Only once did an outsider hear
him say, aggrieved, "In the States, I couldn't make fifteen
thousand dollars a year, and you couldn't have two maids.
Here in Belo, we can."

At the office, Mitrione's routine ran smoothly. His duties
were clear-cut: to assist the police of the state of Minas
Gerais in making their investigations more scientific, to
improve communications throughout the state, and to develop a new regional police academy.

In Brazil, with its history of military takeovers, the civil
police were under the wing of the army. The Policia Militar (PM) might be only the regular cops on the beat, but

their commander was a political appointee, generally a career army colonel.

Back home, Mitrione had seen the effect of the Republican party's stranglehold on the police. It became his announced creed that in Brazil, policemen must be apolitical, and he expounded to the Brazilians the virtues of disinterested policemen enforcing the law impartially. His listeners, applauding the ideal, could not always see how Mitrione's sermon applied to life in Belo Horizonte.

Mitrione himself could not at all times meet his own high standards. In the police laboratory there worked a Brazilian chemist who, if not formally a socialist, believed that Brazil's wealth had to be radically redistributed before the social system would be a just one. Conversations with that man invariably left Mitrione infuriated. Although he had learned to harness his hot temper, once back in his own office, he would stew over their latest exchange and complain to Ricard Neubert, "That man's impossible! He's all wrong about it! He's not thinking right!"

Dealing with Richmond's city government had taught Mitrione how to extract increased funds for his department and the off-duty time for him and his officers to further their professional education. In Belo, he refined those skills until, by 1961, the Brazilian police were awed by the equipment arriving for their new police academy and criminalistics lab: $100,000 worth of expensive cameras, projectors and screens, fingerprinting kits, and photographic equipment. At the FBI academy, Dan had acquired an enthusiasm for practice shooting. Now the AID program was sending targets and ammunition. For crime-scene training, there were kits of tools and bags for taking soil, wood slivers, and hair back to the laboratory; and at the lab itself, a new spectrograph, worth thousands of dollars, for analyzing raw material.

The traffic department first received simple gear, such as tubes to lay in the street to measure speed. Within a few months, Mitrione had produced for them electronic equipment, and radios for each of the few police cars. There was not much that could be done for the cop on the beat. He still had to call headquarters from the public phone on the corner.

Mitrione had kept his faith in the value of appearances. When the police in Belo received new uniforms, he considered the news worth writing home about. He had been sending occasional letters to the *Pal-Item* that could be converted to news stories, a way of keeping his name alive in Richmond should he want to return when his tour ended. Now he told the folks at home that in their new uniforms, the Brazilian police "will look like Richmond's finest."

He added, "Our public relations program includes changing the traffic uniforms from a plain sack-type cloth to blue, made of a better material. The public will have more respect for the police and we expect morale to be higher."

Other advisers, visiting Belo, very occasionally lured Mitrione out to explore the local night life, but left to himself, he preferred to stay home with his family. Though Hank now had maids, she was one of the rare U. S. wives without a Brazilian cook. This was the result of her desire to please her husband. In Richmond, she had mastered the succulent dishes that Maria Mitrione had brought from Bisaccia, and Dan wanted her to continue doing the cooking.

As a result, Mitrione was getting stout in the languid Brazilian sunshine. To his Brazilian hosts, he remained the model of professional behavior: a democrat who never failed to greet the elevator operator by name; a Catholic who never missed Sunday mass; a family man, and yet not above taking a peep with the other men into the windows across the street from his office.

Oscar Niemeyer, the architect who designed Brasília,

had begun his career in Belo, and the curved walls of one of his futuristic apartment buildings seemed to undulate like waves of the sea. To preserve the line, and disdaining prudery, Niemeyer drafted tiers of unshielded bathrooms, and all work stopped in Mitrione's office whenever a woman worth coveting decided to shower during office hours.

About this time, political tensions were rising elsewhere in Belo, unnoticed by Mitrione, who did not read the local papers. In the fall of 1961, a division commander of Brazil's First Army gave a speech in Belo before a conference of the state's Commercial Association. Although the First Army was based in Rio, its crack fourth division made its headquarters in Belo, and its commander, João Punaro Bley, was a figure to contend with.

The meeting of businessmen and factory owners had been underwritten by a right-wing chain of newspapers, the *Diarios Associados*. Their publisher, Francisco de Assis Chateaubriand, was being given funds by the CIA to promote anti-communism; predictably Punaro Bley gave an anti-Communist speech. But its partisanship went beyond even what a conservative audience expected to hear publicly from a general on active duty. Punaro Bley claimed that Communists had penetrated every level of Brazilian society and posed a serious threat to democracy.

A fierce young socialist, José María Rabello, published a weekly paper in Belo Horizonte called *Binomio*, Two Names. Intrigued by the coverage given the speech by *Estado do Minas*, the leading newspaper of the chain sponsoring the conference, Rabello assigned a reporting team to check into the general's background.

Binomio attracted young leftists reveling in the freedom that the press had been enjoying since the Vargas dictatorship. Rabello's police reporter for a time was Fernando Gabeira, a nineteen-year-old from the provinces, who was using Belo as a way station on the road to a newspaper career in Rio.

As a boy, Fernando had watched the men of his town who owned small looms forced out of business by the textile corporations. One by one, the men had to sell their tools and go to work in the factories. Sometimes they struck for higher pay; always the police took the side of the mill owners.

In high school, one of Fernando's teachers had mused aloud about how it happened that some men were rich and other men poor. If you were to put them all on an island, the teacher said, the same men would become rich again because they worked hard. The poor were lazy.

Fernando had raised his hand and said, "I can only say that in my town, the poor work very hard."

That was the shared attitude at *Binomio*, and the reporters sent to investigate the general undertook the task gleefully. Among other things, they found that in the early stages of the Second World War, he had been active in the fascist Integralists. *Binomio* published the details of the general's background, including the fact that as governor of the state of Espirito Santo, he had constructed concentration camps for his political enemies—the liberals and the anti-Nazis. The dispatch was headed: "Who Is the General Punaro Bley? A Democrat Today, a Fascist Yesterday."

Soon after the story appeared, the general rang Rabello and demanded to see him. "You have published an article injurious to me," he said. "The affair must be resolved."

Rabello agreed to meet him but only at the newspaper office.

General Punaro Bley arrived within the hour. Rabello had prepared some remarks on the freedom of the press. The general interrupted him. "I don't want an explanation," he said. "I've come to give you a lesson."

With that, he bolted around the desk and grabbed Rabello by the neck.

The general, at fifty-three, was a bull of a man. He

seemed to expect that the twenty-four-year-old editor, with horn-rimmed glasses and an intellectual brow, would be intimidated by his age or his rank or at the least by his indignation. Instead, when the general threw a punch, Rabello returned it, blackening Punaro Bley's eye and cutting his lip.

The general had left an aide in the hall. Now, alerted by the tumult, the captain burst in, followed by Rabello's editorial staff. All of them became witnesses to Punaro Bley's ignominy. Worse still, the presence of photographers guaranteed that the general's wounds would be on the front page of every newspaper he despised.

More cursing followed, and more shouts. When Punaro Bley finally retreated, Rabello called the police. He wanted to be sure that they understood that the general had been the aggressor. He had not been reassured to hear the captain vowing as he led his bloodied superior to the elevator, "This is going to continue."

It took about two hours before three hundred junior officers from Belo's army barracks surrounded the block around *Binomio* and stopped traffic in every direction. Shock troops raced up the stairs, threw open the door, and set about destroying the office. It was nearly Christmas; they ground the staff Christmas tree into the floor. When the typewriters were demolished, they broke the toilets. Outside on the street, bazookas had been set up near the machine-gun installations. The entire military action took two hours.

The governor of Minas Gerais, an elderly and conservative politician named Magalhães Pinto, wanted to avoid a showdown with the army, but he did promise the *Binomio* staff that Belo's police would protect them against further reprisals. The damage had run to $150,000, but Rabello knew he could never win a judgment against the general or his troops.

However, he had one ally, who proved better protection than a pledge from the governor. Shortly before the episode, João Goulart had unexpectedly become president. When any Brazilian president spoke, especially Goulart, he could not take for granted that the nation's generals would heed him. Still, he decided to move against Punaro Bley. To punish the general's abuse of power, Goulart transferred him to a less prestigious post and somehow made the demotion stick. Punaro Bley chose instead to take an early retirement.

For the leftists of Minas Gerais, the *Binomio* affair had been an ugly reminder of the hostility the military felt toward them. Yet there was one redeeming aspect: Brazil was still a democracy, and Brazil's president had acted to uphold the rights of one civilian.

When a team of undergraduate scientists journeyed up from Rio to Minas Gerais, Dan Mitrione was already deep in his efforts to improve the Belo police. The students composed another sort of advisory mission: they wanted to find ways to make the state's iron-ore deposits, the largest in the world, turn a healthier profit for Brazil.

One team member was a small, round-faced, wavy-haired student named Marcos Arruda. Enrolled in the school of geology at the University of Rio de Janeiro, Marcos did not look like either a revolutionary or a martyr; and certainly during the years of the Goulart regime, his questioning of Brazil's social order was tentative and very respectful.

For example, Marcos and some friends mentioned to the director of their school that because geology courses always ran from 7 A.M. to 5:30 P.M., poor students, those who had to work to sustain themselves, were automatically barred from the profession.

"Yes," agreed the director, Othon Leonardos, "it is elitist. But geologists must be cultured. They must have money enough to travel.

"You talk about the poor," the director continued, pursuing a favorite subject, "they are good for nothing, consuming and never producing. They should jump from the hills, kill themselves.

"But," Leonardos concluded, chiding them for the question, "geology has nothing to do with politics. Our role is to go up in the hills and see how beautiful the Earth is and say, 'I understand it.'"

Lofty words, but to Marcos not inspiring. Nor could he quite accept the distinction the director drew between geology and politics. Leonardos was both a member of the commission within the Ministry of Education that laid down policy for the teaching of geology throughout Brazil and a director of Mannesmann, the German mining company.

What to make of this? When Petrobras, the federal petroleum company, offered the school two scholarships, Leonardos made the selection and gave one grant to the son of a general and the other to the son of Brazil's vice-president. Once again a student delegation called on the director and asked why he had chosen those recipients. "They need money, too," the director replied, no doubt being mischievous, "to put gas in their cars."

That answer drove Marcos into student politics. He joined his classmates in making independent mining studies; and by the time they traveled to Minas Gerais, they had uncovered some troubling statistics: 97.3 percent of Brazil's iron ore was being mined by companies controlled abroad—from the United States there was Hanna Mining, U. S. Steel, and Bethlehem Steel; from Germany, Mannesmann; from Belgium, Belgomineira.

In Minas Gerais, Marcos's assignment was to survey the iron-ore deposits. At first look, the ownership in Minas belied the earlier findings, for the bulk of the deposits belonged to a Brazilian municipal company. Probing deeper, Marcos and his team discovered that the best ore, the ore of the middle layers, had been bought up by Hanna. For the past ten years, the United States had been sending geologists to the region. During that same period, the foreign companies were bidding on concessions. Hanna had selected areas that the Brazilian government seldom visited, areas not known to contain ore at all. When the survey was finally released, it turned out that Hanna controlled the choicest deposits. Marcos could only conclude that the U. S. companies had enjoyed access to surveys in progress while the Brazilian government had not.

Armed with their findings, Marcos and the other students campaigned for a state monopoly, like Petrobras, to be called Mineirobras. It would mine the nation's ore for the good of all the people. Even in the Goulart era, that idea sounded radical. It was true that the group included two or three members of the Communist party. For that matter, Marcos, as a practicing Christian, considered himself an equally legitimate heir to heretical opinions.

CHAPTER

3

IN MID-OCTOBER 1961, Lincoln Gordon, his wife, and their youngest daughter finally arrived in Brazil. From the day that Goulart made his first cabinet appointments, Gordon had begun to take heart. He considered several of the new ministers mediocre—Tancredo Neves, for example—but others, particularly Roberto Campos, a former student of his, looked extremely promising.

Had the professor been grading Goulart's appointments publicly, Brazilians might have noticed that the further to the Left a nominee leaned, the less chance he had of receiving a passing mark. The apolitical Democrat from Massachusetts was suspicious of reformers with too much zeal.

Despite the creation of Brasília, foreign diplomats had proved loath to leave Rio. The U. S. embassy continued to operate in a ten-story building with a heart-stopping view of Guanabara Bay and Pão de Açúcar, the mountain the Brazilians saw as a sugarloaf. But President Goulart was in Brasília, and after a few days Gordon traveled there to introduce himself.

Whereas Goulart has never published his opinion of the ambassador, Gordon has given freely of his first impressions of Goulart. His countrymen called him a *primitivo*. Gordon's translation would have been closer to lout. The

Brazilian president may have had a law degree, but Gordon sniffed to himself that he had probably bought it.

Goulart was extroverted. He was crude. He was a *gaúcho*. Such was Gordon's first summation, and he never found reason to change it. Gordon also detected that pleasure in manipulating men which had made Goulart so valuable to Vargas. In short, Gordon found the president of Brazil just the sort of ignorant political boss he despised.

Even had Goulart been more polished, those early conversations would still have been rough-hewed. Gordon had just begun Portuguese lessons; yet Goulart, trusting to intimacy and fellow feeling, preferred to talk without an interpreter.

For Gordon, even the president's cordiality could be awkward. "I'm coming down to Rio, and I hope you'll come and call on me," Goulart told the ambassador. "I really want to talk with you, not just as president but as the leader of a great popular political party."

Gordon took that last remark for a touch of presumption, as though Goulart were comparing himself to John Kennedy and suggesting that the workers' party (PTB) was comparable to the Democratic party. The invitation also suggested that Goulart wanted to confide candidly in the ambassador about the political considerations that would be guiding his administration, and Gordon was leery about being drawn into that sort of intimacy.

Perhaps most important in shaping Gordon's attitude was the fact that Goulart was not trusted, either by Washington or by those proven friends of the United States, the Brazilian military. Gordon consequently held the president at arm's length while, at the same time, striving to be correct with Goulart's enemies.

The opposition lost no time in making itself known to the new ambassador. One foe, a right-wing admiral named Sílvio Heck, had a social connection to Gordon. In 1946, his niece had met Gordon at a United Nations meeting on atomic energy, and they had renewed acquaintance thirteen years later when Gordon toured Brazil on a Ford Foundation assignment. Now she called to say that her uncle wished to meet with him privately at a party she was giving. Gordon agreed.

At the right moment, the ambassador and the admiral withdrew to a side room, and Heck came quickly to the point. "You know," he said, "when I was the Navy Minister with Quadros, I opposed Goulart. He's a Communist, and he wants to deliver the country to them. To you, he may appear as a moderate. But the sooner he's thrown out, the better.

"We've polled the services," Heck continued, "and seventy-five percent of the army, much of the air force, and eighty percent of the navy feel that way about him. We are organizing. We do not need help. But we are hoping that when the day comes, the United States will take an understanding view."

"That's very interesting," said the new U. S. ambassador. Admiral Heck, having had his audience, did not press then for a commitment.

The next day, Gordon called in his deputy and the CIA station chief, and told them to check the validity of Heck's estimates. They reported back that there was no powerful coup brewing, that Heck represented a handful of officers. Gordon filed that information. He did not then, or later, as the approaches became more frequent, inform Goulart or any of Goulart's advisers about the conspiracy being plotted against Brazil's democracy.

It had been predictable that the sort of Brazilians Gordon had met over the years would oppose the government to which he was now accredited. His acquaintance with a man named Paulo Ayres, Jr., dated from 1959, when Ayres was head of the Brazilian-American cultural center in São Paulo. He was also a businessman, young and very personable, with the added grace of speaking good English.

When Gordon was asked to suggest a Brazilian delegate to a multinational business conference, he remembered his young friend, and he and Ayres had a pleasant reunion in Washington.

Now, back as ambassador, Gordon looked up Ayres and met his friends from São Paulo's corporate life. In good time, Ayres described to Gordon a political organization he was sponsoring with the cumbersome but innocuous name of the Institute for Social Research Studies (in Portuguese, IPES).

Had Gordon's interests at home been more political, the structure and goals of IPES might possibly have sounded familiar, for in 1958, a Massachusetts candy maker had founded an organization of businessmen who were concerned about communism, especially three years later, when a new administration replaced the old. That was Robert Welch's John Birch Society and the administration was John Kennedy's.

In Brazil, the motivating spirit of IPES was Glycon de Paiva, a clever mining engineer from Minas Gerais. From the day of Goulart's inaugural, de Paiva had known that the new president was a menace who must be removed.

De Paiva was often said to look like a Protestant minister, a comparison meant to underline his austerity and zeal. As he made the rounds of Rio's major industrialists, spreading his warning, he made many converts, but he never deluded himself that these men, although they made lavish gifts to his crusade, shared his ideological hatred for communism. Theirs was a different motive, and he got his best results by keeping the message simple and pungent: Goulart and his kind want to take away what you have.

Sounding that alarm, de Paiva had no trouble raising each month the equivalent of $20,000. He began to expand the scope of his organization. Paulo Ayres, Jr., became a chief IPES representative in São Paulo. In Belo Horizonte, as notoriously conservative as Dallas, Texas, de Paiva also recruited fruitfully.

De Paiva's greatest inspiration was to hire as his chief of staff a retired army general, Golbery do Couto e Silva.

Taking over half of the twenty-seventh floor of an office building in central Rio, de Paiva encouraged the general to compile dossiers on everyone he considered an enemy of the nation. Before they were done, they had files on 400,000 Brazilians.

Their standard method was to put informers on the IPES payroll, many of them soldiers on active duty. Given the army's role in Brazilian politics, de Paiva wanted to be sure that key men throughout the services remained loyal to the abstraction called the Brazilian nation rather than to the president who temporarily led it.

De Paiva also paid informers in factories, schools, and government offices. Petrobras, the state oil company, was his special target because he suspected Goulart of riddling its organization with his own supporters. As for the universities, they suffered from an affliction that de Paiva diagnosed as "too much freedom."

The priesthood was another disappointment to de Paiva, largely because of the influx of foreign clerics. By his calculation, half of Brazil's 13,000 priests were not Brazilians at all. They were outsiders from countries like Belgium and France, which could not support the number of priests their seminaries were graduating. These men brought alien ideas to Brazil. At the very time that the Brazilian masses seemed to be losing their devotion to the Church's high spiritual principles, these radicals arrived to hasten the process. Sadly, de Paiva had come to conclude that in his struggle against the forces of communism, religion was a negligible ally.

To evade detection and possible reprisals against IPES, its directors tried to represent it as an educational organization and, in fact, gave money to a campaign to reduce illiteracy among poor children. Such donations were only to shore up its façade. IPES's real work was organizing against Goulart and maintaining dossiers.

De Paiva acknowledged that his reaction against state socialism was largely visceral, and as IPES flourished he felt the need for a crash course in economic theory. To instruct him, he occasionally imported Delfim Neto, a distinguished economist from São Paulo. For airfare and fifty dollars, Delfim lectured one hour on the merits of the free enterprise system.

IPES could afford the tutorial. In Brazil, printing the telephone business directories was a lucrative private business; and its owner, Gilbert Huber, Jr., was one of the men who supported de Paiva handsomely. Huber was also financially involved with American Light and Power, of which 80 percent was owned by U. S. interests. Brazil's banks and large construction companies were equally open-handed.

Nor did de Paiva meet resistance from the most significant embassy in Brazil. Through Paulo Ayres and General Golbery, de Paiva was introduced to Ambassador Gordon, and the two men would meet from time to time. Gordon found de Paiva a smart fellow who was managing IPES with great skill, whereas de Paiva decided that Gordon was a very simple man who, pressed too hard over cocktails or dinner, was sure to retreat into, "Put yourself in my place. I'm the ambassador here." De Paiva felt Gordon meant that he would be helpful so long as he was not embarrassed publicly.

Aristoteles Luis Drummond, a student in Rio and an aspiring comrade-in-arms to de Paiva's cause, tapped an even wealthier treasury than Gilbert Huber's. By chance, Drummond stumbled on the Central Intelligence Agency.

Skinny, intense, proud of his middle-class heritage, Aristoteles was an ardent conservative, and his hero was Silvío Heck. If de Paiva brought to mind a sharper Robert Welch, Drummond had his parallel in the William F. Buckley, Jr., of the 1950s, the precocious young man who attacked Yale University as a morass of liberalism and rose to the defense of Senator Joseph McCarthy.

At eighteen, Aristoteles founded an organization of like-minded youth, Grupo de Ação Patriotica (GAP). Its natural enemy was the national student union (UNE). Since students world-wide leaned toward the political Left, GAP was not a magnet for new members. Aristoteles found it wise to pass out his leaflets selectively, and when he used spray paint to cover walls with the message *GAP with Heck*, he did it at night. Although it was calculated that GAP had 130 "hard-core" members and about five thousand "sympathizers," these persons seldom donated money to their cause. While de Paiva was taking over expensive suites in a skyscraper, Aristoteles was operating from his parents' apartment on Ipanema Beach.

One day a local radio show interviewed him for ten minutes, during which time he expounded on GAP's determination to defend liberty and property, and his conviction that only the military could be trusted to secure either commodity. The Voice of America re-broadcast the interview.

That exposure brought Aristoteles a call from the U. S. embassy requesting an appointment. Two men duly arrived at the Drummond apartment; and although in Latin America CIA operatives were seen and sworn to in the least likely places, Aristoteles had no doubts that these particular men were from the agency. They questioned him closely about his political views, then they went away. A few days later, they returned. Aristoteles observed that they committed nothing to paper and considered them worthy of 007, the popular fictional spy.

"Can we help you?" one man asked. Aristoteles said he would appreciate their help. "We'll get books for you to distribute."

It was a commitment less trifling than it sounded. A few weeks later, a truck delivered to the Drummond apartment a load of 50,000 books. True, they were not thick—paperback tracts with such titles as *China: Communists in Perspective*, by A. Doak Barnett; *The Political War: The Arm of*

International Communism, by Suzanne Labin; and best of all for paying off intracollegiate enmities, an attack on the national students union, *UNE: Instrumento de Subersão.* GAP put this free literature into the hands of high school and college students throughout the industrial triangle.

As Aristoteles labored to change the complexion of the campuses, de Paiva was beginning to recognize that housewives were particularly receptive to warnings that godless communism was destroying Brazilian society. He set up women's societies in the major cities. In Rio, it was the Women's Campaign for Democracy (CAMDE). He gave the women rumors to spread, stories about outrages that Goulart and his cronies were supposed to be planning. "Good gossip," de Paiva called it.

Although de Paiva concentrated on disaffected military men and pious housewives, civilians were also enrolling in the conspiracy against Goulart through a front, organized by the CIA, called Instituto Brasileiro de Ação Democrática (IBAD). Writers on the Goulart era later puzzled over how much Ambassador Gordon knew of the CIA's varied activities. The agency rule called for providing an ambassador with as much or as little information as he showed a willingness to tolerate. Some operations could not be disguised; during this period, the United States increased the number of its consulates around Brazil to provide cover for the CIA's expanded operations.

Certainly, Gordon knew all about IBAD, which, founded in 1959, was older than either IPES or GAP. He was aware that not only was IBAD the CIA's means of channeling money into local political campaigns but that such clandestine contributions were an absolute violation of Brazilian law.

IBAD passed on money through its two branches, Democratic Popular Action and Sales Promotion, Inc. During the elections of 1962, Popular Action underwrote the campaigns of more than one thousand candidates. In some cases, IBAD actually recruited candidates to run for office. They were given to understand that their loyalty was to IBAD, not to the political ticket with which they might be associated.

Most of the CIA's candidates, some six hundred, ran for state deputy. Another 250 ran for federal deputy, and fifteen for the federal senate. Eight ran for governorships in one of Brazil's twenty states. In Pernambuco, IBAD underwrote João Cleofas de Oliveira's campaign for governor. It was an important race because the alternative was a leftist, Miguel Arraes; and the hardscrabble northeast, while no prize in itself, was the sort of impoverished region that Washington regarded as ripe for revolution.

One indication of the Kennedy administration's concern had been a visit in June 1961 by the president's youngest brother, Edward Moore Kennedy, a twenty-nine-year-old assistant district attorney from Massachusetts. Kennedy was scheduled to meet with representatives of the Peasant Leagues, although the best-known organizer of the leagues, Francisco Julião, was out of town.

Francisco Juliano Arruda de Paula had been born into a family of sugar plantation owners, but he was no typical *senhor de engenho*, gentleman of the mill. In his adolescence, he had read a book by Friedrich Engels, and from that time on he considered himself a "man of the Left." As one of the few lawyers in the northeast who would represent the poor, the young man, nicknamed Francisco Julião, built a following and went to his state legislature in 1954 as the Brazilian Socialist party's sole successful candidate.

Landowners in the northeast still took the kingly view that God had decreed them to be wealthy, and they resisted any effort to organize the workers on their estates. The more harassed and threatened the peasants felt, the more radical their league became.

During the Eisenhower years, politicians from Brazil's

large southern cities had persuaded U. S. foreign-aid officials that the northeast was so destitute that any money
spent there would only be wasted. To Lincoln Gordon, the
best solution was a massive resettlement that would lure
farmers hundreds of miles south and west to better land.
The ambassador's wife encountered the prevailing spirit at
a dinner party when she heard wealthy Brazilians speak of
a town in the northeast. "It doesn't exist!" they said and
laughed contentedly.

The U. S. intelligence apparatus took Julião's constit-
uency more seriously. Equally suspect was an educator
named Paulo Freyre, who, under the guise of teaching
farm workers to read, was instigating them to question
their condition as chattel on the land. Were these men more
Fidel Castros? Lincoln Gordon agreed that there was no
reason to mix literacy with politics.

CIA operatives began to distribute leaflets promoting
Julião's appearance at rallies he knew nothing about. The
farmers would come out in droves to see their champion
but he would not appear, and somehow a fight would
break out. Rumors were also circulated painting both Julião and Goulart as cuckolds. Ambassador Gordon was not
averse to gossip and readily passed along stories about Goulart and his wife: that he had blackened her eyes, that she
was having an affair with an air-force major. Gordon knew
how such stories wounded a man of Goulart's honor. As
for Julião, although he and his wife, Alexina, living in a land
that did not recognize divorce, apparently had agreed on
what came to be called an open marriage, stories of her
affairs had never circulated until Julião became a security
risk to the CIA.

(Years later, a Brazilian journalist traveling in Pernambuco heard of the CIA's compiling and printing of false
documents to prove that Julião was a Communist. Other
events overtook that particular strategy.)

For the CIA, there were many enemies in Pernambuco
besides Freyre and Julião. By early 1962, the agency had

two full-time men working out of the consulate in Recife, the state capital. Other CIA agents were placed within such seemingly straightforward groups as the Cooperative League of the United States of America (CLUSA) and the American Institute of Free Labor Development (AIFLD).

AIFLD was a creature of the early sixties, a merger of talent and funds from the CIA, the AFL-CIO, and some sixty U. S. corporations, including the Anaconda Company, I. T. T., and Pan American World Airways. Its purpose, according to President Kennedy, was to stop Castro from undermining the Latin American labor movement. Yet, at least one U. S. embassy labor attaché, a veteran of the union movement in the United States, felt a pang in watching AIFLD disrupt Brazil's progress in labor organizing under the guise of protecting the workers from communism. By 1963, in addition to its field work, AIFLD was arranging a training session in Washington for thirty-three trustworthy labor leaders, who then returned to Brazil and took clandestine roles in the anti-Goulart conspiracy.

The farm workers of the northeast, then, had reason to be suspicious of outsiders and particularly of all police, whom they regarded as the agents of their enemies. During Ted Kennedy's visit, their spokesman asked that his brother withdraw the U. S. police advisers.

When Miguel Arraes won the governorship the next year, he let it be understood that he did not want Byron Engle's men in his state. The Office of Public Safety took a mild line officially: We don't have enough advisers to cover all of Brazil in any event. Of course we shall limit them to more friendly states. But in Washington, the incident confirmed Arraes as an enemy.

Despite differences in age and occupation, most plotters against the Brazilian president shared a common estimate of their fellow citizens. Aristoteles Drummond said

gently that Brazilians did not understand politics. De Paiva
was blunter: Brazil was not ready for democracy.

The military, whether on active duty or in the reserve,
found de Paiva's thinking congenial. At Listas Telefônicas
Brasileiras S. A., printers of the Yellow Pages, Heitor Herrera, a retired general active in the campaign against Goulart, felt it was inevitable and only proper that he and his
fellow army officers lead the nation to its destiny. Perhaps
it was only an accident of history, but they were better
equipped for the task than any other element in society.
Herrera did not maintain that military officers were
smarter, merely that they were better trained; and that
training, which fitted them best to cope with the modern
world, they owed largely to the United States. Herrera was
proud enough of his stint at the U. S. Command and General Staff College at Fort Leavenworth, Kansas, to keep his
diploma framed on an office wall.

Few Brazilians would dispute that training at the hands
of the United States left Latin American officers, whether
from the army or the police, with a new sense of direction
and authority. One reason was the care and attention that
U. S. training programs lavished on their political thinking.
For instance, under Byron Engle's direction, a student at
the police academy devoted 165 class hours—about one
third of his total studies—to internal security and methods of investigation. Of those hours, fifty-five were given
over to warnings about the Communist party and its techniques.

In Belo Horizonte in 1963, a group of nationalistic high
school students were amazed to find the young policemen
in their neighborhoods, once the butts of so many jokes,
returning from the Inter-American Police Academy in
Panama with a new swagger. One such student questioned
a recent graduate and found that he now saw himself as
marching in the front line against communism. He had also
brought back a profound distrust of President Goulart.

These attempts by Washington to instill pride and duty

into Brazil's uniformed forces dated back more than forty years, from the moment the first U. S. Naval Mission in Latin America was established in Brazil in 1922. Until then, Brazilian officers had trained either in Germany or with the French, who maintained a mission in Brazil between 1919 and 1940.

The Second World War gave Washington a justification for expanding its influence even more widely in the Brazilian forces. Military planning was coordinated by a Joint Brazilian–United States Military Commission (JBUSMC). By the war's end, Brazilian training and equipment so thoroughly followed the U. S. model that nationalists protested that the only thing Brazilian in their Independence Day parade was the flag.

In the first years of peace, the United States unloaded surplus infantry and air-force equipment on Brazil at about 10 percent of cost. Among other things, the Brazilians bought more than one hundred combat aircraft. At that discount, naturally they could hardly expect the latest models, and it had been standard practice from the early days of the Krupp dynasty for munitions makers to dump their obsolete equipment on the dictators of Latin America. The weapons, after all, were more likely to be a caudillo's means for keeping his own people quiescent than for waging war across his borders.

In 1949, the Pentagon helped Brazil to set up and staff a copy of the U. S. National War College, the Escola Superior de Guerra. JBUSMC had outlived the war; and in 1954, it was registered with the United Nations as a permanent agency for the handling of military sales and assistance.

At the same time, the U. S. began creating a military-training infrastructure for the continent as a whole. In 1949, the School of the Americas opened at Fort Gulick in the Panama Canal Zone, giving courses exclusively in Spanish and Portuguese. So many of its ambitious graduates went home imbued with a fervor that brooked no civil interference that the school became known throughout the continent as *escuela de golpes*, school of coups.

In 1952, a jungle warfare school was opened at Fort Sherman, also in Panama. Training courses for Latin American flyers at Albrook Air Force Base in Panama dated back to 1943, though student pilots had to await the onset of the Vietnam war to be instructed in the dropping of napalm.

The most prestigious of all training went on at Fort Leavenworth, and many of the officers who were conspiring now to challenge Goulart had trained there. "Those men left Leavenworth," remarked a U. S. general who once served there, "with a burning ambition to identify with the United States and to be loved by their American counterparts."

With such support from the world's strongest power, serving in the Brazilian army or navy became a desirable middle-class way of life. After the home-grown military academies, a promising officer went for graduate work to a Brazilian military college or one in the United States, where he would be exposed to economics, social sciences, and administration. Men like Herrera never questioned that those years of training outstripped anything a man could receive at the civilian universities, which were hidebound, traditional, stuck in the liberal arts of the last century. Only the military was training men for today and tomorrow; the proof was the speed with which a retiring officer could find a well-paying job in industry, either Brazilian or foreign-owned.

Even when an officer did not get to the top school at Leavenworth, training in the United States could change his life. Alfredo Poeck, the son of a physics professor, went to the Special Warfare School at Fort Bragg in 1961, after he graduated from the Brazilian military academy. His three-month course in propaganda and psychological warfare at Bragg opened a whole new career to him.

Poeck was tall for a Brazilian officer, the inheritance of

German parents. He had a receding hairline, his eyes were weak and his chin negligible. He was also methodical and hard-working, and he found the twelve hours of training each day at Bragg pleasurable, even at their harshest.

Poeck was especially struck by the competence of the CIA men he met, then and later. He decided it was the best intelligence service in the world and regretted that Brazil had no counterpart. Poeck was starting to believe the adage "Man is an unviable social product," but in the chaos of Goulart's democracy, it was hard for an officer like young Poeck to see how he could use his psychological warfare training and his dedication to better his country.

The strong government that appealed to many military officers was not the sort that Goulart had in mind. He had always warned that he did not intend to be a Queen of England, a mere figurehead; and by 1962, he had resolved to sponsor a referendum that would restore his full powers. To marshal support, or at least to defuse Washington's hostility, Goulart went to the White House in April to call on Jack Kennedy.

In their talks, Goulart and Kennedy discussed the ballot initiative to return his full authority. Goulart also put forth a plan for the peaceable buying up of the foreign utilities operating in Brazil. He seemed to want to avoid the outright expropriations that had helped to sour relations with Cuba. When the talks adjourned, Kennedy agreed to a visit in July.

Upon Goulart's return to Brazil, he may have felt that his politics of conciliation with Washington had gone too far, and he compensated with a rousing May Day speech that caused any small hope around the U. S. embassy to wane once more. Nonetheless, Lincoln Gordon had to go on meeting with Goulart; it was his job. And he found the Brazilian president, if seldom admirable, full of surprises.

At the time of the Missile Crisis in October 1962, Gordon went to brief Goulart on the presence of Soviet missiles in Cuba. He took along Lieutenant Colonel Vernon A. (Dick) Walters, the new military attaché. Through his service with the Brazilian Expeditionary Force during the Second World War, Walters was the best-connected U. S. official in Brazil, being particularly close to an army general named Humberto Castelo Branco.

Walters possessed a natural flair for languages. He had been Richard Nixon's interpreter during the trip to South America that saw the vice-president insulted and stoned. Sometimes Walters would worry aloud to his friends that his extreme facility as an interpreter had slowed down his promotion to more substantial assignments.

Goulart listened to the ambassador's report, interrupting only to say "I thought Rusk said lately that those arms were purely defensive."

Gordon thought, So he is aware of what's going on. "Yes," he replied, "but now we have evidence to the contrary."

"Well, Ambassador," Goulart said, "if that's true, it's not just a threat to you; it's a threat to all of us. Be assured of our solidarity in this matter."

This momentary rapport was not enough to temper Gordon's conviction that the Brazilian president himself was the greatest danger to his country's democracy. Goulart might not be a Communist, but he would try to emulate Vargas and stage a coup within his own government to obtain even greater powers. Since he was so erratic and inept, that move would only open the way for a Communist takeover of the country.

Because men who already hold their country's highest office rarely overthrow their own government, there was no word Gordon and his advisers could find to describe what they accused Goulart of plotting. It fell to the ambassador to invent a term, and he took pride in its aptness and ingenuity. Anyone working from beneath a government to overthrow it was engaged in "subversion." Therefore, Goulart's plot was "superversion."

John Kennedy chose not to repay Goulart's visit. Instead, he sent his brother Robert to Brazil in December of 1962. Gordon sat in on the meetings between the attorney general of the United States and the president of Brazil, and he saw that Bobby Kennedy had neither the time nor the talent for Latin indirection.

It's been a turbulent period, Kennedy told Goulart. But now with your plebiscite, you'll have a fresh start, a real opportunity for moving ahead. (A few weeks later, by a margin of 4 to 1, the voters returned full presidential powers to Goulart.)

Kennedy continued: We can offer our cooperation and support. However, should you flirt with romantic left-wing causes and give weight to the Communists and their friends—should that mood dominate—then it will be difficult for us to cooperate. That will be bad for you and bad for Brazil.

In a Brazilian phrase, Goulart asked for particulars: "*Da nomes de bos,*" he said. Give names to the bulls.

Kennedy and Gordon mentioned Almino Afonso, the labor minister, whom the U. S. embassy considered radical, and a general at Petrobras, the national oil company.

When Goulart shuffled his cabinet early the next year, he left in office the men whom Gordon had considered too far left. At dinner, Goulart asked the ambassador, "You remember the visit of Roberto Kennedy? How do you think he'll like my new cabinet?"

"It's a mixed bag," Gordon replied dryly. Once again he listed the men his embassy regarded with suspicion.

"Oh," Goulart said cheerfully, "I can keep an eye on them."

With the help of the CIA, however, Gordon had begun to put together his own file—a prosecution brief—against Goulart's government. He kept track of those unions that

Goulart was seeding with suspected Communists: the petroleum workers, the merchant marines, the railroad unions, the communications workers, the bank clerks; and Walters kept him informed of potential subversion within Goulart's military household.

Thus began a time of intense rumor. Gordon was told that Goulart confided to visitors how enormously he envied Juan Perón because in his day the Argentinian dictator was supposed to have had a button on his desk that he could push and send the port workers, for example, out on strike. And there was another button to send them all back to work. Gordon granted that the story might be apocryphal, but what a potential for despotism it revealed!

On the surface, the antagonism seemed to be one-sided. As late as mid-1963, Goulart was still sounding out the U. S. ambassador before he went forward with any reform. "What would you think," he asked Gordon, "if I were to decree that all of ten or twenty kilometers adjoining any federal public works—roads, dams, anything—would be expropriated and subdivided among the people?"

Gordon replied at measured length that if the president was truly interested in land reform, that method would seem both arbitrary and inadequate. "You'd just be left with some peculiar patterns," Gordon concluded.

Goulart agreed, but he explained that the plan would infuriate his political opponents. It was the gleeful remark of a reformer paying off old scores against his conservative opposition. All Gordon saw, with considerable disgust, were Goulart's limitations: that he would weigh an issue for its political advantages.

Meantime, Goulart's enemies continued to meet with the ambassador, not only Gordon's personal friends like Ayres and de Paiva, but others whose language seemed extremist to the ambassador, even though Gordon himself had mastered the vernacular of the Cold War, and these days was regularly tossing off phrases like "parlor pink" and "playing footsie with the Communists."

Within the Brazilian military, traditional political terms were being redefined to satisfy Goulart's opponents. By any usual measure, General Pery Constant Bevilacqua, the commander of the Second Army in São Paulo, was a conservative. Yet word soon passed through the higher echelons that he was critical of the scheming of men like Silvío Heck. Goulart might indeed be a menace, General Pery told his fellow officers, but he had been voted into office, and it was up to the people, not the army, to put him out. That earned General Pery a reputation for being disloyal.

Increasingly, the lines were drawn: the Brazilian military officers on one side and, on the other, Brizola, the labor unions, the Peasant Leagues, the majority of enlisted men, the Communists.

The showdown came in March 1964. Though the U. S. military attachés respected Silvío Heck, they knew that a successful coup could not be led by the navy but would require the army. It would especially require those commanders who were either friendly to Goulart or hesitant to see democracy overthrown.

One key figure was General Amaury Kruel, who had replaced General Pery as commander of the Second Army. Kruel's intimacy with Goulart created a problem, since São Paulo's forces were essential to the success of a coup. Walters was quoted as telling Brazilian officers that if they really wanted to be helpful, they should prevail on Kruel to join the conspiracy.

In February of that year, Philip Agee, the conscientious CIA officer from Notre Dame, had been in Washington preparing for a change of assignment. He had received two promotions in Ecuador, bringing him to GS-11, about the rank of captain in the army. His successes in Quito had included bugging diplomats' houses, suborning and bribing local officials, and disseminating lies through the Ecuadorian press. He was being rewarded with a transfer to Montevideo, with the bonus, for a Floridian like Agee, of its famous beaches.

During his stopover in Washington, Agee spent the night in McLean, Virginia, at the home of the chief of the Brazil branch of the CIA's Western Hemisphere Division. The chief, Jim Noland, briefed Agee on Brazil, the most serious problem the United States was facing in Latin America.

One pressing concern was the Brazilian parliamentary investigation into the CIA's corruption of the 1962 elections through IBAD and ADEP. The CIA had spent as much as $20 million, and everyone involved at the U. S. embassy, from Lincoln Gordon down, was worried about the incriminating evidence that might be made public.

A scandal was averted only by three lucky developments: five of the nine members of the investigating committee had themselves received CIA funds; three of the banks involved—First National City Bank, the Bank of Boston, and the Royal Bank of Canada—refused to reveal the foreign sources of money deposited in the IBAD and ADEP accounts; and best of all, President Goulart, still hoping to get along with Washington, saw to it that the final report was laundered. The offices of both IBAD and ADEP were closed. But to the disappointment of the leftists, no detailed indictment of the foreign agents who had broken Brazil's election laws was supplied.

Throughout the spring of 1964, a Pentagon specialist on Brazil was astonished at the impatience of liberal Democrats around Washington who kept nagging at him, When will your army people finally get going? But the Kennedy years had already proved that distinguished liberals, given authority overseas, could surmount their domestic principles. For example, as early as 1961, John Kenneth Galbraith had urged President Kennedy to undercut President Diem in South Vietnam and prepare the way for a more efficient regime headed by the army.

The embattled Goulart tried to hang on to the presidency with his only weapon, the support of the people. He scheduled a series of public addresses to reassure the population that rumors about his tyrannical ambitions were false. Whatever effect that strategy had on his countrymen, it only further alarmed the intelligence operatives in the Department of Defense, who saw him borrowing his tactics from Fidel Castro. "Going out to the rabble," one influential DOD analyst called it. "Inciting them. Practicing public-square democracy."

The president's brother-in-law tried to buttress Goulart's position by announcing the formation of Groups of Eleven. These groups would be armed, and should the military attempt a coup, they would be prepared to resist it.

Fernando Gabeira, the former police reporter for *Binomio* in Belo Horizonte, had come to Rio to work for *Pamfleto*, a newspaper published by Leonel Brizola. Fernando joined one of the Groups of Eleven and saw at once that Brizola's movement was all bluff. If a coup comes, each cell was told, try to resist it. But how? With what? The groups had been quickly organized; they lacked both training and equipment; and like the Peasant Leagues, they were immediately swarming with informers. Fernando was sure that the embassy knew how ill-prepared and ineffectual the Groups of Eleven were; and when he heard later that Gordon had cited them as one more excuse for the military takeover, he marveled at the ambassador's cynicism. When Gordon first arrived in Brazil, Fernando and his socialist friends had underestimated him. Just an academic, they thought, puffing on his pipe to hide his befuddlement. Now he was at the center of a plot to overthrow the government of the fifth largest nation in the world.

Goulart called a public meeting for March 13. Besides delivering a speech, he was expected to use the occasion to sign his patchy land expropriation bill. For two weeks, the opposition papers attacked the coming rally as perilous to the public order. In Rio, anonymous callers were spreading the message: "Don't go to the Communist meeting."

Out of Washington came news of the creation of the Business Group for Latin America, a linking of U. S. business and U. S. government, with David Rockefeller, president of the Chase Manhattan Bank, presiding over thirty-seven executives of such corporations as Standard Oil, United Fruit, U. S. Steel, Ford Motors, and E. I. Du Pont de Nemours and Company. The group would not be official nor was it seeking publicity. Rather than involve itself only with AID projects, it would attempt to deal with the continent's "political troubles." Late in January 1964, the members had met at the White House with President Johnson; AID Director David Bell; and Johnson's Latin American coordinator, Thomas Mann, who was no partisan of the Kennedy administration's Alliance for Progress. The businessmen reported being received with a warmth they had not felt at the White House for three years.

In the press, Goulart's enemies were now finding it ominous that he had chosen Friday, March 13, for his rally. Not, however, for superstitious reasons. Congress adjourned on March 7 and would reconvene on March 15; and the possibility existed that Goulart, in his demagogic speech, planned to declare a state of siege and keep Congress closed.

One concern of the conservatives was that if Goulart intended to inflame his audiences with the injustices of their daily life, he did not have to search for evidence. Every day the newspapers had fresh examples. The minimum wage was $23 a month; the old and disabled had to get by on even less. One pensioner who had lost his leg in a railroad accident won a slight increase in compensation when Rio's zoo director testified that it cost five times more than the man's monthly pension to feed an adult chimpanzee.

Prior to the rally, Goulart was floating new proposals: requiring corporations to make loans in order to expand credit for workers; pegging rentals on apartments to the level of the minimum wage; launching an inquiry into all government-controlled business. He had also signed a decree compelling manufacturers to add a line of shoes and fabrics priced low enough for the poor to afford. Carlos Lacerda, now the governor of the state that included Rio, protested that the result would be a uniform look, like that of women in Russia. "Choosing colors at will," Lacerda said, "is one of the rights of a democracy."

Everyone seemed to understand that a battle was looming. A spokesman for Rio's Industrial Center proposed to train families in the use of arms, since in the state of Guanabara alone, he said, there were nine thousand Communists. Other reports noted that Goulart intended to speak from the very grandstand where Vargas had proclaimed his dictatorship.

At last the evening of March 13 arrived. Brizola spoke first and attacked the Brazilian Congress as "do-nothing." This statement was designed to contrast with Goulart's action taken before the rally—his signing of the land expropriation bill. Besides the swaths along railroads and irrigation dams, the bill applied to holdings of five hundred hectares or more but only if the land was not being properly used. He also announced plans to take over the last seven private oil refineries, all Brazilian-owned, which had not yet been brought under federal control.

In his speech, Goulart reached out to his opponents on the Right, observing that General Douglas MacArthur had carried out a more radical distribution of land in Japan after the Second World War than anything in the Brazilian plan. To his supporters on the Left, Goulart pledged that this was only a first step. To all the Christian crusaders, especially de Paiva's housewives, Goulart remarked that "Christendom should not be used as a shield for privilege."

Watching Goulart's address on television, Lincoln Gordon was not mollified. First of all, those oil takeovers might not be legal. Secondly, the man standing directly behind Goulart was Darcy Ribeiro, the former rector of Brasília University, head of Goulart's domestic policy advisers, and a dangerous man. Ribeiro had amassed a number of black marks with the embassy. He had attacked the *clube dos contemplados*, the privileged ones, whom he estimated made up five million Brazilians. The other seventy-five million, Dr. Darcy said, were excluded from that club. He also announced that while he himself had no intention of joining the Communist party, it should once again be legalized in Brazil. Furthermore, he had shown the effrontery at diplomatic receptions to let Gordon understand that he felt the ambassador's meddling in Brazil's affairs had overstepped proper diplomatic limits.

Now there he was at Goulart's side. It was perfectly obvious to Gordon that Ribeiro had even written the president's speech. Gordon was flying to Washington for consultations over the weekend. As he listened to the last two thirds of Goulart's speech over the radio on the drive to Galeão Airport, he decided that the situation had finally become untenable.

In the final days before the coup, Washington was being kept well informed. Walters wired a report to the Pentagon, and Secretary of Defense Robert McNamara called in his advisers, including a senior analyst from the Defense Intelligence Agency with good contacts in Brazil. McNamara was not debating the merits of a military coup against a civilian president in a Latin American democracy. He was convinced that many confirmed Communists—or socialists; it was not important what these leftists called themselves—had a powerful influence over Goulart. McNamara was worried, however, that Goulart had already "superverted" the military, having packed it with so many of his supporters that the army would not be able to rise up against him. Gordon had recently coined another phrase for that process: "overmining" the government.

McNamara's only other misgivings seemed to concern the success of the coup. Six months earlier, the United States had collaborated with the anti-Diem forces in South Vietnam to bring down a civilian government and substitute a military man. The first, and regrettable, choice had been the hulking, easygoing general Big Minh, who was popular with his people but an anathema to the more energetic and heads-up U. S. advisers. It took a second small coup three months later to transfer power to a U. S. favorite, Nguyen Khanh.

In Brazil that particular problem would not arise. Walters had remained extremely close to Humberto Castelo Branco, who would head up the proposed coup. But would it succeed? McNamara's analyst from the Defense Department assured him it would.

The secretary then turned to General Joe Carroll for guidance. Did this fellow from army intelligence know what he was talking about? The analyst spoke up again, pointing out that in any case the United States did not want to be openly involved.

Yes, McNamara agreed, that's the ideal. Let them do it. But I'm getting gloomy reports—this general has a Communist wife, that one is a Goulart hack.

It was decided that the Brazilian military should proceed as planned. Tentative arrangements were made for secret help if that became necessary: clandestine arms dropped in by air, tankers docking at Santos with U. S. oil if the Communists succeeded in seizing Petrobras. There was even a contingency plan in the unlikely event the Russians made a move; and a Chilean journalist later reported another commitment: during his stopover in Rio in early March, General Andrew P. O'Meara, the commander of the U. S. Southern Command, had promised to fly paratroopers out of the Panama Canal Zone and drop them into any pockets of resistance left. Washington officials later stressed that two possibilities were never considered seriously: the clandestine use of U. S. troops and an attempt to talk the military out of the coup.

In Brazil, the generals themselves were getting jittery as the time neared. Goulart was obviously popular among the enlisted men, the mechanics, and technicians of the air force. What if the officers found themselves with no flightworthy aircraft? For that matter, how loyal to their commanders were the army sergeants? Or the navy's seamen?

The generals believed that the civil war they were planning could drag on for three months, even longer, but they believed their assurances from Gordon and their other U. S. contacts: if they could hold São Paulo for forty-eight hours, Washington would recognize them as Brazil's legitimate government.

The week of the coup saw a huge march against Goulart, organized by IPES. In São Paulo, tens of thousands of people walked from Praça de Republica to Praça de Sé in a March of the Family with God for Freedom. The march ended with a manifesto of São Paulo women on behalf of Christianity and democracy. However, not every Christian joined in; the archbishop of São Paulo forbade his bishops to join the march because he said it had been organized by McCann Erickson, the U. S. advertising agency.

Goulart's temperate speech had neither brought him friends nor bought him time. At a Labor party lunch on March 19, some party members asked him to close the Congress. Goulart refused categorically.

The next day, Goulart pledged to the liberal wing of the Social Democrats that he "would not agree to be a dictator even for a single minute." He wanted only to hand to his successor "a new Brazil."

But the rumors kept engulfing him. On March 22, Goulart was forced to assure the public that he was not planning to alter the constitution to extend his term. And Glycon de Paiva churned emotions further with an unproved charge that Goulart had appointed twenty-eight hard-core Communists to key positions in his government.

On March 23, when Gordon returned from Washington, Goulart's days were nearing their end. But Goulart had one last pluck at the eagle's feathers. He asked Brizola to become president of the Brazilian Labor party, perhaps hoping to bank his fire with responsibility. Brizola's faction was to form a front with the country's workers and students to retain mining concessions for Brazilians, extend the vote to illiterates, legalize the Communist party, put all foreign aid under federal control, nationalize foreign banks and insurance companies, and create a monopoly for coffee exports.

The conservatives responded by announcing an immense anti-Communist rally in Rio on April 2. That was also the target date the military had chosen to depose Goulart.

By the night of March 27, Walters was able to remove any doubt about Castelo Branco and assure the State Department that the general was firmly committing his prestige to the plot: "It is now clear that General Castelo Branco finally accepted leadership of forces determined to resist Goulart Coup or Communist takeover . . . Mar. 13 meeting and tremendous response to São Paulo March for God and Freedom have instilled new vigor into plotters."

The president was spending the Easter holidays at his vast ranch in Rio Grande do Sul. Gordon had always been a bit nettled that Goulart so clearly preferred fishing and hunting with his sons to the duties of office, that he favored the company of uncouth *gaúchos* to the conversation of diplomats. In Goulart's absence, thirty sailors had been arrested for making political statements, and three hundred marines were dispatched to arrest their protesting comrades, which they could not or would not do.

Upon his return from his ranch, Goulart set the sailors free. They marched through the streets, shouting: "Long Live Jango!" To the senior military men it verged on mutiny, and the navy minister, known for his discipline, resigned in protest.

Then, unrepentant, Goulart met on the night of March 30 with a party of more enlisted men and used the forum to attack the international oil trusts, the greedy owners of apartment houses, the dishonest tradesmen, and the foreign drug manufacturers. Those were the interests, Goulart said, like Vargas and Quadros before him, which were financing the campaign against him.

That happened on a Monday night. Early the next day, Gordon, Walters, Gordon Mein, the deputy chief of mission, and the CIA station chief gathered in the ambassador's office. The army generals of Minas Gerais were unwilling to wait another day. At 9:30 A.M., Tuesday, March 31, 1964, the U. S. embassy got word from an army contact: "The balloon is up!"

The generals marched their troops down from Minas Gerais to join what surely would be a bloody war. Some units of enlisted men were told they were heading for Rio to secure the city against Goulart's enemies, and they marched willingly, nervously, to preserve democracy.

In Washington, an array of the top representatives of the United States government (USG), were also edgy. The March 31 telcon to Gordon came from Dean Rusk, Robert McNamara, General of the Army Maxwell Taylor, General Andrew O'Meara, CIA director John A. McCone, George Ball, Thomas Mann, and special presidential assistant Ralph Dungan. The message granted that such an "opportunity" might not recur but urged the embassy not to "get the USG out in front on a losing cause."

The telcon also posed some belated questions: "Who are the possible civilians who might lay claim to presidency of new government? This does not rule out possibility of military junta as last resort but that would make U. S. assistance much more difficult. What information do you have as to military plans for action? What plans are there for interdicting possible 'break-out' of First Army from

Rio? We assume interdiction should occur in the escarp-
ment area on road between Rio and São Paulo and also on
road between Rio and Belo Horizonte. Do you have any
information as to what friendly governors and army commanders in northeast area are planning?"

The final question removed any possible misconception
about which side the United States had chosen: "Would it
be necessary for U. S. to mount large materiel program to
assure success of takeover?"

Later "Top Secret" communiqués from the Joint Chiefs
of Staff indicated how much the Pentagon was relying on
Gordon and his staff to direct the U. S. role in the coup.
One message stated that a 110-ton package of arms and
ammunition was being held at McGuire Air Force Base
pending Gordon's determination that the Brazilian military
or police required early U. S. support. In addition, a carrier
task force was continuing toward the South Atlantic
awaiting Gordon's word that port calls or other U. S.
demonstrations of naval power were definitely not wanted.
The ambassador was also asked to determine how much of
the petroleum shipment should be continued.

That night, March 31, Gordon called on Juscelino
Kubitschek. For all the accusations of corruption and the
indisputable inflation during his regime, Kubitschek remained a popular politician. Now with Goulart on his way
out, Gordon wanted Kubitschek to lobby with the Brazilian Congress to give an appearance of legality to the new
regime.

An hour before midnight that same night, General
Kruel, the most reluctant of the coup makers, finally joined
with his colleagues. Had he held out any longer, very likely
he would have been arrested by the officers around him.

If Goulart knew that the United States government was
not seamless, if he appreciated the deep division between
speeches by Kennedy or Johnson supporting social reform
and the resistance to those reforms by the U. S. business
community, the intelligence services, the Pentagon and the

police advisers, he may have assumed that a president in Washington spoke for the stronger impulse. On the night of March 31, Goulart learned otherwise.

That division was a long-standing puzzle to the politicians of Latin America. Rómulo Betancourt of Venezuela once tried to convince Ché Guevara that the United States had two faces. One could look repressive and imperialistic, Betancourt maintained. The other face was friendly and devoted to social justice. No, said Ché, there is only one face, and it is the repressive one.

On April 1, as the coup became general knowledge, Gordon worried about securing the embassy. Situated only a couple of blocks from the large square in front of the opera house, it could never be protected completely. Gordon remembered hearing that when Quadros resigned, a crowd hurling rocks had broken a dozen of the irresistibly large green-tinted windows. These windows were always sealed, and because there were equally tall buildings on three sides, Gordon ordered the blinds drawn against snipers.

Although it was a hot, humid day, he ordered the air conditioner turned off. Otherwise, if the rebels—anyone loyal to the civilian president—succeeded in starting a fire on a lower floor, smoke would spread throughout the building much more rapidly.

The ambassador also sent home most of the staff and prepared to await reports from the battlefield with a handful of men he called his "executive action group" in his stifling, dark office on the eighth floor. The ninth floor belong to the CIA; the tenth was given over to communications. Gordon ordered that documents be sent up to those three floors, and he posted the embassy's full complement of twenty marines.

But there was no battle. Some students massed to protest the coup in Cinelandia, the square facing the major movie theaters; others gathered at a student cafeteria. One crowd charged up the stairs at the Military Club. The guard shot into their midst and killed two students. The crowd fell back.

Around the country, many commanders were proving watchful and slow to rally to the example of Minas Gerais. But neither the Communists, the labor unions, the enlisted men, nor Brizola's Groups of Eleven mounted a resistance: they were waiting for word from Goulart.

At the main air-force base in Rio, Santa Cruz, the enlisted men, having heard early reports of a coup, seized the base and put their officers under arrest. The chief of the air-force general headquarters was rumored to sympathize with the Communists. Now the mutineers called him, asking what action should be taken. Bomb the army columns coming down from Minas? Some officers were willing to fly, and the others would fly with guns at their necks. But the officer, Major Brigadier Francisco Teixeira, said, Keep organized. Release your officers. Wait and see.

Carlos Marighela, a former deputy in parliament and a leader in the Communist party, ordered Teixeira to bomb the columns coming down from Minas and, at the same time, Governor Lacerda's palace. Teixeira refused to take such an order from Marighela. It would have to come from either Luís Carlos Prestes, the head of the Communist party, or from Jango Goulart.

Prestes did nothing. Earlier in the year, Nikita Khrushchev had reportedly told him that he should work to have the Communist party legalized. The Soviet Union, Khrushchev added, did not want either to finance Brazil or to tangle with the United States over the country.

Goulart proved himself to be more *brasileiro* than fiery *gaúcho*. He flew south to Pôrto Alegre and met with Brizola, who tried to persuade him to stand and fight. Their argument was long and loud. Finally Brizola accused his brother-in-law of being a coward.

No, said the president, I don't want to be responsible for bloodshed among Brazilians.

. . .

For Carlos Lacerda, the coup meant a great opportunity. Under the law, Vice-president Mazzilli could serve 120 days. Then, given Washington's preference for a civilian front man, the military would need someone in mufti to complete Goulart's term. Kubitschek would never take the job. Constitutionally, the interim term would bar him from seeking a full term next year. But the U. S. embassy had allowed Lacerda to understand that he would be a natural temporary choice.

Taking to the airwaves, Lacerda gave one of his most impassioned speeches. He ringed his palace with garbage trucks and urged everyone hearing his voice to rush there and join the barricades against the supporters of Goulart.

At the U. S. embassy, all that Ambassador Gordon and his team could know on the afternoon of April 1 came from the runners they sent into the streets. These agents returned to say that the army had broken up the crowds of students. The siege was ended. It had lasted ninety minutes.

Everyone in the room, aware that a historic moment had passed, looked to the ambassador to provide the fitting phrase. He might fairly have congratulated his staff on their success at "destabilization," but that word did not enter popular usage until Salvador Allende was overthrown in Chile, and it was not coined by Lincoln Gordon.

Still, the ambassador sensed the challenge and rose to it. For years afterward, Walters would chuckle and tease Gordon by repeating his memorable words: "Turn on the air conditioner."

There was one more nervous day for Gordon to pass; but by nightfall on April 2, it was clear that the military had Brazil entirely under its control, and President Johnson had already sent a congratulatory wire to the new government. About twenty people had died in the coup d'état, a low enough figure for its backers to characterize it as bloodless. They also termed it a "revolution."

For Lincoln Gordon, it was as though a nightmare had ended. He went home to the official residence, and for the first time in months he enjoyed a solid night's sleep.

When Gordon returned to Washington, he found the prevailing mood as jubilant as his own. Everyone wanted to share in the credit. William C. Doherty, Jr., director of AIFLD, did his boasting in a radio interview: "What happened in Brazil did not just happen—it was planned—and planned months in advance. Many of the trade-union leaders, some of whom were actually trained in our institute, were involved in the revolution, and in the overthrow of the Goulart regime."

Gordon, who was more discreet, felt that Thomas Mann, in seeking to impress Congress with the administration's sagacity, had bragged a bit in the claims he made for U. S. involvement in the overthrow.

In their responses to Mann's testimony, the congressmen appeared willing to give Mann and his colleagues at the State Department a healthy measure of credit. Representative Wayne Hays, the Ohio Democrat, called the quick approval of the coup the best thing that had happened in Latin Armerican policy in a long, long time.

General O'Meara reminded congressmen of the record in Latin America since John Kennedy was elected president: in nine instances, military juntas had replaced elected governments. But the general was not pointing a critical finger. "The coming to power of the Castelo Branco government in Brazil last April," O'Meara said, "saved that country from an immediate dictatorship which could only have been followed by Communist domination."

Congressman Harold Gross, the Iowa Republican, inquired, "It is a dictatorship today?"

General O'Meara replied, "No."

While in Washington, Ambassador Gordon ran into Robert Kennedy. The attorney general was still grieving over the murder of his brother, but he found cheer in the events in Brazil.

"Well, Goulart got what was coming to him," Kennedy told Gordon. "Too bad he didn't follow the advice we gave him when I was down there."

CHAPTER

4

VERY FEW OF the U. S. citizens in Brazil deplored the coup, the police advisers least of all. The closer their ties to Brazil's business and military circles, the more strongly they believed that the coup was long overdue. Nor did it trouble the advisers that there was an overnight change in their role, that they had been training the police in a democracy and now would be training the police of a dictatorship. That distinction, and the different assignments that might be in store for Brazil's police, also failed to disturb either U. Alexis Johnson or Byron Engle.

In February 1963, Dan Mitrione had been transferred to Rio, where he began to spend more time with the police colonels and thus became less accessible to the average policeman around the barracks. Most junior officers liked what they saw of him, and word spread around headquarters that he got results—more hardware, including reloading machines for revolvers, radios, riot control equipment; and more men accepted at the police academy in Washington. He also introduced the policeman's notebook, standard procedure in the United States, for keeping track of activities on the beat. He urged officers to cut back on ceremony and spend more time on supervision, to get out of headquarters and check their patrolmen.

Mitrione's job expanded even further when the new head of the Guanabara state police, an army colonel, approached him at headquarters. "I've driven a jeep all my life," the colonel said. "Now, they've given me a sedan to drive. Will you show me how?" From that favor, a friendship developed.

Each morning Mitrione spent four hours with the new commander, discussing budgeting, distribution, equipment, the assigning of men. After they had run through the major topics, he would repeat the discussion with the commander's top twelve men. When his lectures were over, he expected the men to take twelve of their own men and brief them with the same material.

Mitrione and his secretary worked out of a small office in the downtown *cuartel,* the police barracks. The office was white stucco, and lights behind an overhead glass gave the cubicle the look of an aquarium. Mitrione's door opened onto a cement basketball court. At its far end rose a small chapel, Nossa Senhora das Dores, Our Lady of the Pains.

That name later took on a sardonic, hurtful meaning for civilians brought to headquarters. Before the coup, however, officers around the barracks believed that the pain was theirs alone. Police the world over, ran the lament, are the same: underpaid, overworked, never supported by the people. Mitrione himself, now sufficiently fluent in Portuguese, joined in the constant griping, whereas his predecessor had never ventured a word in the language.

For months before the coup, the officers had nursed special grievances, each day sharing the most recent outrages committed against them by Goulart's supporters. Their children were abused in school, left-wing teachers grading them low because their fathers were *gorilas,* police or military officers. The policemen did not need W. S. Gilbert to tell them their lot was not a happy one. An adviser stationed with Mitrione in Rio used to say that a policeman was a repository of hurt, and his listeners did not jeer at that striving after poetry.

They all had their stories, *brasileiros* and *norte-americanos:* how the press misused its freedom, how every story about the police was either slanted or snide. There was always room to report that police officer Mauricio Guimarães had been caught stealing a basket of flowers from a florist's shop, or that Severino Bezerra da Silva, a plainclothesman in the theft section, had his pocket picked in the post office. Once, in fact, the police had held a shootout with revolutionaries—dangerous men who had killed two policemen—and the press reported the incident as an assassination of political protestors.

"I'll tell you how that headline should have read," a Brazilian policeman complained to his adviser. "It should have read: 'The Forces of Good Won Over the Forces of Evil.' Instead, the press just murdered us. Why not tell the press to get out of here?"

The adviser hearing that complaint was not the man to defend a free press. Back home, he had once given the publisher of a small newspaper a traffic ticket and subsequently found himself called a liar in print; Dan Mitrione could also remember the bludgeon that Rudy Leeds had made of the *Pal-Item;* and many other advisers had at some time also run afoul of a local newspaper. As the military regime tightened controls over Brazil's press, few U. S. advisers around the police *cuartels* were arguing that the censorship set a dangerous precedent.

As for social programs, most advisers thought that the military regime's leading economist, Roberto Campos, was sensibly ordering the national priorities by favoring industrial development over all other goals. Coming from the world's leading industrial nation, they knew they foresaw better than the impatient Brazilian students the rewards that would one day accrue to every citizen. At police headquarters, one adviser paraphrased approvingly what he took to be the junta's philosophy: "The generals are saying, 'Sure, share the pie. But let's make it a bigger pie before we divide it.' "

Over the early years of the police program, under Kubitschek, Quadros, and even Goulart, most U. S. advisers, unless they were CIA officers using the AID program for cover, had not faced the problem of political subversion. Now there was a new class of criminals, the political rebels; and had their sympathies not lain so totally with the local police, advisers like Mitrione might have faced a dilemma. Officially, the line was clear-cut and antiseptic: police work was concerned with homicides, bank robberies, and kidnapping. The motive was not important.

But in their hearts, policemen from both Brazil and the United States knew better. Subversives were trying to infiltrate the established institutions: schools, labor unions, the Church. One officer returned from a raid on a monastery suspected of harboring dissidents, and reported seeing a photograph of Ché Guevara superimposed over Christ's face. At headquarters, it was hard to determine whether the outrage over that blasphemy was more religious or political.

The danger might be clear, but the means for dealing with it was not. General Golbery had gone to Brasília with his hundreds of thousands of files to set up Brazil's first national intelligence service, the SNI. But sometimes the material in those dossiers was hard to prove, and court procedures were still cumbersome and slow. Thousands of men and women, according to the police, were escaping their just punishment in the wake of the coup. Was there no recourse?

As it turned out, there was a solution at hand. In Washington, students at the International Police Academy would later be shown Gillo Pontecorvo's *Battle of Algiers.* The film portrayed policemen loyal to France regrouping at night into secret squads that wreaked reprisals on Algerian nationalists, bombing their homes and killing their families.

Brazilian police already had a similar blueprint in the actions of their own less scrupulous members. For years, in the tough suburbs of Rio, like Caxias, gangs had contested for control over drugs and whores. When a gang leader needed to eliminate a rival, he sometimes paid a policeman to do the job for him.

The U. S. advisers knew of that practice; and in the years before the 1964 coup, they used it as one more argument for raising a policeman's pay. Mitrione and the others had argued that if the rookie was given more money, headquarters could demand a higher standard of performance.

Yet the practice of off-duty murder was never stamped out, only channeled to new purposes. The year of the military takeover, a Rio policeman named Milton Le Cocq was murdered by a criminal nicknamed *Cara de Cavalo*, Horseface. Le Cocq's friends on the force vowed to avenge him by killing ten gangsters. In a short time, it became clear that their zeal outran mere vengeance. The bodies of thirty petty criminals—*marginais*, in Brazilian slang—were found dumped at roadsides and in remote fields. Pinned to the bodies were hand-lettered notes of explanation: "I was a thief." "I sold drugs." All were signed E. M., for *Esquadrão da Morte*, Death Squad.

Even under a military regime, which was substituting army trials for civil ones, the police found justice lagging and capricious, so the quick, sure judgments of the E. M. spread to other cities, where the police pooled their intelligence. This was not a competitive effort; on a wall at police headquarters in Rio hung a flag, a fraternal gesture from the Death Squad in São Paulo.

Le Cocq's killer, Horseface, was finally trapped on a farm. After he was shot to death, each policeman in the posse stepped forward and fired into his corpse. Such a ritual killing had been clean, in its way: but bodies began turning up with marks of torture—cigarette burns on the skin, knife marks in the flesh. The Death Squads also started courting publicity for their executions. In Rio, a man calling himself Red Rose alerted newspapers to where

they could find the latest "ham." In São Paulo, public relations were handled by an officer with the code name White
Lily.

Although some members of the Death Squads maintained a formal fiction that they themselves were not involved, they let their identities be known among elements
of the public they believed would admire them. One such
officer was Sergio Fernando Paranhos Fleury, thirty-one
years old at the time of the coup and very ambitious.

The son of a coroner who had died when the boy was
eleven, Fleury, with his slicked-down hair, remote eyes,
and mouth like a purse's clasp, was not prepossessing.
Through the Death Squad, however, he made himself famous, as word of his exploits circulated through São Paulo
and then all of Brazil. Fleury seemed to enjoy the attention,
although he protested to the newspapers that he was not
a violent man, that he cried at the movies.

The São Paulo police was only one of several branches
of government in the city that had begun to collect information about subversives. Each of the armed forces had
been expanding its own intelligence unit until some conservative businessmen became concerned that the competition
among these offices was leading to duplication and, worse,
inefficiency.

Henning Albert Boilesen, the president of a liquid gas
company, acted on these concerns. Boilesen had come to
Brazil from Denmark as an official of the Firestone Rubber
Company. Seventeen years later, he became a naturalized
Brazilian citizen. He moved easily through São Paulo's
prosperous society, picking up a host of influential friends:
former minister Hélio Beltrão; Ernesto Geisel, the president of Petrobas; General Siseno Sarmento. He occupied
a house on Rua Estados Unidos, and for years it was widely
believed that this was not the only sense in which Boilesen
lived on the United States.

The suspicion that Boilesen was a CIA agent grew when
he began soliciting money for a new organization to be

called Operação Bandeirantes (OBAN), in honor of the
bandeiras, the explorers and treasure hunters who had once
trekked across Latin America. OBAN united the various
military and police intelligence services in a crusade that
went beyond normal jurisdictions.

Boilesen and his cohorts put heavy pressure on fellow
businessmen for money to support OBAN. Their message
was not so different from de Paiva's. But Boilesen could
draw on a squad of volunteers from the military and police;
he could guarantee results.

It was not long before the United States subsidiaries
based in São Paulo were calling the U. S. consulate asking
for guidance. Should they contribute to OBAN? Use your
own judgment, the political section replied. We're staying
out of this. Despite this show of neutrality, at least one
U. S. businessman, after making such a call, did receive a
follow-up visit from a consular officer, who told him approvingly about contributions that other U. S. companies
in São Paulo had made to the cause of civil peace.

In 1965, another development helped to reinforce the
interest of Brazil's military in the Communist threat to the
hemisphere. At Lyndon Johnson's urging, Castelo Branco
joined the United States in sending troops to the Dominican Republic. Among the Brazilian units to go north were
two marine battalions, the Riachuelo and the Humaita.

Since the U. S. military command understood the difficulty Brasília would face in explaining casualties, the Brazilian role was largely defensive. U. S. troops were to hold
and expand an international corridor, while the Brazilian
marines were to do their part by demonstrating hemispher-
ic unity for the invasion. They were kept well back of
those boundaries.

To the young Brazilian troops, the situation soon
became demoralizing. They had come to save a sister
republic from the communism they themselves had
averted only the year before. Yet instead of welcoming
them with flowers, the people were inexplicably hostile.

Even when a woman seemed friendly, a Brazilian marine had to be cautious. From the U. S. camp came stories of GI's who would go out dancing with attractive women and be found the next morning with their throats slit.

One incident involved a band of Dominican boys who came to an edge of the Brazilian encampment and pelted the marines with stones. At first the Brazilians ignored the volley. The second day, when the boys returned, the troops called out to them with friendly jokes. They were only children of nine and ten; they could be won over. But the boys shouted back insults and ran away. The third day the boys returned with grenades. Several Brazilian troops were killed. At home, they were listed as military accidents or traffic deaths. From that time on, the Brazilian marines opened fire on any stranger who came too close.

Whatever other effect on the Dominican Republic, the 1965 invasion led to an outpouring of U. S. aid to the right-wing government, some $100 million, and to an expansion of the Public Safety program. Within three years, one third of the eighteen police advisers there were CIA officers operating under OPS cover.

In Washington, the Office of Public Safety had remained immune to public embarrassment as it went about two of its chief functions: allowing the CIA to plant men with the local police in sensitive places around the world; and after careful observation on their home territory, bringing to the United States prime candidates for enrollment as CIA employees.

Besides the courses at the IPA, the CIA was sending foreign police officers to its own clandestine center, a four-story townhouse on R Street in Washington. There, under the name International Police Services, Inc., Asian, African, and Latin American policemen were trained in surveillance, the use of informants, and other police methods. They were processed as though this course were also administered through U. S. AID. Along with foreign students, the institute trained U. S. officers destined for South Vietnam.

As head of the Office of Public Safety, Byron Engle was more sensitive than his CIA colleagues to the need for keeping his program uncompromised by the overt spying. His new associates at OPS heard him arguing heatedly with CIA officers at the agency's headquarters in Langley, Virginia, as he tried to retain a measure of respectability for the IPA.

Throughout the early sixties Engle succeeded, although his efforts did not end the campaign within U. S. AID against his police program. One AID official was sufficiently concerned about the first reports of torture in Brazil to start checking the requisition orders from the Office of Public Safety. Electric shocks, he knew, were usually administered with military field telephones, and over those he had no control. But he could try to prevent generators being sent out with the U. S. AID decal if they were going to be used for torture.

This official soon came to believe that his watchfulness was useless. There were many legitimate purposes for small generators, and to ban them on the assumption that they were going to be abused would be to cripple the AID program. Ultimately, he decided, one had to trust the humanity and discretion of the police advisers. They had been raised under the Bill of Rights, and they could be expected to respect it.

But when put to the test during the Kennedy administration, the Office of Public Safety quickly demonstrated that there were few hesitations about breaking a rule or two if success was at stake. Since the irregularities were in the best of causes, Engle had not feared reprisals from either the president or his liberal advisers.

In 1962, for example, a group of Venezuelan leftists, inspired by Castro, formed the Armed Forces of National Liberation (FALN) and set out to discredit the elected

president, Rómulo Betancourt. The FALN wanted to persuade voters to boycott elections the following year. Although the group never totaled more than five hundred
members, by fanning out they were able to bomb a luxury
hotel, burn a Sears Roebuck warehouse, and attack the
U. S. embassy. When Franco loaned several Impressionist
paintings for an exhibition in Caracas, the FALN carried
off one work each by Cézanne, Van Gogh, Picasso, Braque,
and Gauguin, choices that contributed to the suspicion that
the FALN might include artists as well as students and
writers.

The Venezuelan police seemed helpless to act, even
when patrolmen were being shot down on the street. Under pressure from the Kennedys, Engle borrowed four
Spanish-speaking officers from the Los Angeles Police Department and quietly sent them to Caracas to give intensive
classes in police work. Had the mission been exposed, the
Kennedy administration might have been forced into a
round of excuses and apologies. Had any of the Los Angeles cops been killed, there would have been no provision for
compensating their families. Engle was thus much relieved
when the secret operation ended and the men were back
in California.

That was behind the scenes. The public image of Engle's
program remained positive. Robert Kennedy, now a senator from New York, had been happy to address the first
class that completed its training at the Washington police
academy. Graduation came one month before the military
coup in Brazil; and in his remarks, Kennedy warned the
class that "the world today is buffeted by winds of change."

At the academy, however, most of the actual training
seemed aimed at preventing that change, although that
intention was seldom committed to paper. The training
syllabus, which was not classified, had never been released
to the press; and one IPA official explained that "the Communists might even pay a little more for it. And we don't
want to help them." Yet, any Soviet or Cuban agent who

did pay out cash for the printed materials might have felt short-changed. More perhaps to protect the IPA from on-slaughts by the U. S. Congress and the liberal press than to preserve its secrets from foreign enemies, the training sheets were relentlessly high-minded and vague.

The foreign policemen themselves understood why they were being sent to Washington. Even before the coup d'état, in July 1963, one Brazilian officer described the academy program to the governor of São Paulo as "the latest methods in the field of dispersion of strikes and strik-ing workers." He would learn, he said, how to use dogs and clubs and "to modernize the mechanism of repression against agitators in São Paulo."

The basic academy course ran fifteen weeks and was offered twice a year in French, several times in Spanish and, for Africans and Asians, in English as well. The first two and a half months were spent in a standard introductory course, whereas the last four weeks offered advanced train-ing in any of ten specialties, including immigration and customs control, protection of dignitaries, and "Criminal Violence Control," which dealt with airline security, bomb threats, kidnapping, extortion, and assassination.

Candidates were expected to be between the ages of twenty-one and forty-five, and—a provision often waived —to be high school graduates. Women could be accepted at the IPA, but their selection was discouraged. If a coun-try nominated one female officer, it was told it must send two of them.

In Belo Horizonte, and later in Rio, Dan Mitrione had become skilled at screening applicants for the program. His successor in Belo was not so adept. An amiable and lazy cop from the Southwest, he assured every Brazilian police-man who inquired about the program that he was sure to be accepted. When the adviser was finally transferred, the Brazilians found his desk drawers stuffed with applications he had never bothered to forward to Washington.

Brazilian officers attending the IPA often came away

believing that the courses, like those which had been offered in Panama, were beneath them. Sixty percent of the student body came from Central and South America, and some Brazilians felt degraded to be grouped together with Costa Ricans and Guatemalans.

If the training was not always valuable, it could be entertaining. The highlight of each course was an exercise first developed during the school's days in Panama: Operation San Martin. San Martin was an imaginary country with an equally nonexistent capital, Rio Bravos. Its neighbor and enemy was called, somewhat less mythically, Maoland. Few foreign students recognized that the map of Rio Bravos was only an aerial photograph of Baltimore with an overlay of imposing government buildings and its streets renamed in Spanish.

The warm-up exercises were simple. A dignitary was arriving from a friendly country. How would the students deploy their policemen to protect him during his visit? The final problem offered more chances for miscalculation. Infiltrators from Maoland were staging a national disturbance. The villains—and every semester this delighted the students—were instructors from the IPA faculty, their mug shots emphasizing their sinister aspect. Resisting fashion, one instructor kept his hair crewcut, and every semester he was nicknamed The Nazi. Other instructors passed for Communists or university rebels.

A dozen IPA students were divided into three groups: one joined the instructors in creating the problem, writing the Communist propaganda, plotting the disruption; one faction made the decisions for putting the insurrection down; and the other group was composed of onlookers and judges. The chief of police from Somali, an accomplished player, complained afterward that the exercise was harder than any comparable situation in real life because at the IPA he was judged by his peers.

The exercise was held in the Police Operations Control Center, a room of muted grays and greens with four raised rows of seats. The magnetic map of San Martin covered the front wall. Students chosen to suppress the demonstration were connected by telephones and teletype to a control booth. Such direct communication they found to be a burden. One line connected directly with the "Prime Minister," who demanded action, provided it did not embarrass his party in the forthcoming elections. If an operation was going too smoothly, the instructors called from the control booth with snags: "My problem is the reporters on the scene. They're getting in the way and interfering with our police work."

"Do the best you can," said one student commander.

From the control booth, the instructor called two more times about the reporters, and finally he exploded, "God damn it! You've got to do something!"

"All right," said the student chief. "Arrest them! Bring them in!"

That answer won him only a ten-minute respite. Then the Prime Minister was on the line: "What in hell is going on?"

No one had to instruct a police officer how to stall for time. "What do you have reference to, sir?"

"I'm getting calls from AP and UPI. I'm catching hell."

As the Prime Minister passed along some of that hell, the student police chief had to improvise a way out of his bungling. In one case, the student telephoned for a bus, ordered the reporters released, briefed them on the rioting, then drove them back to the scene to let them see it for themselves. His fellow students agreed that for a makeshift remedy his had not been a bad one.

Besides the training exercises, San Martin was the locale of a film shot in Panama, *The First Line of Defense*. The instructors memorized a short introduction in Spanish: "The events you will see take place in the mythical Latin American republic of San Martin. But they are not fictitious events; they 'really happen.' You will see that the people of San Martin are mostly favorable to their govern-

ment (else it could not stand), and that the police work with
the people and are truly the first line of defense."

In the film, the center of subversion was the National
Committee for Agrarian Reform (CONTRA). Once an
organization of student reformers, it had fallen into the
hands of strangers well past college age. Across town, more
strangers, possibly Communists from Cuba, disrupted a
meeting of striking workers from a fertilizer factory. The
plot involved a police spy, a Czechoslovakian gun smuggled in a box marked SUGAR, and a riot outside the factory
that became too frenzied for the police to handle alone.
The chief ceded responsibility to the military, and the
army dispelled the protestors with tear gas, flying wedges,
and fire hoses.

At the film's end, two policemen drew the moral for
several smiling children: "A new day dawns over the city
of Rio Bravos." If other subversives were plotting against
the security of the people, they were not likely to succeed
as long as the civil police enjoyed the people's confidence
and had "confidence in their own ability to enforce the
law!"

IPA officials anticipated that some students might object
to the film. To cope with them, the instructor was told to
break in at any sign of restiveness and assure the class that
the film presented only suggestions on how to proceed, not
absolute directions. In most cases, if any objections were
raised at all, they pertained to the amount of equipment at
the disposal of the Rio Bravos police chief.

The inequality between U. S. supplies and what the
students had at home was even more glaring when the
students were taken outside of Washington to Fort Myers
for field training in riot control. Invariably, they came
back impressed by the plethora of gas masks, shields and
batons, riot guns that fired pepper shot and rubber bullets;
and they would grumble about their own meager means.

The instructor was expected to turn any shortcoming
into a challenge. "You don't have radio cars for your po-

lice? Class, any suggestions?" A student might say, "How about putting up a light bulb at the highest point in town and telling the patrolmen that whenever it was lit, they should call headquarters for instructions?"

The academy also showed more conventional training films: a twelve-minute film, *The Police Baton,* from the Los Angeles Police Department; *The Third Challenge,* made by the Department of Defense; *The Use of Tear Gas to Preserve Order,* a bit of public relations by the Lake Erie Chemical Company. In Brazil, local advisers also used a film on interrogation made by the FBI. Until they could have it dubbed into Portuguese, U. S. advisers turned off the soundtrack and offered their own pungent commentary.

During class hours at the IPA, discussion of domestic politics was discouraged. The academy's officials liked to point to the time the Somali Republic was fighting Ethiopia, yet policemen from each country had roomed together.

Given the films and the tone of the courses, few students missed the purpose behind the IPA. The academy had been set up to train the police to fight communism wherever it existed. Even students not considered sufficiently qualified to be passed on to the CIA for professional intelligence work were instructed in what Jack Goin called "preventive law enforcement."

You're a rural policeman, Goin's illustration went, and you've stopped to talk with a farmer about his sick cow. In the course of your conversation, he mentions that lately a stranger has passed through his pasture. That could be a matter of internal security. It's up to you as a policeman to recognize that it could be important.

Overseas, the U. S. advisers had coped with local customs with varying degrees of ingenuity, and foreign policemen coming to the United States similarly found the native practices confounding. At first, grading at the academy was a problem. One police colonel arrived with his aide, a major. The junior officer sat in on the classes with him and outshone him in every category until the colonel did not want to go home at all. That was in 1965, and grades were abandoned soon afterward.

A Third World student was arrested for shoplifting from a self-service drugstore. He later said that he had waited some time for a clerk to approach him. When none did, he stuck a few items in his pocket and left. He intended, he claimed, to return the next day and pay when everyone was not so busy. Officials from the academy had the charges dropped, but it took hours of persuasion to keep that affronted student from taking the next flight home.

Once an African student was picked up on a rape charge. During a line-up, the white victim made a positive identification. The District of Columbia police investigator then asked what the rapist had sounded like. "Just like any other nigger," the woman replied. The IPA student was asked to say a few words, which he did in his decidedly British accent. Once again the case was dropped. This time the African policeman was more amused than embittered.

Yet many black students arrived at the IPA certain that racism was going to blight their stay. Most were agreeably surprised by the welcome they received in Washington, where the population was becoming increasingly black. But having the academy in the capital irked some of the white instructors who felt that the visitor would get a more representative picture of the United States had the academy been located somewhere in the Midwest.

"We're only here," one said, " because the civilians in the State Department don't trust us."

That much was true. The Office of Public Safety had been sending police-training teams to South Vietnam; and as the years passed, the stories that reached Washington were increasingly disturbing. Around the U. S. embassy in Saigon, there were allusions to the torture and murder of political prisoners, sometimes in the presence of agents of the United States. Similar reports had started to come in from Iran and Taiwan, then from Brazil and Greece.

Torture ran counter to the official instruction at the IPA. A number of instructors fervently spoke against it, less because it was morally indefensible than because they considered it self-defeating. Their students, however, sometimes had different opinions. Interrogation was a crucial subject and a source of lengthy debate among students and staff.

Before discussing the procedure of questioning, students were briefed on what were the best physical surroundings in which to conduct the interrogation. The room should have one door and no windows. If a window was unavoidable, there should be no view. The room should be sound-proofed. The telephone should not ring but signal instead by flashing lights seen only by the questioner. All of this, including the blank walls, were to emphasize the prisoner's sense of isolation.

Important interrogations were to be recorded, the microphone hidden somewhere in the room, perhaps in a "live" telephone. The room should have a two-way mirror. If the interrogator wore civilian clothes, he was more likely to inspire confidence.

As the questioning proceeded, the interrogator should look for changes in his prisoner that might indicate lying: sweating, loss of color, dry mouth, racing pulse, heavy breathing.

That had been the preliminary instruction. But during the mid-sixties concerns began to shift. Until then, interrogating a murder suspect had required only experience and a few timely tricks:

INSTRUCTOR (off-handedly, as though it didn't much matter): Would you like a cigarette?
STUDENT SUSPECT: Yes, thank you.
INSTRUCTOR: May I use your lighter?
SUSPECT (fumbling): I don't seem to have it.
INSPECTOR: Where did you leave it then?

But simple ploys like that worked only with amateurs. Policemen arriving at the academy now had tougher questions about defiant rebels and dedicated subversives.

The instructors, particularly those who had served in a country fighting an insurrection, knew that most political activists would try to stall for twenty-four hours, to give their colleagues time to move to safer quarters. The students wanted to know what to do about those professionals. "If a man thinks he's smart," one instructor answered, "bluff to make him think you know even more than he does."

"No," another instructor told another class, "act dumb. Keep him talking. He may try to justify himself. If he does, just go on listening. In the midst of his tirade, something may come out that will be helpful to you."

"Or," another instructor suggested, "bait the prisoner a bit."

But the same question always arose: "Why not beat the shit out of the guy?"

Although the official response was negative, the students could detect which instructors were genuinely opposed to beatings and which were a bit more realistic.

One instructor argued that any torture was ineffectual because some people did not feel pain. Others, he suggested, could be reduced to pleas and trembling without a hand laid on them. Another instructor, a former policeman from the Southwest, advised students to say clearly, "Bring in the transformer and the electric wires." Of course, he added, there were no transformers or wires. It was merely that people responded differently to different stimuli, and the interrogator had to find out what turned the key.

"The first man who hits a prisoner is a coward" was the opening statement of one adviser to an IPA class. He seemed to believe what he said. A Latin American student then asked, "Even if he spits in your face?" It was moot which was the more intolerable, being spit upon or being called a coward.

The adviser nodded emphatically. "Even if he spits in your face."

"Jesus Christ," said another student. "That's a pretty strong statement. There are circumstances—"

"No, he's in your custody and he's your responsibility."

Another time, a Brazilian policeman interrupted that sort of sermon: "Let's cut out the bullshit. If I can get you to swear that no policeman in the United States ever slapped a prisoner, I'll kiss your ass." The instructor could not guarantee that every policeman in the United States lived by the rules.

By the mid-sixties, enough of the students had been exposed to U. S. intelligence methods in their own country to take the IPA's instruction about nonviolence more lightly. Given the difference in signals that IPA students received from their advisers, it was not surprising that when they were asked near the end of their course to sum up what they had learned, their essays were guarded.

Nguyen Van Thieu, a South Vietnamese police officer, began his list of three methods of interrogation with torture, but he said it did not usually bring satisfactory results. But he thanked the free world, "the U. S. most of all," for making interrogation more effective with "technical and equipment aid."

Milciades Espita Ovalle, a detective in Colombia's Security Department, said that a government must kill or capture guerrillas in order to reassure the population that the rebel cause would not prevail. He did grant, however, that Communist propagandists would make the guerrillas out to be victims of the police.

Inspector Madhav Bickrum Rana of Nepal wrote that an interrogator could extract valuable information either by getting a subject drunk or by injecting him with a truth drug, such as sodium pentathol. He also discussed starving a man, hitting him, or subjecting him to steady drops of water on his head. But he concluded that the use of threat and force was justified only as a last resort, when every other technique had failed.

Kula Nand Thakur, also of Nepal, reported to the IPA faculty that he had beaten suspects after he became district inspector for Nawakot in 1964. He had seen other interrogators grow careless, though, and hit tender parts of the body so that the suspect died and "thereby created another trouble."

One Brazilian officer sent to the United States in 1967 brought along memories of a discussion he had had in his police *cuartel* the year before. A police squad had just brought in a young mulatto suspected of belonging to Leonel Brizola's resistance group. The suspect had been beaten during his capture, though not severely enough to require hospitalization. In 1966, this particular police barracks did not use equipment to torture a prisoner, but if a suspect refused to speak, he could expect more kicks and punches.

The Brazilian officer watched the bloody man being brought in and knew what was in store for him. Visiting his office that day was an official from the United States, a pleasant sandy-haired man in his forties who spoke excellent Portuguese.

When he first began to call, he had introduced himself as a political officer from the U. S. embassy. He had not asked about anything at all sensitive. Instead, he seemed willing to talk for hours about soccer and movies. He had come back three times, never in a hurry, never with anything specific on his mind.

Now the Brazilian policeman said to him, "I don't like seeing a prisoner brought in with a black eye and cuts on his head. It reminds me too much of what I heard from my father about life under Vargas."

"I agree with you," the embassy man said. "But you policemen have a very bad job. Other people just don't know. They want protection from men like Brizola and his gang, but they won't see how dangerous they are. This man they brought in could have a lot of information that would save innocent lives."

"Yes," the Brazilian agreed, a little surprised. He had only made the remark because the sight of the prisoner had left him feeling uncomfortable. He had no intention of interfering with the arresting officers or of offering them unsolicited advice about doing their jobs.

"I was in the military police stationed in Germany after the war," the embassy man said. "We used to talk about what we'd have done if we'd ever got hold of a Nazi."

"That was war," the Brazilian said.

"So is this," said his guest.

Bull sessions similar to that discussion went on regularly at the IPA. After class, an instructor talked only for himself, not for the academy. Some of the faculty stuck to the IPA line. If they were not personally outraged at the thought of torture, they argued that word of it always got out and hurt the cause of the men who practiced it.

It was apparent that the men who espoused that soft line, even over a beer several blocks away from the Car Barn, were rarely men who had been stationed in a country with a serious threat to its internal security. They were also— it was a feeling about them—not going far in the hierarchy of the Office of Public Safety. On the other hand, there was the adviser who returned from South Vietnam with sympathetic stories about the perils of the Saigon police. On the ground in South Vietnam, U. S. advisers complained loudly about the timidity of the Vietnamese policemen and repeated their demeaning nickname for them, the White Mice. Part of the name was inspired by their white uniforms, part by their uncombative attitude.

Since Vietnamese and other Asian police came to the IPA as students, the instructors held back on jokes and insults, and spoke instead about the viciousness of the Vietcong, how they planted bombs in crowded restaurants and movie theaters, where they did not kill U. S. troops but their fellow countrymen. The Vietnamese police were entitled to take any measures, no matter how severe, to prevent that slaughter. At least, that was the message some Brazilian students took away with them.

Other Brazilian police had begun to wonder whether there was a decent way to resolve the conflict facing their own country's intelligence services. Indisputably, a rebel movement was growing in Brazil. The government of Artur da Costa e Silva, the hard-line general who had assumed the presidency on the retirement of Castelo Branco, was depending on his intelligence network to break up the movement before it became a real threat to the military regime.

Inevitably, that new intelligence apparatus, SNI, turned for help to its powerful counterpart from the north. In the police barracks, it was well known that many Brazilian officers worked closely with the CIA and were suspected of accepting pay from their CIA liaison officers. That exchange of money, more than the exchange of privileged information, could infuriate those officers who had not been recruited by the agency.

Sometimes these officers would remark—even in front of political prisoners—that it was too bad certain *brasileiros* had sold out their patrimony. The complaints never went far, since the commanding officers seemed to favor cooperation with the CIA, which brought praise, promotions, and an access to the CIA's special stores of equipment. A well-connected police commander who wanted new supplies of tear gas did not have to fill out the involved U. S. AID requisitions. Within a few days his friend in the CIA could obtain what he needed directly from the Panama branch of the Technical Services Division (TSD).

In that gray area between AID's open program and the CIA's special needs, Mitrione had functioned so capably that many Brazilian officers thought he was a CIA officer working under the cover of the OPS. By 1968, the rumor had traveled far enough that when an East German publisher named Julius Mader brought out a book entitled

Who's Who in CIA, he listed Dan A. Mitrione. This was a case where common knowledge was mistaken. Mitrione was merely smart and ambitious enough to cooperate with the CIA to the fullest. Brazilian police officers at his head-quarters were alert to the distinctions within the U. S. hierarchy, and they took reflected pride in their adviser's evident closeness with the men who came by his office, ostensibly from the embassy's political section. Mitrione's predecessor in Rio had not enjoyed that rapport, nor had he spoken Portuguese.

In 1966 and early 1967, Brazil's police were hard-pressed for information about subversives. Though the Brazilian navy had amassed comprehensive files, they were not shar-ing information with the other services. It was about this time that the police and army began to use coercion on their prisoners.

Older policemen briefed the younger officers on the ways in which they had extracted information during the first Vargas years. Their techniques, often brutal and effec-tive, usually involved beating a man until he was near death, at which point he either talked or died. One police-man remembered that when Mitrione heard a story like that he had commented that a dead prisoner could not tell anyone very much. Yet what was the alternative? The U. S. advisers who had become close enough to their coun-terparts to hear these discussions now had to settle the question for themselves. The CIA and SNI were pressing the police for results, and nothing loosened a prisoner's tongue quicker than pain.

Some police advisers argued that intense but not lethal pain was more humane than indiscriminate beatings. Their CIA contacts endorsed that view. At least in one case, when Brazilian intelligence officers began to use field telephones to administer electric shocks, it was U. S. agents who in-formed them of the permissible levels the human body could withstand.

Word was passed that the CIA could supply more than

tear gas, that the laboratories of the TSD in Washington, and its branch in Panama, were developing devices to make the pain so sharp that a prisoner would break quickly and not force a police interrogator to hurt him repeatedly. But the Brazilian police who heard those reports did not immediately receive the new mechanisms, and those who gave in and used torture had only their field telephones to work with.

The men charged with getting information knew that they were not sadists. They had been given a responsibility, and they would meet it. They did not want sermons from their U. S. advisers, and Mitrione was not one to lecture them. He was their guest. He always told new advisers not to forget that.

From the point of view of the policemen, however, Mitrione was also their patron, their mentor, the keeper of their professional conscience. Stories came up to Belo Horizonte from Rio about the torture of prisoners, and his former Brazilian colleagues debated what Mitrione would do if a police officer began to abuse a prisoner in front of him.

"He'd leave," said one officer.

"Leave the country?" another asked.

"No," said the first. "Leave the room."

In the middle of 1967, Mitrione was called back to teach at the IPA. It was a lucky time to be leaving Brazil. The rebel movement was growing and counter measures would have to be more severe.

Mitrione had spent five years in Brazil. Among his Brazilian students and his fellow advisers, he was leaving as a widely known and well-regarded professional. Later, the Office of Public Safety would claim to have taught 100,000 policemen in Brazil, one sixth of the country's total police force, and Mitrione had trained hundreds of them.

He knew what some of those policemen had started to do. They discussed the problem with him and told him what they had seen—the wires, the water used for near-drownings. His very success as an adviser had won him that intimacy and trust. Hearing of the torture, he was—at least as they remembered it much later—noncommittal.

There would, however, be no torture at the IPA. In Washington, an instructor could talk about police work as it should be done, not about the methods forced on a conscientious cop in a compromised world.

But Mitrione was to find that in conversation over coffee during each IPA term, the question of torture persisted. Another popular instructor settled the queasiness of one Brazilian student with an anecdote. The police officer, who was promoted many times since his student days, remembered it years afterward.

"If anyone ever asks you what you do to prisoners," the U. S. adviser began, "tell them this story: Right now, as we're talking, my fellow policemen are holding a man involved in a kidnapping. He and two of his accomplices took a little five-year-old blonde girl who belongs to a businessman in this city. They're saying that if they don't get two million dollars, they will kill that little child tomorrow at noon.

"We picked up the man while he was leaving instructions. We've had him now for ten hours, and he's told us nothing. The businessman doesn't have two million. He's wealthy but not in that league. The deadline is getting closer. What do we do next?"

"There is no little girl," the Brazilian student said.

"The person who asked you the question can't be sure of that. Somewhere every week or month if not every day, police officers have to face that kind of problem. It might not be a little girl. It might be a policeman standing on a corner that some nut has decided to shoot. But it's the same principle.

"And if the man who asked you about torture doesn't agree that you should use any means to find out where that little girl is being held, then don't answer any more of his questions, because he'll never understand what you tell him anyway.

"He's got his mind made up, and he hates the police so much that he'd sacrifice an innocent child to put you in the wrong."

CHAPTER
5

FOR LINCOLN GORDON, the coup had first seemed to fulfill his every expectation. Mazzilli, the civilian vice-president, was a dignified lightweight. If the military agreed to let him serve as president for the four months specified by law, that would have satisfied the ambassador. Instead, Gordon was informed that the new president would be General Humberto Castelo Branco, which seemed to satisfy Dick Walters, the military attaché, even more.

The first clue that things might take a bad turn came when Francisco Campos, a lawyer whom Gordon regarded as an unintelligent old fascist, drew up the First Institutional Act. Under its provisions, the government, by decree, could create *cassação*, a political death, a deprivation of all political rights for ten years. Its victims would have neither a hearing nor an appeal. Moreover, they were being identified by General Golbery's SNI. The SNI very much resembled the CIA, except that since Brazil's enemies were inside her borders, Golbery was not burdened by those restrictions the U. S. Congress thought it had placed against domestic activity by the CIA.

Gordon was displeased with the act but took comfort from Castelo Branco's inferences that it was distasteful to him as well. Then, just as the act was about to expire, it was invoked against Juscelino Kubitschek, which was a shock to the U. S. embassy, or at least to the civilians there. According to one U. S. scenario, Kubitschek was to be elected to the next full civilian term as president.

As it turned out, there were not going to be any more true elections. The military decreed that Castelo Branco's term would be extended for an additional year, which frustrated Carlos Lacerda's hopes of becoming president of Brazil for that year by appointment. The bitterness of his disappointment led eventually to his being made *cassado*, too.

Gordon sought out a friend in the new government, Milton Campos, to protest the military's high-handedness. Since the ambassador had urged Castelo Branco to appoint Campos as justice minister, Campos was obliged to hear out Gordon as he denounced the Institutional Act. What would Washington say? Gordon demanded. Or the world? "At least create a special court," Gordon told Campos, "to preserve the appearance of legality."

Campos promised Gordon that something would be done. Two weeks later, Campos resigned from his post.

Hearing of the ambassador's disquiet, Castelo Branco called him into his office in Brasília. He had been president slightly more than two months. He assured Gordon that the *cassação* of Kubitschek also troubled him, but he pointed sorrowfully to a massive document on his desk. Gordon took it to be a bill of indictment against Kubitschek.

"If we were to publish the reasons for this *cassação*, the degree of corruption is so shameful that it would be devastating to Brazilian pride."

Gordon accepted the explanation. As a diplomat, he felt he had little choice; and Dick Walters, whom the ambassador considered a sophisticated student of Brazilian political history, did not seem much troubled by the Institutional Act.

Eighteen months after the coup, there was a Second Institutional Act. This time Gordon made notes in Portuguese of his long protest so that he would not forget a trope.

I was uncomfortable with the first act, he told Castelo Branco, but it had been for a limited duration. I assumed that when the emergency powers expired, we would get back on the road. Now, after a year and a half, there is this Second Institutional Act, and as a precedent it is very dangerous.

Castelo Branco said he was not happy either, but the ambassador had to understand that he had accepted the emergency powers only from the highest democratic principles. Two politicians from the token opposition party had recently been elected to governorships. If Castelo Branco had not agreed to accept these new powers, he said, the hard liners within the military would never have allowed those two men to take office.

Gordon took his leave. By the time of the Fifth Institutional Act, which shut down Congress, suspended habeas corpus for political crimes, and gave full autocratic power to the president, Gordon was no longer ambassador to Brazil. From the United States, he signed a telegram of protest.

Gordon's successor, John W. Tuthill, considered a number of reprisals against that latest act. One, which was not taken, would have withdrawn all U. S. police advisers from Brazil.

Robert Kennedy visited Rio in 1965 and agreed to meet with students at Catholic University. By that time, few Brazilian officials would risk visiting a campus, and Kennedy got good marks for courage. Otherwise his rally drew a mixed response. Looking on, Jean Marc Von der Weid observed that the more his classmates knew about Brazil's recent history, the less susceptible they were to Kennedy's undeniable presence.

Jean Marc was a bookish boy whose only previous burst of political ardor had been touched off the night of the 1964 coup, when Carlos Lacerda asked his supporters to rally at the governor's palace. Sure that Goulart intended to become another Vargas, Jean Marc had dashed to the palace, where he had been chagrined to find no sign of a threat to Lacerda's life or property, only a few hundred retired military men joined in sedate revelry.

Jean Marc's conservatism came naturally to him. His father, a Swiss chemical engineer who worked for a Brazilian subsidiary of U. S. Steel, had lived in Brazil for many years, married a Brazilian woman, and raised four children in Rio. Jean Marc's mother came from a prominent political family, the Sodres. Her father had been a deputy during the early Vargas years and later a political exile in Argentina.

But although as a high-school boy he had welcomed the coup, Jean Marc's college experiences were leaving him disillusioned with the military government. He had resisted blaming the United States for Brazil's dictatorship, but when the leftists around him called the new influx of foreign capital and control a proof of "U. S. imperialism," Jean Marc asked himself whether they might not be right.

For all his intelligence, the young man was somewhat retiring, following along his father's path by studying chemical engineering at the federal university. He was working with a select unit, charged with studying a means of developing Brazilian mineral oil; and by 1966 it was apparent that if he avoided political involvement, he could look ahead to a decidedly profitable and possibly distinguished career.

Instead, Jean Marc was drawn into his first student demonstration. Out of curiosity, he showed up at the scene and someone put a placard in his hand: AMERICANS OUT OF VIETNAM. Jean Marc laid it down. "That's not our problem," he said and chose another: DICTATORSHIP OUT OF THE UNIVERSITY. In the course of that protest meeting,

Jean Marc was clubbed by a couple of the police, whom
U. S. advisers were teaching to be more efficient.

Jean Marc's next political lesson was bloodier still. A boy
named Edson Luis de Lima Souto was shot to death during
a demonstration that had first seemed trivial but proved to
be a turning point in Brazilian politics. Edson Luis died for
better food.

The locale was Calabouço, a student café in downtown
Rio owned by the state's student union. Its food had never
been appetizing, but then few three-star restaurants served
seven thousand meals a day. Whenever Jean Marc ate at
Calabouço, he considered the meal another sacrifice to his
growing political commitment.

In 1967 the state of Guanabara decided to close the
restaurant for reasons that had nothing to do with the
quality of its meals. The International Monetary Fund was
due to convene in Rio at the Museum of Modern Art.
Hardly a stone's throw away stood the café, which was
also an informal headquarters for those student critics who
believed that the fund was more interested in protecting
foreign capital than in feeding the world's hungry. It was
not surprising then that the governor should abruptly find
the Calabouço unattractive and unsafe.

To prevent the café from being closed, the students
resolved to occupy it. The leaders set two limited goals: to
keep the restaurant open and to serve better food. The
governor tried to send in the police, and each day there
were clashes between the two groups. Both sides understood that the issue was not half-baked meals at one café.
The government was simply not about to submit to the
protestors; and that intransigence led to more pamphlets,
more protest meetings, and finally to demonstrations that
brought out the Guanabara state police in force.

At this point, the police either panicked or merely followed orders. In any event, they opened fire on the students; and Edson Luis was shot to death. There was a
struggle for his corpse, and the students won. Hundreds of

young people then bore Edson's body through the streets. One of them was Angela Camargo Seixas, a first-year engineering student at Catholic University in Rio. Like Jean Marc, Angela was new to political protest, but this day's demonstration would not be her last.

The students carried Edson's body to the steps of the state legislature and took over the building. Some members of the opposition party supported the demonstration, and their influence kept the police at bay.

Jean Marc arrived at the scene to find the mood hysterical. Most students had been in high school when Goulart's government fell. The 1964 coup had produced at least forty casualties and many vengeful reprisals, particularly in the northeast; but the generals had always boasted of their victory as a bloodless one. Now there was blood everywhere and the corpse of a seventeen-year-old boy to make the students aware that this was no light-hearted game the government had been playing.

The students proclaimed a day of mourning, shut down the schools, and prepared a mass demonstration for the day Edson would be buried. The leaders knew nothing about Byron Engle or his theory of a Communist master plan to create martyrs. Instinct warned them, however, that the police might break in during the night to seize Edson's body so that the sight of it would not inflame passions even more.

They resolved to keep vigil with the body, while a delegation toured the city alerting people to the horror that had been committed. Some went to the cinemas. Jean Marc went to six legitimate theaters around Copacabana and Botafogo beach, interrupting the performances to tell his story. Other students spent the night canvasing *boites* and street-corner bars throughout the city. Rio has no fixed hours for its clubs; they close when the last customer leaves. The students continued until dawn, soliciting money for the burial and for printing pamphlets about the killing. They returned to the parliament building having collected over one million cruzeiros.

One disturbance had occurred during the vigil. An intrepid policeman in plainclothes had infiltrated the wake and was somehow identified. The mob shouted, "String him up!" indicating the nearest gallows, which was a lamp-post on the street. Jean Marc and five colleagues linked arms and held the crowd inside the building, while other students surrounded the infiltrator and hustled him out onto the street.

The next day, April 4, five thousand students marched the three miles to the cemetery of St. John the Baptist in Botafogo. There, packed among bone-white tombstones and ornate marble crosses, the mourners were waiting. Edson Luis's family, who lived along the Amazon in Manaus, were poor and could not afford the flight to Rio. But 60,000 of the boy's countrymen had turned out to pay their respects as his body was lowered into its grave.

The police did not try to intervene. In an ill-advised peace gesture, the governor had sent a car and police escort to bear the coffin to the cemetery, but the sight of the uniforms inflamed the crowd, and the officers backed away.

The day of the shooting had been emotionally draining for the students; the day of the funeral proved devastating to the police. Until that afternoon, the public had treated them with good-natured contempt. To the average man, the army, not the police, was to blame for the repression. But the day the state police killed a high-school boy, they became a target for civilian frustration and hatred.

(Three years later, a police psychologist told Jean Marc that the week after Edson Luis's funeral there were officers lined up outside the psychologist's office. Some men wanted transfers to desk jobs; others wanted to resign from the police entirely. Jean Marc paid heavily for that gratifying information; he was in prison at the time, and the psychologist was part of the team interrogating him.)

The day after the funeral, President Costa e Silva, the hard-line general named by the military to succeed Castelo Branco, used the rally as his reason for banning a political

movement called The Front. It had been put together by
Carlos Lacerda as one last attempt, should civilian presidential elections ever be restored, to win the power denied him
after the 1964 coup.

Lacerda responded that the ban demonstrated that Costa
e Silva's regime was a "military dictatorship in the worst
Latin American tradition." His invective was officially si-
lenced as he was made a *cassação*. Ambassador Tuthill also
came under attack when it was revealed that he had been
meeting with Lacerda and listening to his fervent, belated
protests against close ties between the U. S. government
and the Brazilian military.

Jean Marc now enrolled in a drive to change Brazil's
entire system of higher education. In 1968, only 250,000
students from across the nation—1 percent of all children
who began the first grade—were entering the universities.
In May of that year, Jean Marc and his colleagues called
a strike in which they were asking for more money for the
school of engineering. That strike was nearly as parochial
as the Calabouça demonstration.

To generate support, Jean Marc was chosen to speak on
television. At that time, television and the press were not
yet totally censored. On their screens, viewers were confronted by Jean Marc's long, ethereal face, his delicate yet
resolute manner. He now spoke warmly about opening the
university to the poor, increasing its funds, keeping it free
from government intervention.

That last point interested the former union organizers,
who were forbidden to speak so directly. Jean Marc's
group attracted a wider and more aggressive following,
until, by the end of May, students from the other faculties
voted to expand the protest into a general strike. Before
calling their walkout, however, the students tried to pe-
tition the minister of education with their grievances.

The police blocked them at the ministry steps. When the

students came back in force, they found 20,000 police from all over Rio at the ready. The city looked on, edgy but exhilarated. Drivers snarled in traffic beat rhythm on their horns to show support for the demonstrators.

Jean Marc had been organizing the rear guard at the university and arrived late to a clearly tense situation. Across the main square from the ministry lay Cinelandia, the sector of large first-run movie houses. That wide street was jammed with students and their sympathizers, perhaps seven thousand. Before Jean Marc could reach them, they rushed the police and took control of the ministry steps.

Jean Marc fretted that the students had not adequately explained their position. Climbing up the steps in front of a movie house, he tried to spell out the grievances. Few people heard him.

Meanwhile, the police brought up their reinforcements and gave an order to disperse. Most people obeyed, but some three hundred demonstrators elected to stay. In the milling and confusion, an army jeep was rolled over and set on fire.

Both sides in a political dispute know the power of a symbol: during this same period, anti-war protestors in the United States were sewing the Stars and Stripes to the seats of their blue jeans. The jeep was the first piece of army property attacked during a student demonstration. To Jean Marc, the soldiers at that point seemed to lose control. Although he had not been near it when it was set afire, Jean Marc now stood alongside the smoldering jeep, trying to persuade jubilant students to go home. He was clearly one of the leaders; and when the soldiers and police finally broke through the crowd, he was among those they wanted to arrest.

But being born to a prominent family in a class-ridden country gave him a certain manner. Tall for a Brazilian, Jean Marc drew himself up when the first policeman approached. To that small and timid man, Jean Marc presented his credentials as a reserve officer in the Brazilian marines. Improvising, he said, "I can be arrested only by a marine officer of the rank of captain or above."

Perplexed, the policeman went away. When he returned, he was accompanied by a less gullible police captain, who arrested Jean Marc on the spot.

The arrests made that day provoked another demonstration at which those who blamed the United States for Brazil's despotism led a march on the U. S. embassy. There, throwing rocks at the embassy's inviting windows, they once again identified plainclothesmen in their midst and spotted other armed men on the embassy roof. From the ground, no one could say whether those security guards were from Brazil or the United States. Whatever their nationality, they began sniping at the crowd.

The number killed that day was never resolved. Jean Marc's friends later showed him where two victims—a public official and a shopkeeper—were buried. Medical students and workers at the morgue calculated that perhaps three dozen others had been shot to death. Their estimate became more credible the next autumn, when an air-force officer said that the Parachuting and Rescue Service of the air force had killed many demonstrators that day, collecting their bodies and disposing of them in the ocean.

After the shootings, the student leaders retreated to the university. But most of the demonstrators, including some of the wounded, rioted through the streets, shouting that the government was guilty of murder. From noon until 9 P.M., fighting raged through the center of Rio. Cinelandia, the museums, the opera house, the imposing office buildings, all were in the hands of the demonstrators.

The police were equally out of control, shooting up at office windows along Avenida Rio Branco, the route each year for Rio's joyous carnival. Wherever the police went, people flung down ashtrays, lamps, chairs. One U. S. police adviser never forgot the sight of a policeman, sitting on the curb, crying because he had been stoned. Here it was, the adviser thought, the earliest, the Biblical, way of killing, and the Brazilians were doing it to their own policemen.

Eventually, with the police driven entirely from the center of Rio, the demonstrators went home for dinner, and Bloody Friday was at an end.

Jean Marc heard about the riot from his jailors at the army's First Armored Brigade. All day, the brigade had been on alert. Then the wires to the headquarters were cut and the officers, with no outside contact, considered themselves in a state of war. But headquarters issued no call to arms.

It was a restraint, Jean Marc learned, that disappointed some army officers. During his imprisonment, he was questioned at length by an army colonel, Helvecio Leite, who was notorious as a torturer. Leite threatened Jean Marc with beatings and worse, but on that occasion he was only blustering. After the interrogation, he stayed on to discuss politics.

According to Leite, President Costa e Silva had proved too weak to purify the country. Brazil needed a blood bath, which should have come in 1964, when Leite and some fellow officers were ready to kill the Communists. However, because Goulart and his supporters had refused to fight, that opportunity had been lost. It would come again.

In the week after the rioting, Rio's professors called their first protest meeting and sent their own delegates to the minister of education. The students set their largest demonstration yet for Wednesday. Mindful of the impact of de Paiva's Women's Campaign for Democracy, the students rounded up 1,500 mothers to join their protest. There were also movie actors and musicians and bank employees, along with a few union leaders, although after four years of dictatorship most unions were staffed with docile men.

The demonstration, which lasted five hours, brought 100,000 people into the streets. At the police *cuartels*, at the army barracks, at the U. S. embassy, it looked as though Brazil was finally on the verge of civil war.

Aristoteles Drummond, a little less lithe four years after the coup but still fighting leftists where he found them, received word that the president wanted to speak with him. He took it for a joke, the only humor on that menacing day. Then Costa e Silva himself called. Come to Brasília tomorrow and speak with me, the president said. At 9 A.M., Drummond boarded a military aircraft and flew to the capital with several other conservative spokesmen. They spent an hour with the president, during which time Drummond assured him that Jean Marc and the other student leaders were Communists who did not represent the majority on their campuses.

The next week was quiet, each side weighing the strength and probable response of the other. Believing the future of his government to be at stake, Costa e Silva agreed to meet with a delegation: one priest, one professor of psychology, one tractable student. The group drew up four proposals. Their vagueness caused Jean Marc in his jail cell to despair.

After a month in jail, Jean Marc was released pending his trial, the result of normal legal procedures, not a gesture by Costa e Silva to the demonstrators. Four months later, Jean Marc went on trial in a military court.

The government had one star witness: the driver of the jeep, who testified that he had heard Jean Marc exhorting the students while the jeep burned. The defense had something better: television films of the jeep being set afire with Jean Marc nowhere in sight.

When the court adjourned to deliberate, Jean Marc was ordered to return for the verdict. From the tenor of the preliminaries, he was convinced there would be only one outcome. Besides, he was now running for the presidency of the national student union, and that alone guaranteed a guilty verdict. Consequently, he decided to disappear. His fellow defendant, who was also not guilty, demonstrated his faith in military justice by showing up for the verdict; he was sentenced to two years in jail. In absentia, Jean Marc drew the same. By then it was September of 1968.

A month later, the outgoing UNE leaders decided to hold a clandestine meeting at a farm near Ibiuna, a town outside of São Paulo. Jean Marc argued against the secrecy. Let the meeting be public, he said, and let the police, if they dared, break it up. The resulting publicity would only win the students more converts. But the vote went against him.

By this time, the students had reached a private pact with the governor of São Paulo, a Sodre and a distant relative of Jean Marc's. The governor had opposed the crackdown on the universities, and he promised the students security for their congress. So, from all over Brazil, a thousand delegates streamed into Ibiuna. They faced a three-hour walk to the farm, but for a secret march there was much singing and laughter.

Army intelligence managed to locate them. The local commander called Governor Sodre and told him that the students were armed guerrillas. He was not entirely wrong, for ten or fifteen students had brought along handguns, mostly .22 caliber revolvers. Since the farm abutted a forest, they thought those guns could hold off any raiding party long enough to let the delegates gain cover in the woods. Jean Marc argued unsuccessfully that bearing arms conflicted with their role as students.

The army was threatening a massacre. To avoid that, Governor Sodre decided to arrest the students with his own police, whom he dispatched to Ibiuna. When the students heard of the impending raid, there was panic at the farm. But the São Paulo state police were even more terrified. They believed the propaganda about these fanatical guerrillas, who would fight to their last man.

The police approached the farm shooting. Yet as they drew closer, there was no answering fire. The students had decided that they were not gunfighters after all. Finally holding their fire, the police rounded up the students and poured out stories of how scared they had been. One officer confessed that before he got into the police van, he had drawn up his will.

In the uproar of marching so many prisoners three miles

to the road, the police had no time for identity checks. Once in jail in São Paulo, the students learned that their arrests were already setting off street demonstrations in every state capital. President Costa e Silva tried to lower the fever by announcing that although the students would all be charged, the maximum possible number would be set free immediately, pending trial. Then, too, Governor Sodre was eager to defuse the potential for a riot in São Paulo by getting the prisoners from other states out of his jail. He ordered his men to work round the clock, identifying the students and packing them on buses for home.

Prior to the raid, Jean Marc had been elected UNE's new president. Because he was also the only one among the thousand delegates who was a fugitive from the police, his situation required some inventiveness. In case informers were describing him, Jean Marc traded clothes with one student within the jail. Another gave him a pair of glasses, and he combed his hair into a different style.

The police knew he had been caught somewhere in their net, and officers flew in from Rio with his photograph. As they approached the cells, the students banged on the bars and shouted so ferociously that the Rio team decided not to enter the cells but wait instead until squads of students were led out to the buses.

It was 4 A.M. before Jean Marc was brought from his cell for processing with forty-nine other students. He had concocted a false name to match his new appearance, and he claimed to be from the state of Paraná, south of São Paulo. The governor there was reported to be reasonably liberal.

While the students were being questioned, Jean Marc heard an officer from the Rio detail vow, "He's here somewhere, and I'm going to find him." But as he said it, the policeman yawned, and he passed by Jean Marc without recognizing him.

Once Jean Marc reached the bus, he knew that in a few hours better-rested intelligence officers would be taking up the search. He napped during the ride. Then, as the bus pulled into Paraná's capital city and stopped for a red light, he pushed open the emergency exit, jumped off the bus, and ran down a side street.

During the trip south, he had accumulated the names of people who might help him. His first calls let him know that CENIMAR, the navy's intelligence section, had discovered that he had boarded the Paraná bus. Officers were already checking all traffic out of the city.

Jean Marc considered the size of the town. It was small. His was not the native accent. It would take all his wit to stay a step ahead of the police.

The next day, striking bank clerks had called a mass demonstration in Paraná, to be joined by professors, workers, and the city's poor. A cadre of students surrounded Jean Marc and called on him to address the crowd. He was a wanted man, but he was also a celebrity, and though not the most passionate of Latin orators, he had become diffidently eloquent.

Twice Jean Marc tried to speak, and each time a plainclothes officer in the crowd took a shot at him. Seeing the danger he was posing for the other demonstrators, Jean Marc slipped away to a friendly house, where he borrowed a suit and tie. From another student, he borrowed a car and, newly respectable, drove to the airport.

Some habits resisted even the new technology. Police were stationed at the train and bus depots, and along the roads they were making motorists get out of their cars to open the trunks. However, they were not watching the airport, where Jean Marc boarded a plane for São Paulo. Once lost in its teeming industrial quarter, he lived the next year underground.

Throughout the world, 1968 was a year of demonstrations. Back in Washington, Dan Mitrione was finding the United States far different from the country he had left eight years earlier. Brazilian students at the IPA sometimes asked him why he had not stayed in Brazil, and Mitrione joked with them, "I had to come back so as not to forget I'm American."

But the lawlessness he was finding at home troubled him deeply. IPA instructors in Brazil agreed among themselves that the streets at night were less dangerous than the streets of New York, and Mitrione could feel that he had contributed to the quiet that had fallen across Brazil.

The contrast was so strong that three years later, when Senator Frank Church's foreign relations subcommittee began to probe the rumors of torture coming out of Brazil, the senators called in Brazil's chief U. S. police adviser and asked him where he had felt safer, in Washington, D. C., or in Rio.

The adviser, Theodore Brown, took the bait: "I would feel safer in Rio."

"If that is the case," Senator Church asked, "then how is it we are so well qualified to instruct the Brazilians on adequate police-protection methods?"

It was a debater's point, and the perfunctory committee hearings turned up no hard evidence against the Office of Public Safety, its Washington academy, or the U. S. advisers in the field.

If Nelson Rockefeller wondered what sort of young hooligan organized the protest demonstrations against him in the spring of 1969, one answer was the studious and well-mannered son of a Swiss chemist.

Rockefeller was still governor of New York when Richard Nixon sent him to Latin America to prepare a policy report. The governor was scheduled to spend only a few hours in any one capital, but even the short duration of each stay did not mollify the protestors. In Latin America, the governor was not widely perceived as the beaming egalitarian who ate blintzes and pizza on the streets of New York City. For two generations, long before the prison riots at Attica had tarnished Nelson Rockefeller's liberal standing at home, his family's name had been handy political shorthand throughout South America for imperialism and repression.

The average U. S. taxpayer might find it mystifying that since the 1964 coup, Washington had pumped $2 billion into Brazil to protect U. S. investments totaling only $1.6 billion. But in Latin America as a whole, the stakes were much higher. U. S. investors controlled 85 percent of Latin America's sources of raw material. U. S. investment had doubled from $6 billion in 1960 to $12 billion nine years later, and the Rockefeller interests remained among the most visible of those investments.

At the time of the governor's trip, Standard Oil of New Jersey, part of the trust put together by Rockefeller's grandfather, controlled 95 percent of Venezuela's largest oil company, Creole Petroleum. Below the equator, another Rockefeller family corporation, IBEC, showed assets of well over $50 million. There were also Rockefeller-controlled industries, banks, and supermarkets. Not unexpectedly, then, Rockefeller met riots in Colombia. In Ecuador, the police killed six students demonstrating against him. Faced with public protests, the governments of Chile and Venezuela withdrew their invitations.

Given the scope of Rockefeller's inheritance and the hostile reception he received, the liberals of Brazil were not surprised that his report to Nixon followed a very hard line. According to Rockefeller, workers were largely under Communist domination. The same was true of students, but perhaps they were merely dupes. The report praised the hemisphere's police and its armed forces. The army had enabled each country to deal with "a growing, covert Communist threat to their internal security." As for the police, the Rockefeller report chided the people of the United States for not appreciating the importance of their role. True, the police had been used for political repression, and that was "unfortunate." But if anything, Rockefeller's report concluded, the Latin American police must be strengthened.

That spring, there was more than the Rockefeller mission to occupy Jean Marc. In February, the government had issued Decree 477, forbidding all political activity within the university. The authorities also closed most student centers. In Rio, only Catholic universities were exempt. Many student leaders were expelled, and Jean Marc found growing company in the underground.

Torture was also becoming more systematic. In the earliest aftermath of the coup, a number of men and women had disappeared; their bodies were later found in fields and gullies. The cases of torture had been isolated—a couple of actors; a former army sergeant, Raimundo Suares, tortured to death. Even the leftist students were inclined to blame that torture on a few brutes among the police and military. Their respect for the presidency died hard, though the office was now occupied by usurpers, and torture was far removed from the Brazilians' own view of themselves.

But in June 1969, people in São Paulo were speaking guardedly of a paramilitary organization called OBAN, apparently a collection of intelligence agents from the police and the military. In the war against the Left, OBAN considered itself to have a free hand, and its financing came from industrialists around the city who funneled their money through a man named Boilesen.

Jean Marc spent many months underground without being forced to resort to false documents. Challenged for identification, he would either show his Swiss passport or his card as a marine officer. With a glance at either of those elite documents, policemen would wave him past. Twice when Jean Marc's name was on "wanted" lists, he was scooped up by a police dragnet; but the officers failed to check each name against their lists, and he was let go.

Life underground affected the hunted differently. For

some, the constant movement and daily fears weighed so heavily that they sighed with relief at the clasp of the police hand on their shoulder. Jean Marc was not one of those. When his night came, he was no half-willing accomplice in his own capture.

It was August 31, 1969. Such were the tangled loyalties of that era that Jean Marc was hiding in the house of a physician who was also attending the president of Brazil. In that way, Jean Marc heard that Costa e Silva had suffered a stroke, which the military high command was covering up while his potential successors jockeyed for his position.

It was news too explosive to hoard for himself. Jean Marc set off for the house of friends. They were not at home. Still excited, he broke one of his own security rules and went to a house where fellow revolutionaries were living. Before, he had always met them on the street.

As Jean Marc approached, instinct warned him that something inside the house was not right. Listening at the door, he heard strange voices. Quietly he began to back away.

It was a trap. Minutes earlier, the house had been raided. Now police on the street were watching the door. When they seized him, Jean Marc told the officers that he was simply a student who had come to the wrong address. The police may or may not have believed him. Under the procedure that was evolving, it did not matter. The government had discovered that random beatings created a climate of quiescence at the universities, and the generals much preferred that stillness to the riots of the previous year.

Jean Marc was taken first to the headquarters of the Departmento de Ordem Politíco e Social (DOPS), where he found six other suspects already waiting. They were all told to stand with their feet far from the wall, then to lean forward and press their palms against it. For half an hour they were beaten on their kidneys with clubs. It was not punishment for refusing to answer questions. No questions had been asked. It was a preliminary lesson, to impress on them the consequences of being arrested.

During this first round of beatings, Jean Marc was not blindfolded, and looking around he saw twelve men in the room. Later, he learned that half were from CENIMAR. The other six were civilians from DOPS who specialized in torture.

The main CENIMAR prison was in the basement of the Ministry of the Navy, near the docks of Rio's lovely harbor. Whenever possible, the intelligence agents on the fifth floor of the ministry waited to do their torturing at night, when the staffs were gone from their offices. U. S. Navy officers based at the naval mission in the building sometimes heard screams from across the court. Their attitude was one of wry distaste; but none of them, not even missions commanders—like Rear Admiral C. Thor Hanson, who told aides of overhearing the screams—raised the matter with their hosts. It was an internal matter and none of their business.

Sometimes they saw men, obviously fellow countrymen wearing civilian clothes, around the intelligence office. If anyone was to object to the torture, it was they. Since the screams indicated that the torture was continuing, the information being gathered must be extremely vital to Brazil's security and, by extension, to the security of the United States.

Occasionally Brazilians who had undergone torture at CENIMAR managed to interest a foreign journalist in their ordeal. Once, their story reached William Buckley, Jr., the conservative columnist, as he toured Rio. They complained to him that they had heard English-speaking voices next door to the room in which they were being tortured. If they could hear conversation, why had the North Americans not heard them screaming?

Buckley, who had once worked for the CIA in Mexico City, reported later to his readers that there were radio monitors in the ministry. He said that what the prisoners had heard were not U. S. intelligence officers in the next room but rather transmissions from U. S. ships moored in the harbor.

Jean Marc, when he heard Buckley's explanation, thought that an excuse so transparent would only confirm the accusation in any neutral mind. But who was listening? Either to the charge or to Buckley's rebuttal?

After being held at CENIMAR, Jean Marc was shipped across Guanabara Bay to a prison on the Isle of Flowers, a dot of land in the Atlantic Ocean as beautiful as its name. A battalion of Brazilian marines kept the low white buildings and the grounds immaculate. Also on hand were interrogators who specialized in torture.

For twenty-four consecutive hours, Jean Marc was beaten with clubs and shocked with electric wires. At first the torture was simply administrative, the first stage in the prison's routine. But on the third day, his captors discovered his identity, and the brutality of his beatings intensified.

The island's commander was Clemente José Monteiro Filho, a marine commandante and graduate of the U. S. course in military intelligence in Panama. Monteiro came only twice to watch Jean Marc being tortured. The prisoners were blindfolded, but Monteiro's distinctive voice gave him away. Women prisoners said he looked in more often on them, especially when they were stripped naked.

Among the torturers themselves there was a division, an acknowledgment that a few were sadists and the others merely career men who were following orders. One man who enjoyed his assignment was an agent from DOPS named Solimar. Half admiringly, the other guards called him Doctor Bottleopener for his skill in extracting the last bit of information from the most stubborn prisoner. Solimar was very small, but his energy was prodigious. Jean Marc wondered whether he used drugs. Other torturers often complained of being tired, but Solimar could go on for six and seven hours.

Yet he was not the leader. That man was Alfredo Poeck, the navy commander who had been so impressed by his U. S. training in psywar at Fort Bragg. Poeck tried to protect his reputation by using the alias Doctor Mike.

The fury of the assault of these men on Jean Marc astounded him. He saw how unprepared Brazilians of his generation were for a political war. In Vietnam, fighting had gone on for a quarter of a century; to be a young Vietnamese meant arming oneself for war. But after the first Vargas regime, Brazil had enjoyed nearly twenty years of peace and democracy. Torture had no place in Jean Marc's universe. Until the Isle of Flowers, his greatest pain had come at the hands of his dentist. Now he found himself isolated in a room with men who let him know that they hated him and felt not a trace of compassion for his suffering.

These men routinely wrapped wires around his penis and his testicles, betraying no embarrassment at the intimacy of handling his genitals. With the end of one wire attached to his sex, Jean Marc had the other stuck into his ear, and both were connected to a battery-operated field telephone. Jean Marc recognized the telephone. His marine reserve unit had used equipment like it, supplied by the United States through the military assistance program.

When the crank was turned, voltage leapt between the wires, shocking Jean Marc's tenderest skin. When they wanted to apply the shocks to his mouth, a torturer first put on a rubber glove to hold the wire in place.

Other times, wires were attached to Jean Marc's fingers or, with clothespins, to his nipples. Brazilians called the pins crocodiles because of their wooden jaws. Jean Marc found it disturbing to see those harmless adjuncts to the family wash now appear as instruments of suffering. It was one more proof that the world was mad.

There was another torture Jean Marc hated even more.

The guards took paddles—flat pieces of wood with holes drilled through them—that were normally used to discipline schoolboys. A swat or two left a nasty stinging, like a nun's knitting needle, but until the Island of Flowers the paddle had been nothing for Jean Marc to fear. Now the torturers used them hours at a time, repeatedly beating his head, his kidneys, his sex.

Those beatings and shocks went on for seven days, the first four without interruption. Jean Marc was sure he would not live. What offense justified this fury? Setting fire to a jeep? Giving a few speeches?

On the seventh day, blindfolded and beaten on the ears until his eardrums seemed about to burst, until the inside of his head ached worse than any bruise on his body, Jean Marc learned the answer. He heard Commander Monteiro translating into English the questions put to Jean Marc: "What groups did you belong to?" "Where are its members?"

Jean Marc also heard a man speaking to the commander in English with a United States accent. At the time, Jean Marc was hanging upside down, trussed like a roasting chicken, his wrists and ankles tied to a pole called the parrot's perch. The guards were giving him electric shocks on the inside of his ears. Yet he heard the astonishing news and understood the frenzy that went into his beating.

The U. S. ambassador to Brazil had been kidnapped.

CHAPTER

6

CHARLES BURKE ELBRICK, recently appointed as ambassador to Brazil, was a diplomat of the old school with an air and interests that led younger political officers at the State Department to find him stodgy and unimaginative, to find him, in the words of one very junior colleague, "an old fart." To the more earnest men of his own age at State, everything about Elbrick's life was an irritant. He seemed to them a caricature of the impeccably dressed careerist who selected his political opinions with a bit less care than his neckties.

Elbrick's family, comfortably fixed in Louisville, had sent him off to Williams College. He graduated the year the stock market crashed. Joining the diplomatic corps two years later, he edged his way upward—through Panama and Haiti, and just before the war, Poland. At each of his stations, Elbrick and his wife, Elvira, were indefatigable patrons of the ballet, the local symphony orchestra, and the opera.

As an adult, Elbrick shifted his undergraduate allegiances from Phi Delta Theta to the Metropolitan and the Chevy Chase clubs in Washington. Abroad, with fewer such retreats available, he was a conscientiously good fellow about showing up at embassy picnics and joining in the group sings. He could very nearly seem to be enjoying himself.

During Lyndon Johnson's administration, Lincoln Gordon's service in Brazil had been rewarded with the job of assistant secretary of state for Latin American affairs. John Tuthill, his successor as Brazil's ambassador, was less complaisant about Brazil's dictatorship and had seriously antagonized the country's generals. Now, to ease Elbrick's way, Gordon took him in hand before his departure from Washington and administered a cram course in Brazilian history. Gordon, older now but no less loquacious, talked until Elbrick felt the facts were coming out of his ears. On July 8, 1969, not remembering a thing Gordon had told him, Burke Elbrick arrived in Brazil.

At the embassy, Elbrick's reputation had preceded him, and the fears of his new staff were not eased when Mrs. Elbrick explained firmly that a charity reception previously scheduled for the residence would have to be canceled. "Oh, my dear," she was quoted as saying, "my house is not a public place."

Yet Elbrick and his wife could be gracious indeed, when it pleased them, and there were few qualities that most Brazilians valued more. Perhaps, his staff thought wishfully, when he settles into the job, he will work out after all.

Although Brasília had now been the nominal capital of the country for a decade, the embassies were still loath to relinquish Rio's glitter for the new city's bleak geometry. Elbrick went on living in the official residence in Rio's Botafogo district: 388 São Clemente was the address, and he would return there each noon for an unhurried lunch.

On September 4, 1969, a Thursday in the Brazilian spring, the ambassador followed his habit, dined agreeably, and a little before 2 P.M. set off in the ambassadorial Cadillac to return to the embassy. At the wheel was his Brazilian chauffeur, Custodio Abel de Silva.

The residence was set in the middle of narrow one-way

streets. Making its way down one of them, the Cadillac was suddenly blocked by a Volkswagen that seemed to be stalled. As Elbrick looked to see what was wrong, four men yanked open the doors of the limousine shouting, "We are Brazilian revolutionaries!" They pointed .45 automatics at the ambassador and pushed the driver to the middle of the front seat. In the back, they forced Elbrick to lie down on the floor. To everything he asked, one man kept repeating, "Shut up!"

They reached a deserted spot in the hills above Botafogo beach. The man told the ambassador to close his eyes. They are going to kill me, Elbrick thought.

The year before, John Gordon Mein, Lincoln Gordon's deputy who had been promoted to ambassador to Guatemala, had been assassinated fighting off rebels from his embassy car. Elbrick would not fight, but he would not close his eyes either. Instead, he raised his hand, a reflex, to push away the gun from his face. When he did, another of the men hit Elbrick with a gun butt. The blow stunned him and sent blood running down his face.

His captors prodded him out of the Cadillac and into a Volkswagen bus. Again, he was ordered to lie on the floor while they covered him with a tarpaulin. The man who had told him to shut up sat over him with a .45.

The men spoke to each other but not to Elbrick. They drove for fifteen or twenty minutes. Under the tarpaulin Elbrick began to relax. He puzzled over their intentions, but he no longer thought they were going to kill him. If that had been their plan, they would have done it at the deserted spot in the hills.

The kidnappers drove into a building and stopped the engine. The four of them got out of the Volkswagen. One said to Elbrick, "You can get up now, and if you face forward you can sit on the seat. But if you turn around, we'll shoot you."

Elbrick raised his head. It looked as though they were in a tiny box of a garage. Two men had stayed with him, one on the seat behind him, one just outside the garage door.

It was hot. Very gingerly, careful not to look around, Elbrick slid out of his jacket. He asked for water to wash his wound. Someone brought a bucket and a pitcher of filtered drinking water.

Elbrick assumed that they were waiting for it to get dark so that they could smuggle him safely from the garage. It was only a little after 3 P.M. With springtime's late sunset, Elbrick prepared for a long wait. He pondered his circumstances. Who were these men? What did they want with him?

One of the kidnappers inside the house was Fernando Gabeira, the former police reporter for *Binomio* in Belo Horizonte. Fernando was now twenty-eight, and his rapid advancement as a journalist in Rio had been matched by his evolution as a man of the Left. He had been working as research editor of *Jornal do Brasil*, an influential conservative daily in Rio and teaching journalism at the federal university. He had watched the military coup brewing for years in Belo; yet, when it finally came, it demoralized him.

After 1964, Fernando saw Brazil's Left fall into three major movements. The PCB, Brazil's old-line Communist party, still looked to the Soviet Union for direction. The Partido Communista do Brasil (PCDB) leaned toward Mao Tsetung. Politica Operaria (POLOP) recruited among the Trotskyites. As often happens with articulate revolutionaries, there were many other splinter groups.

The conservative PCB leadership preached that Brazilians must win back their rights through elections. The other groups all saw the only choice as armed revolution. But revolution of what sort? The Catholic Popular Action, the PCDB, the National Liberation Action (ALN), and others favored a revolution of national liberation. MR-8 was different. Movimento Revolucionario do Outubro 8 had been named to honor the day that Ché Guevara was shot. It was an offshoot of the Communist party's student group, and it favored a socialist revolution. Fernando was a member of MR-8.

In his heart, Fernando believed that he and his fellow Brazilian Communists were far from being ideologists. They were Catholics who had lost their formal faith and were now trying to justify Christian concerns by passing them off as Marxist. If they owed their allegiance to any manifesto, it was the Sermon on the Mount.

The members of MR-8 expressed contempt for the idea of working to restore elections to Brazil. One chief grievance against the Communist party was that the Communists in Goulart's day had cooperated with him in peaceable reforms rather than organize an effective resistance against the inevitable military coup.

At its zenith, MR-8 never attracted more than a hundred men and women. The previous July, navy intelligence had swooped down and arrested twenty-seven of them. The small size of the remnant explained the attempt for a grand effect.

Fernando had been steeling himself for this moment by testing his nerve with lesser dangers. He got up mornings at 5 A.M. to leave his expensive apartment in Leblon and race through factories outside Rio, hurling down political tracts. To be caught would have meant arrest, jail, torture, the end of his career.

Then someone in the group proposed a political kidnapping. In 1969, it was not a shopworn idea. They would abduct an important man and hold him for ransom. But not for money. That would not stir the hearts of the average *brasileiro* whom they were trying to reach. It would be better to kidnap a man and demand in exchange the release of political prisoners who were being tortured while they were held for months without a trial. It was a good demand; humane. But how many prisoners? It had to be a reasonable figure. They settled on fifteen.

That much of the planning took six weeks of discussion. As the hectic debates continued to spin out over the same ground, Fernando would think to himself, "We are, after all, intellectuals."

Suddenly it was drawing near to September 7, Brazil's national independence day. Everyone agreed they should take advantage of the symbolism, and the abstract discussions became more urgent. They realized that they had no jail for their victim. However, they had rented a house on Barão do Petropolis in a northern section of Rio to serve as headquarters for an underground newspaper Fernando was supposed to edit. An MR-8 member, Elena Bocayuva, was taking her small children there every day so that the neighbors would think it was a normal household. As soon as her presence was taken for granted, Fernando would launch his paper. Now, with no better place at hand, they decided to use that house to cage Burke Elbrick.

Not that Fernando or most of the others knew Elbrick's name. They knew only that the United States maintained an ambassador in Rio and that kidnapping him would guarantee the largest headlines and the greatest willingness on the part of the Brazilian government to negotiate his release.

(Later, when abducting diplomats became commonplace, Brazilians, joking about the relative status of the victims, agreed that to get one prisoner released, the Haitian ambassador would have to be kidnapped twice.)

To familiarize themselves with the U.S. ambassador's routine, the plotters took a venerable approach. They sent to the embassy a pretty girl who flirted artfully with the young Brazilian in charge of security.

"Oh!" she exclaimed. "I'm fascinated by the way your complicated embassy runs." The security man puffed up and answered her every question.

All at once, it was the night before the kidnapping. Since they did not have much experience in political action, the MR-8 cell had voted to contact the ALN in São Paulo. That group, founded by Carlos Marighela, a legendary figure among the Brazilian Left, also comprised alumni of the Communist party. ALN had agreed to send half the twelve-member crew needed for carrying out the action. Of that dozen, six would actually seize the ambassador on his morning ride to the embassy. The others would stay behind at the house. Fernando had begun living at the address, so he was among those chosen to wait.

It was night when the ALN reinforcements arrived from São Paulo. Marighela was not with them. Later some Brazilians argued that his absence showed cowardice; others saw it as proof that he had never approved of kidnapping as a tactic.

Although Marighela had not come, another revolutionary almost as renowned did join them. Toledo was the code name of Joaquim Câmara Ferreira, a seventy-eight-year-old veteran of the Spanish Civil War who had broken with the Communist party in 1964. Within the ALN he ranked second behind Marighela. Toledo would pretend to be Fernando's father.

There were last-minute arrangements to attend to, including the procurement of four freshly stolen cars. Several men left the house and rounded up three cars and a Volkswagen bus. The revolutionary tactic was to point a pistol at a driver and tell him, "We're going to need your car for an action."

In the early days of the resistance, there had sometimes been room for negotiation. "Do you really need this car tonight?" one young man had protested. "I'm supposed to take my girl to the movies." That would send some rebels moving on, looking for a driver with a less legitimate excuse. License plates were always changed immediately.

Most MR-8 members had been kept ignorant of the kidnapping. They had only been told: Tomorrow, be a little careful. Something is going to happen. But the others, the dozen, went to bed exhilarated by their secret. They knew that tomorrow all of Rio would be talking about them. Or they would be dead. But they did not think seriously about death, and certainly not Elbrick's. Of course, they might have to threaten to kill him. That was the way their hand was to be played.

The next morning, the six set out on their mission. One would linger up the street and signal when the ambassador's limousine approached. Another would block the narrow street with the stolen Volkswagen. Four would leap in with drawn pistols and subdue Elbrick and his chauffeur.

But nothing went right that morning. The kidnappers had scarcely left the house when there was a loud crash on the street. One car had banged another, and the accident blocked the garage so that nothing could get in or out. Then, upon leaving the residence, Elbrick's driver apparently acted on caprice and took a different route. The desperate men of the ALN and MR-8 waited an hour for a car that never came.

So it was important there be no mistake in the afternoon. The tension was too great to be endured another night. Later, talking over why an ALN man—Virgilio Ferreira, code name Jonas—had given Elbrick the crack on the head, the rebels agreed that Virgilio had probably thought Elbrick was making a move to escape and that he had been even more scared than his victim.

At the house, two hours passed. Then four of the six men came tramping up the stairs; and from the exultant look on their faces, Fernando knew that this time everything had gone as planned.

When dusk finally settled, Burke Elbrick was blindfolded and led out of the garage and into the house. "What's happening?" he kept asking. "I want to get in touch with my wife. What's become of my chauffeur?"

The revolutionaries had anticipated Elbrick's concern for his wife. The night before, they had agreed that one agonizing aspect of their life was to have a comrade disappear and not know his fate. Was he dead? In the hands of

the police? Had he acted on a tip and fled the city? They
resolved to spare Elbrick's family that particular anguish.
Immediately upon the ambassador's arrival in the garage,
Fernando had gone to a pay telephone on the street and
called William Belton, the minister-counselor at the
embassy, to assure him that Elbrick was all right.

Fernando could not know that their plan for buying
time had misfired. After they placed a threatening note on
the front seat of the Cadillac, the kidnappers had taken the
driver's keys away from him. His walking down from the
deserted hill they thought would take an hour. But Custodio carried duplicate keys. As soon as the van pulled away,
he drove down to the first house with a telephone. Within
minutes the embassy knew of the calamity, and Belton was
contacting the intelligence office: "The ambassador was
kidnapped seven minutes ago."

Within half an hour, Belton and the staff had copies of
the three-page manifesto the kidnappers had left on the car
seat. It was not reassuring. The rebels demanded the government meet two conditions: the release of fifteen political prisoners, their names to be supplied after the
government had agreed in principle; and the reading of the
entire manifesto over all radio and television networks.

By censoring the press, the military had tried to keep the
population ignorant of the rebels' bank robberies and raids
on the arms caches at military barracks. Now, on the night
of its most daring strategem, MR-8 was demanding its due.

If they received no answer within forty-eight hours, the
kidnappers said, they would execute Burke Elbrick. "Each
of them," the manifesto added, referring to the fifteen political prisoners, "is worth one hundred ambassadors. . . ."
The message ended with a broader threat: "Finally, we
would like to warn all those who torture, beat, and kill our
comrades that we will no longer allow this to continue. We
are giving our last warning. . . . Now it is an eye for an eye
and a tooth for a tooth."

Reading that statement on the air would prove no real

problem, distasteful as the government found it. But the broadcast would satisfy only the simpler of the two requirements: the prisoner exchange looked all but insurmountable. Thus, from the time of the driver's call the entire embassy staff was, in the words of one ranking diplomat, "crapping in our pants to get Elbrick back."

Elbrick, meantime, had no idea that his life had been threatened. In his makeshift cell, he was getting his bearings. They had taken him up many twisting stairs to a top floor and shut him in a room about nine feet by twelve. The shutters were closed, but from the cracks he would be able to tell night from day. Hanging from the ceiling, a single electric bulb burned continually. The furniture was a folding cot and one stool.

The kidnappers told him that he had only to ask permission when he wanted to cross the hall to use the bathroom. Then they took off his blindfold and left him alone. One armed man took up sentry duty beyond the door, left slightly ajar.

Downstairs, Fernando was reproaching himself for not laying in provisions for dinner. For the first time in his life he was responsible for feeding a prisoner, and he did not know what the ambassador might like to eat. Fernando decided on pizza.

In Brazil, pizza is the ubiquitous snack at the small corner bars, their version of the hot dog. For fifteen cents a man can buy a wide slice of pizza fresh from the oven to eat with his glass of draft beer.

The nearest pizzeria was far enough away that Fernando had to take a cab. He picked up the pizza and hailed another taxi for the trip back. As he got in, the driver said, "Do you know that they got that man?"

"Which man?" Fernando asked.

"The man! The boss of everything! The American ambassador!"

"Oh," said Fernando, "I didn't know."

"It's a pity," the driver reproached him, "that you are so

unconnected with reality. Many things are happening in the world."

At the house, the rebels were consulting about the ambassador's head wound. When Elbrick complained of a headache, they called in a revolutionary in his final year of medical school.

"It looks all right," the young man told them. "But if complications develop, you must bring a doctor here."

Although the others wanted to believe that the headache was more likely the result of tension than a concussion, they agreed to frequently check on his condition. Now, however, they wanted to question him. Here he was, the boss of everything, in their power. They would collect the proof for what until today they had only suspected.

Upstairs, Elbrick was growing equally impatient. He called to his guard, "What in the world are you up to?"

The man said, "You'll see, you'll see."

After an hour, Elbrick was ordered to re-tie his blindfold. When it was in place, two men entered the room. Their voices sounded older to Elbrick than those of the men who had grabbed him, and when they spoke it was in the fusty language of Karl Marx. Elbrick asked himself whether one of them could be Marighela. It was tempting to speculate that he was in the hands of the country's most notorious revolutionary. However, it was Toledo who led the questioning. If his intention was to terrify the ambassador, he succeeded.

"Mr. Elbrick, we know all about you," he began, speaking in Portuguese. The rebels had agreed before the abduction that even though several of them spoke English, they would not make the work of the intelligence services easier by using it with Elbrick and narrowing the list of suspects.

"We've studied your career," Toledo went on, "and we know you have long been a prominent member of the CIA."

Elbrick took it for a bluff, a way of unnerving him. "No," he said, "I've been in the diplomatic service for thirty-eight years."

"We know otherwise."

The truth was that in the two months Elbrick had been in Brazil he had not yet requested his briefing from the CIA station chief. Others might call it indifference to duty. Today it looked most fortuitous. Elbrick really did not know much. Even if they were to torture him, he could not betray any profound secrets.

But would they torture him? "We don't like to treat our prisoners the way the Brazilian police treat theirs," one man said. Was that supposed to be reassurance or a threat?

Whatever their intention, whenever Elbrick replied that he did not know an answer, one would say, "Come now, Mr. Ambassador, you don't expect us to believe that. Tell us who the CIA men are."

It was after that repeated hectoring that the ambassador committed an indiscretion. For some time, the CIA station chief in Brazil had been, as Elbrick put it primly, "misbehaving." The CIA man was maintaining a wife and child in Rio and a girlfriend, also from the United States, in Brasília. In Elbrick's view, the man had simply been stationed in the country too long. He had not been seduced by its women, but he had certainly succumbed to its mores.

A few days before the kidnapping, Elbrick had called this station chief to his office. They both understood that such philandering ran counter to CIA rules. But when Elbrick told the chief that he would have to recommend a transfer, the man had pleaded so plaintively that Elbrick had said he would think it over.

Now, pressed by his captors repeatedly for CIA names, Elbrick said, "One officer in the political section maintains contact with the intelligence services, and he briefs me." He meant the CIA station chief. Naturally his questioner said, "Who is he?"

Elbrick gave them the name. The man, after all, had already made a muddle of things. But as soon as he had spoken, the ambassador regretted it. What if they got that man too? With their knowing about his CIA connection, the man would surely be finished. What Elbrick had done made him sick with remorse.

His regret, could Elbrick have known it, was wasted, for his earlier answers had been so uninformed that the kidnappers had stopped paying much attention to what he said. To the Brazilians, Elbrick appeared to be a well-meaning man, even a liberal, who was as contemptuous as they were of the ruling generals. When they kept coming back to the CIA, Elbrick suggested names of Brazilians who might be CIA agents, but it was merely the same speculation they had engaged in among themselves. It was clear that unless he was playing an extremely clever game, Elbrick was simply musing aloud.

The kidnappers decided to open Elbrick's briefcase. Fernando saw that as taking a considerable liberty with the ambassador, but they all agreed that they would read only his official papers, nothing that was personal. Here they had better luck than with their direct questions. Elbrick was carrying no documents stamped SECRET, but he had been planning a trip to São Paulo the following week; and the embassy's political section, drawing on CIA files, had put together a series of profiles on the businessmen and politicians he was due to meet. Elbrick heard the kidnappers going through those papers, and from their exclamations he knew they had found the dossiers engrossing.

For one thing, the language and attitudes of the Cold War permeated the biographical sketches. Was Elbrick going to meet with the minister of mines? Then it behooved him to know that the man's sister was a bit left-wing. Other ministers were described as being flexible; in CIA terms, that was a compliment. Hélio Beltrão, one example, was praised for being very open to U. S. advice.

With that ammunition, the rebels went back to soliciting the ambassador's personal opinions. What did he think of José de Magalhães Pinto, the foreign minister?

This was not idle conversation. Several days before Elbrick was abducted, President Costa e Silva had suffered the stroke that sent Jean Marc Von der Weid rushing to imprisonment. With the president disabled, the country was being run by a military triumvirate.

Elbrick was new to Brazil, but he had no special fondness for generals; and he thought that the vice-president, a law professor and civilian named Pedro Aleixo, had been slighted. Elbrick went to the Foreign Office and asked Magalhães Pinto, "Isn't the vice-president supposed to take over?"

The minister had seemed disconcerted by Elbrick's bluntness. Casting about for an answer, he finally explained that the country was being ruled by Institutional Acts, under which the military triumvirate was perfectly legal.

Elbrick had found it an odd reply. Now, trying to strike a sympathetic chord, he repeated that he had not been satisfied with it. He did not know that the rebels were recording their questions, as well as his answers, on tape.

It was about 11 P.M. before they left him. When Elbrick removed the blindfold, he was sweating, and it was not simply from the warm spring night.

In his briefcase, the rebels had also come across a roll of tablets. These they carefully put on the window sill next to his cot. They think I have a heart condition, the ambassador decided, amused that there was at least one thing he knew that they did not. They were just antacid tablets. Tonight, strangely, he did not feel a need for them.

Elbrick habitually smoked little cigars, cigarillos by Robert Burns, and had been carrying a box of five in his briefcase. He had run through them in the first hour of his interrogation. Now he found that without consulting him, one of his kidnappers had run out and bought him a supply of little Brazilian cigars from Bahia.

The ambassador lit one. It was strong. Strong but good. His captors were peering in the door to watch him, and they seemed gratified by his enjoyment.

Elbrick felt like reading in bed. He called for reading material, and one rebel disappeared and returned with a copy of *Manchete*, the Brazilian picture magazine. He also brought an English-language edition of Ho Chi Minh on revolution. They had given Elbrick a T-shirt; and wearing that and his own undershorts, the ambassador settled down for his first night in captivity.

He read for a while. Then he turned on his side, away from the light bulb burning at the ceiling, and with no trouble at all he fell asleep.

At the U. S. embassy, the mood was not so tranquil. At 5 P.M., the staff official deemed to have the closest ties with the ruling junta went to see Magalhães Pinto. The foreign minister would only say, "We're taking appropriate action." His response was purposely vague because at the moment, the military triumvirate was racked by dissension.

One year earlier, with their riots in the streets, Jean Marc Von der Weid and the student union had come closer than they realized to bringing down the government. Only the police, their U. S. advisers, and the highest embassy and military circles recognized the disarray among the leaders of the junta and the thinness of popular support for Costa e Silva. Tonight, those U. S. agents close to the ruling generals were alarmed that Elbrick's kidnapping would strain once again the uneasy agreement among the military services and reveal to the world their dissension.

It was the army minister, General Aurelio de Lyra Tavares, on whom the embassy rested its hopes and brought the greatest pressures. At sixty-three, a veteran of the engineer corps, he had a reputation for detached analysis, and the embassy trusted that he would foresee the propaganda defeat for the junta in the U. S. Congress were Elbrick to die because of Brazil's intransigence.

The other two ministers, Admiral Augusto Rudemaker Grünewald of the navy and Brigadier General Marcio de Souza e Mello of the air force, were regarded as spokesmen for the hard liners within their commands. Of those two services, the navy seemed the more unbending. In fact, the hard line was demanding that until Elbrick was released, a political prisoner already in custody be taken out every hour and publicly shot. No doubt the kidnappers would retaliate by killing Burke Elbrick, but that sacrifice would be preferable to the humiliation of meeting the rebels' demands.

The U. S. embassy staff saw matters differently. There was no precedent to guide them; nothing like this had happened before. In the absence of any contrary instruction from Washington, they were bringing to bear all their leverage, calling in every debt, to get Elbrick freed.

Once MR-8 had decided to set the number of prisoners at fifteen, the group wanted to free those men and women who were being tortured most savagely. They made room on their final list for one sick seventy-year-old Bolshevik, Gregório Bezerra, to show respect for his twenty years of imprisonment under various regimes. Bezerra had also been one of the first political prisoners abused after the coup of 1964. A Brazilian army major had tied him to the back of a jeep and dragged him bleeding through the streets of Recife.

Jean Marc Von der Weid would almost certainly have been on the MR-8 list, although he and Fernando Gabeira, in their few contacts, had never found each other simpatico. But the same anonymity that had served Jean Marc well in the past now worked against him. Those three days it took the military intelligence to learn his identity were enough to prevent word of his arrest from reaching the outside. By the time his imprisonment became known, Fernando had already dropped the fifteen names into the suggestion box of a supermarket in Leblon.

On his first morning as a prisoner, Elbrick woke up ready to talk. He had found Ho's tract fascinating, and he wanted to discuss it with his guards. Wasn't it a blueprint in reverse for what these young men were doing? Ho wrote about rural warfare, and they were engaged in urban war. There were so many interesting points to cover.

The kidnappers found Elbrick's naïveté as he spoke of Ho hard to believe. As revolutionary ideas they had not been startling for twenty-five years or more. Yet here was a veteran U. S. diplomat eager to probe and debate them as though Mao had never lived, as though Ché had never written, as though Ho himself, who had died just the preceding week, had published his manual yesterday.

Elbrick's colleagues in the State Department could have assured them that his guilelessness was genuine. And in Elbrick's defense, the *Minimanual of the Urban Guerrilla*, Carlos Marighela's contribution to revolutionary literature, had only circulated within the ALN three months earlier.

Marighela had dedicated his booklet, which later won support among revolutionaries in the United States, to three victims of the Brazilian military and police, and to the prisoners "subjected to tortures that even surpass the horrendous crimes practiced by the Nazis."

The ideas themselves, whether from Ho or Marighela, struck Ambassador Elbrick as misguided but eminently worth discussing. The rebels had agreed among themselves that Elbrick's guards would stand outside his door, not in his room, and would speak the minimum to him.

Fernando watched as one by one they succumbed to the temptation to air their opinions before their distinguished visitor. Well, he thought, resigned to it, we are Brazilians. But much more of this behavior, and we'll be inviting him out to dinner.

After Fernando's first excursion for pizza, Toledo had cooked up a mess of rice and beans and macaroni, and that was what they were ladling out to the fastidious ambassador. *Feijoda*, the Brazilian national dish, is a mixture of beans and meat so heavy that many restaurants serve it only at Saturday noon, when their patrons can go home immediately afterward to sleep off its effects. Properly prepared, *feijoda* is a delicacy.

What the ambassador found on his plate was an abomination. Eating the same slop, Fernando and the other rebels agreed with him. Sympathetically, one said, "You don't eat much."

"I don't seem to have a revolutionary appetite," Elbrick answered. Those who heard him laughed loudly and repeated what he had said. The camaraderie that was developing among them would change Elbrick's life more than his kidnapping.

One young man, six feet four inches tall and exceedingly handsome, was the ambassador's favorite guard. Not only did he have a *brasileiro*'s full complement of charm, but he spoke English far better than Elbrick spoke Portuguese and was willing to breach the ban on speaking English in the hope of making the ambassador understand.

Elbrick asked the fellow whether he ever saw his family.

"No," he said, "I couldn't possibly. They disapprove of what I'm doing."

As they talked further, it became obvious to the ambassador that this boy came from what people once termed— and Elbrick still considered—"a good family." He was a natural heir to wealth and position. Yet rather than exercise those options, he was here, existing on beans and rice, sleeping on the floor of this ramshackle house, ready at any moment to have his head blown off.

Fernando was a tradesman's son. He himself might be proud that as he had advanced as a journalist, he had never lost his sympathy for the poor. But Fernando's was not a story to impress the ambassador. It was this other boy—so attractive, so favored at birth—whose sacrifice made Elbrick begin to understand, even to respect, the depth of the revolutionaries' dedication.

That boy and the other guards came in, some with bandanas over their faces, and talked fervently for the duration of their one-hour shifts. "You are in a dangerous business," Elbrick would remind them. "You can be killed at any minute."

"You're right," one young man answered. "But a bullet is better than being in jail. We've declared war on the Brazilian government. It may take ten years or twenty or thirty, but we will win. For every one who falls, there are a hundred to take his place."

Arrant nonsense, Elbrick thought, but they seemed to believe it. None of his young guards was a Communist, they told him, although they granted that there were Communists in their organizations. They seemed particularly proud of Carlos Marighela—for his skill, for his courage, for his having been a deputy in the parliament.

Although he was warming to these boys, Elbrick continued to be put off by their hatreds. He asked about the rash of bank robberies. Over the past month they had averaged almost one a day. "Yes," said one guard, "we're responsible." Elbrick had to laugh at his coolness and nerve.

Before his capture, Elbrick had known in an abstract way about the repression in Brazil. Now here were men who said they would not hesitate to shoot a policeman. "No, no," the ambassador protested. "No, that's not the right way to go about things. You may have legitimate grievances," he went on, still unaware of the tape recorder, "but violence never solves anything."

They answered him: We have no freedom of speech or expression. We have no free press or trade unions to represent the aspirations of our people. We have no elections, no forums, no rights. If we want to change things, this is the only way.

To that, Elbrick had no rebuttal.

While his colleagues stood guard duty, Fernando maintained communication between the house and the world's press. Elbrick had been allowed to write a note to his wife, and Fernando left it at a church, Nossa Senhora da Gloria. Then he called *Ultima Hora*, instructing the editors where to find it. His own paper, *Jornal do Brasil,* lost the scoop because he was sure someone would recognize his voice.

As Fernando was dealing with the press, another of the rebels, Cid de Queiroz Benjamin, ran information between the house and other members of MR-8 and the ALN. That job took him out regularly among the people of Rio, and he was buoyed up by the festive air in the streets. Three months earlier, Neil Armstrong had stepped onto the moon. Now a taxi driver told Cid there were two groups of men he admired: those who had gone to the moon, and those who had abducted the ambassador.

Another MR-8 member overheard passengers on a bus agreeing that for the first time in its history, at least some Brazilians were acting independent of the United States. Everywhere, people walked with radios pressed to their ears as though it were the week of World Cup soccer.

Cid's message-passing all went smoothly. It was the house, never intended to be a people's prison, that gave the intelligence services the break they needed.

Elbrick first knew there was trouble when he heard a whistle up the stairs. His guard picked up his pistol and pointed it at Elbrick's chest.

Downstairs Fernando was answering a knock at the door. On the step were two men in civilian clothes. They asked for someone Fernando had never heard of. He said, "No one by that name lives here."

"That's strange," said one of the men. "We were invited to dinner."

They apologized and left. Fernando wanted to know whether they were truly lost or whether they were intelligence agents. He waited a few minutes, then slipped out of the house and into the garden of the house next door. Through the wall, he could hear one of them talking on the telephone. From the low monotone, it sounded as though he was making a routine report.

Fernando went back to warn the others. It may have been only a house-to-house check, he said, but we have to face the possibility that they know about us and are planning to come back with troops.

They waited. After an hour, the men had not returned. At last, they whistled up the stairs again, and Elbrick's guard relaxed and lowered his gun. But the ambassador realized with a jolt that had it been a police raid, he would have been the first man killed.

Fernando's suspicions had been correct. The two men were agents from Brazilian army intelligence. Neighbors had reported an unusual amount of activity at the house; and after their brief glimpse past Fernando's shoulder, the men decided that the ambassador was probably somewhere inside. What the men did not know was that CENIMAR had received an earlier tip about the house and had sent a car to park across the street and monitor all activity. Those agents recognized the army operatives; and for one heady moment as they watched them approaching the house, the navy men were sure they had unmasked double agents within the rival service.

(The navy agents also photographed everyone who went in and out of the house. Once Fernando went out to place a message for the press, and an agent had cruised along behind him. Later, in jail, that officer reminded Fernando of the episode. When Fernando looked blank, the agent asked, "Didn't you see me?" "No," said Fernando. "Ah, foolish me," the navy man said with a sigh. "I thought you did, and when I came back to change cars, I lost you.")

While this sleuthing was under way, Lyra Tavares, acting for the junta, decided to meet the kidnappers' demand and fly the designated fifteen prisoners to Mexico. Magalhães Pinto's office announced that he would address the nation. The U. S. embassy staff was jubilant. Lyra Tavares received a barrage of compliments on his wisdom and courage.

Then, late Friday, perhaps because of the success of

CENIMAR in locating the house, a rumor spread that the hard liners had forced a reversal of the plan, and there would be no release of prisoners. When Magalhães Pinto canceled his speech, the rumor seemed confirmed. Then CIA agents around Rio picked up the story, and a CIA officer hurried to William Belton with it.

Belton's dedication to embassy security had been less dogged than the military and police advisers would have wished. Once a thief fished out a woman's purse from a stall the woman was occupying in an embassy toilet. The U. S. police advisers used the episode to argue for beefed-up patrolling, but Belton had said, No, when people entered the embassy they should feel a sense of calm and not be surrounded by uniforms. Given that attitude, Belton's desperation over Elbrick's abduction touched few hearts among the police advisers.

By the time the rumor of a deadlock reached Belton, it was 3 A.M., Saturday morning. He called Colonel Arthur Moura, a diminutive and snappy army man who had succeeded Dick Walters as ranking military attaché at the embassy. A veteran of army intelligence, Moura had never been overwhelmed by either the CIA's sources or its evaluations. Now he scoffed at the report and assured Belton that the trade was still on.

Belton kept calling back. By 6:30 A.M., he was agitated enough to tell Moura, "If he dies, it's on your hands."

Moura capitulated to that moral blackmail. Still grumbling, he got dressed and drove to the suburb of Santa Teresa and the house of a friendly Brazilian general who laid the rumor to rest: "When I left the office late last night, they were rounding up the guys. A C-130 is supposed to be warming up to get them off at two-thirty this afternoon."

By Saturday morning, the kidnappers also started believing that the government was indeed going to meet their demands. Some of them wondered why they had not asked for more prisoners, not knowing that to release even the fifteen had strained the military's hard line almost past endurance. It was not widely publicized within Brazil, but forty Brazilian paratroopers had seized a government radio station on the outskirts of Rio to denounce the release.

For the first time, the rebels permitted Elbrick to see a newspaper. To his chagrin, spread across the front page of *Journal do Brasil* was a facsimile of his reassuring note to his wife. The ambassador taxed the rebels with this breach of his privacy, and they apologized. "But if we had sent it through the mail, it would have taken a week."

"Dear Elfie," Elbrick had written,

> I am all right, and I am hoping that I shall be liberated and see you soon. Please don't worry—I am trying not to. The Brazilian authorities have been informed of the demands of the people who are holding me. They should not try to find out where I am, which might be dangerous, but hurry to meet the conditions for my release.
>
> The people, of course, are very determined.
>
> All my love, darling—hoping that we shall be together soon, Burke

Elbrick joked afterward that his only dismay had been the sight of his stiff handwriting exposed for the world to see. Yet, to the Brazilian hard line, his message was somewhat less than a ringing defiance of his captors.

The sight of the letter, like the taxi driver's remarks to Fernando, reminded everyone within the house that this was no private interlude in their lives. All of them now figured in a world-wide drama whose last scenes were yet to be written, and not entirely by them.

Late Saturday, fifteen prisoners were taken from cells at their various prisons. Two men had overheard radio bulletins about the kidnapping and the exchange. The rest left their cells not knowing what new ordeal awaited them.

Magalhães Pinto's speech to the nation was rescheduled for 3 P.M. At 3:30 P.M., he went on the air to announce that the C-130 was in the air and on its way to Mexico. This was not true. Two hundred navy men, shouting that the exchange was a national disgrace, had surrounded the plane and blocked its departure. The navy high command finally called them off, and the plane left a few minutes after 5 P.M. The four-engine turbo prop flew at 360 miles an hour; and with stops for fuel in Recife and Belem, it was estimated the prisoners would travel the 4,700 miles in about sixteen hours.

On Sunday afternoon, Fernando and his group received confirmation that the plane had landed in Mexico City and that the prisoners had been set free. Relaxing with them, Elbrick watched the young men capering around his room. They came to him, patted his shoulder, and said, "You'll be released soon."

Once more they waited until nightfall. As an extra precaution, they wanted to release Elbrick in the midst of a crowd. There was a major soccer game that night, and the logical spot was around Rio's immense soccer stadium. By now they had spent better than three days and nights with the ambassador, and they understood his crotchets. One man cleaned the blood spots from Elbrick's suit and pressed his trousers. He also washed Elbrick's expensive silk necktie. Accepting his tie, the ambassador appreciated the gesture and did not have the heart to say that of course it had been ruined.

When darkness came, they blindfolded Elbrick for the last time and led him downstairs to a Volkswagen. "Now we're going to drive you to a corner," one rebel told him. "You are to stand on that corner for fifteen minutes without communicating with anyone. Then you're at liberty."

"Fifteen minutes!" Elbrick protested.

"You've been here three and a half days," the rebel reminded him. "Fifteen minutes isn't so long."

There were six of them again—a driver, another man in back with a pistol, and four men in a backup car. Sitting in the dark, Elbrick heard a lot of complaining about the heavy Sunday-night traffic. Then the man in the back said, "We're being followed!"

The driver asked, "Should we get out and run for it?"

"I don't think so."

They speeded up, snaking through the lines of cars. At last Elbrick felt the tension dissolve, and he assumed they had lost their pursuers. Behind the blindfold he could not know that this had not been accomplished through a spurt of daredevil driving. When the navy intelligence officers saw Elbrick being taken from the house, they gave chase. Through the snarl of cars they had managed to keep pace with the two-car convoy. Then at a red light the two navy men pulled alongside the backup car. One officer raised his hand until his pistol showed in the window. At that, the rebels stared at his weapon, and then each slowly lifted his own gun. The navy agents were brave but not fanatically so. They dropped back, returned to headquarters, and reported that they had suffered a flat tire.

The lead car pulled to a quiet corner, and the driver told Elbrick to remove his blindfold. They shook hands all around, ambassador and desperados. Clutching his briefcase, Elbrick stepped out of the car. He made out bright lights a block or two in the distance. Feeling disoriented and more than a little foolish, he walked to the intersection and found crowds of spectators on their way home from the soccer match.

Elbrick went up to the first man he saw and asked where he was. Tijuca. It was a cheerless barrio, and the ambassador had not been there before. He asked where he might find a taxi, and the man said, "There's one right behind you."

The driver let out two women fares, circled around, and opened his door to Elbrick.

"Three eighty-eight São Clemente, please."

"You're the ambassador from the United States, are you not? Get in!" He saw Elbrick's head wound. "*Pobrezinho!*" he exclaimed. Poor little thing.

Turning on the radio, the cab driver picked up an announcer saying, "No word yet on the fate of the ambassador." He turned around and grinned: "Do you hear that?"

It took twenty minutes to reach the residence. A crowd had collected outside—the curious, the thrill seekers, and the police. When Elbrick drove up, there was a wild shout. Enough policemen surrounded the cab that they could have picked it up and carried it to the front door.

Elbrick stuck out his head. Newsmen from the U. S. television networks crowded around and pushed microphones through the window. Elbrick said, "Later."

On the steps of the residence, a man from the U. S. Information Service was waiting with a tape recorder; and Elbrick did not feel, as one State Department employee to another, that he could brush him aside. So he said that he was very grateful to the Brazilian government, and he added, to coin an understatement, he was glad to be back. But he could not bring himself to denounce his kidnappers. He could say that they were misguided, that their tactics were wrong. What he could not do was deny their bravery or their dedication or the consideration they had shown him.

At the U. S. embassy, some men who had striven hard for Elbrick's release were appalled by those mild remarks. They knew the strains on the junta, that at any time over the past seventy-eight hours the military rule could have come unstuck. Now the victim was saying that these terrorists, these criminals, were really nice young men who had gone astray. If Elbrick's own staff was disturbed, the Brazilian military command was enraged—and this was before they found the tapes that had been made.

Elbrick did not know that his diplomatic career was over. When an aide told him that there was a message for him to call the Western White House, the term puzzled an old Washington hand like himself. What could that mean? he wondered. Was it the western side of the White House? In due course a call was arranged from São Clemente Street to San Clemente, California, and Elbrick spoke for a moment or two with Richard Nixon. Everyone was curious about their conversation, but all Elbrick remembered was a formal exchange of appropriate platitudes.

With any luck, releasing Elbrick might have ended the chapter for Fernando and his colleagues. Since Toledo was the most notorious of their number, they had let him out in the soccer crowd to make his way back to São Paulo. Their showdown with navy intelligence had resolved any doubts about the house being identified. The two cars would not return there, and the other occupants were out looking for safer lodgings.

One of those young men made a careless move. He was paging through the classified advertisements of *Jornal do Brasil* for a cheap *pensione*. When he found one that sounded right, he tore out the address, threw down the paper, and packed his bag. After they heard that the ambassador was home again, intelligence agents raided Fernando's house. Although it was empty, they found the torn classified section and went to the *Jornal do Brasil*'s office to see what address had been ripped out. Within hours, they arrested the fugitive.

Another young revolutionary had left an old coat behind, a cast-off from his uncle. After a few days the police traced it through the tailor's label, and the nephew was picked up.

For Fernando, Cid, and the others, their ordeal was only beginning. For the fourteen men and one woman who arrived in Mexico City, the suffering seemed to be over.

In small ways, the air-force guards on the flight had shown their disgust for the exchange, not permitting prisoners, for example, to speak for the duration of the flight. If Flavio Tavares Freitas had not smuggled aboard a newspaper to pass silently among his fellow prisoners, most of them would have known nothing about their release.

Tavares was a journalist, and his early exposé of the ties between IBAD and the CIA had earned him a file in General Golbery's office. Later he joined Leonel Brizola's National Revolutionary Movement (MNR), which drew recruits from the PTB and the PSB, the workers' party and the Socialist party, and shared some members with Catholic Popular Action. A prison guard had told Flavio that Christian nationalists such as he were more dangerous to the regime than Communists because their appeal was broader.

Flavio had been arrested by a Death Squad led by a police inspector nicknamed Chinês for the almond shape of his eyes, then taken to Pelotão de Investigaçoes Criminais (PIC), at the police headquarters at Barão de Mesquita in Rio. True to their new procedures, the police tortured him for three days and nights with no serious questioning. Afterward they asked for the names of revolutionary bombers and saboteurs. Flavio knew no names. He was tortured again, by officers from the army, the navy, the police.

In the torture room, the guards administered electric shocks with a small gray generator about a foot and a half long. On the side facing Flavio was a familiar symbol: the red, white, and blue shield of U. S. AID.

His guards wrapped wires around his penis. They stuck wires up his anus. They jammed wires into his ears. Somewhere, they obtained extremely fine wires to fit between his teeth.

The pain was excruciating. What was worse was knowing that when he could not answer a question, he would be shocked again before the burning from the last spasm had subsided.

For those first three days and nights, Flavio was not allowed to sleep or to eat more than a little bread. His torture went forward in shifts. On the fourth day an army doctor came to examine him. For an idealistic prisoner, the arrival of a doctor could be the most dispiriting part of his ordeal. At first the heart filled with hope. Here was a professional man dedicated to healing; he would put a stop to this misery. Then the prisoner learned that the doctor had come only to be sure that the victim was strong enough to endure further torture. He might give a prisoner drugs to make him more compliant, or he might advise the torturers how to keep welts and bruises to a minimum. Despite that guidance, Flavio came off the plane in Mexico City with scars around the little finger of his right hand, burns from the electric wires.

The journalists on the ground sought out Flavio. As a former reporter for *Ultima Hora*, he would speak their language. He tried to impress upon them that for all their air of celebration, the prisoners were entering upon a forced exile.

"I am certainly not here of my own free will," he said, a little stiltedly. "Certainly you realize that I came to Mexico by an imposition." But then his balding head began to bob and his serious expression gave way. With a grin, he said, "But I think this is a pretty happy imposition."

From the questions they were asked, the prisoners knew that the press, while friendly, had no grasp of conditions in Brazil. "Do my parents know I've been released?" one student repeated a reporter's question. "They don't even know I've been arrested."

Soon after his release, Burke Elbrick was summoned back to Washington for consultations with Secretary Rogers and other State Department officials. In their meeting, Elbrick asked them whether the department really wanted him to serve out his tour in Brazil.

His superiors agreed that Elbrick's kidnapping had given the United States a political advantage. Inside Brazil, it seemed to have generated a degree of sympathy, for the embassy had received hundreds of letters apologizing for the indignities the ambassador had endured. Why shouldn't he go back and capitalize on those feelings?

Within the week, Elbrick was flying back to Rio. He was glad at least that he was not giving the appearance of quitting under fire. But once on the job, he found nearly everything unpleasant. The ruling junta was not going to risk a repetition of the kidnapping, so everywhere he went he was encircled by military guards.

Elbrick had always thought of diplomacy as a peaceable occupation. Now here he was, the U. S. ambassador, roaring through the streets like a proconsul with uniforms at every side. Although suspicion had fallen on Elbrick's timid driver because the kidnappers had turned him loose unharmed, Elbrick himself never believed his chauffeur had been involved. Now a huskier man had replaced him, and Brazilian security installed another man in the front seat to keep an eye on Elbrick for his superiors. Behind the limousine followed a car bearing three men with machine guns.

Worst of all, the sympathetic feelings that the kidnappers had aroused in the ambassador would not go away. Elbrick deplored violence. He knew they were going about their crusade in the wrong way, but he recalled their desperation, and he still had no answer to their question, *What other way is there?*

Behind the scenes, the junta was agitating for Elbrick's recall. On his side, Elbrick was not making the slightest effort to atone for his tepid public condemnation of the rebels. Art Moura, as well connected to the Brazilian military as anyone in the embassy, saw the ambassador only at the Friday staff meetings. Elbrick never requested a military briefing.

One day Moura ran into Elbrick in an embassy corridor and seized the opportunity to ask, "Mr. Ambassador, would you consider hosting a luncheon for the commander of the First Army? It might be useful to us."

Elbrick said, "I don't have time for those people."

It could not go on. Within three months, Elbrick was letting friends in the State Department know that while

Brazil was a lovely country, he had developed an irrational feeling about it and would like to move on. When an embassy doctor recommended that Elbrick return to the United States for tests, most embassy officials felt that the doctor was practicing more diplomacy than medicine.

Elbrick went home. As his doctor in Georgetown was examining him, he suffered a stroke along the right side of his body. When he came to, he was in an intensive-care unit. His recovery was complete, but there was no thought now of returning to Rio.

Elbrick retired from the diplomatic service to divide his time between Washington and a house in upstate New York. Occasionally he agreed to appear on television, once along with Reg Murphy, a Georgia editor who had also been kidnapped. Another time, Dick Cavett, the television host, invited Elbrick to share the stage with Steven Weed, the fiancé of Patricia Hearst, after she had been abducted by the Symbionese Liberation Army. There was a slight link between the kidnappings of Elbrick and Ms. Hearst: members of the SLA said they had adopted the tactics of Carlos Marighela's *Minimanual*.

CHAPTER

7

WHILE BURKE ELBRICK was serving out the end of his career, Fernando Gabeira was living underground, trying to organize an effective labor movement. He had eluded the police dragnet in Rio, reached São Paulo, and moved into a house with several workmen. One day in January of 1970, while he was at the corner bar for a Coca-Cola, police raided the house and arrested one of the workers.

As he drew near the house, Fernando saw that it was surrounded. When he tried to edge away, a policeman ran up and put a machine gun to his belly. "Move and I'll shoot!"

Instead of freezing, Fernando reached out and pushed aside the gun barrel. Then he ran. More policemen caught up and surrounded him. He feinted from side to side. They opened fire, and Fernando took a bullet low in his back.

As he lay bleeding, he heard the policemen standing over him debate their next move. "Shall we finish him off or not?"

"No, we want to interrogate him. We'll take him to the hospital."

Fernando spent the next two months in a São Paulo military ward. The first night, intelligence agents came to his room. The military doctor protested: Fernando's condition was far too delicate. They ignored the doctor and began their questioning. They did not know Fernando's identity, only that he had been living with men committed to the resistance. The questions yielded little information, because Fernando was too weak to talk. Nonetheless, the agents continued to return at different hours, sometimes pulling their pistols and pretending that if he refused to talk, they would shoot him.

Fernando believed that they were injecting him with drugs to make him dizzy. He was also being fed intravenously through a tube running up through his nose. It was uncomfortable for him but evidently worse for an officer, Captain Homero. "When you speak, blood fills that tube," Homero complained. "I may be a torturer, but I'm not a doctor. It makes me sick to look at you."

When the police judged Fernando sufficiently improved, they took him to the OBAN jail in São Paulo. Because they were too eager to begin the torture, after one day of electric shocks they had to send him back to the hospital. He had begun to bleed from his penis; and during his stay in the hospital, he had lost thirty pounds from a body with no flesh to spare.

By the time he was returned to the police, they had learned Fernando's name and had stepped up the interrogation in hopes of rounding up the rest of Elbrick's kidnappers; and Fernando had discovered that the police had found the recordings the rebels had made with the ambassador. Although Elbrick's open contempt for the military government enraged them, the police destroyed the tapes because his sentiments could have proved damaging to the regime.

The torturers interspersed their shocks and beatings with a good deal of joking and horseplay among themselves. Lighter-skinned men would tease the mulattos: With your blunt features and dressed as badly as you are, you've got "cop" written all over you. You'll never be able to go out on undercover work. Or they would mock the United Nations declaration on human rights. "Time to apply the declaration again," they would say, tying a prisoner back on the parrot's perch and fastening the wires to his body.

To Fernando, it was a revelation that the men who tortured him were not monsters. Many wore their hair long. Off duty, they went to the same night spots he had known. Some even came to his cell to confide their troubles with women. But they had been trained to detest him. "You are a son of a whore!" a man would shout, while his face clenched with hatred. Then someone would call, "Dr. Paulo, telephone!" As he crossed the room and picked up the receiver, his face would open up again, and he would be smiling and smoothing his hair and murmuring endearments.

Nor could Fernando console himself that the men who applied the wires to his testicles were depraved. They seemed to practice sexual torture only because it was most efficient.

Fernando began to distinguish a hierarchy within OBAN, one that confirmed his Marxist view of society. The poorest men, often also the most courageous, were sent to the streets to make the arrests. The torturers were usually from the middle class. Some had pretentions to culture. Once Homero, the squeamish captain, came to Fernando's cell with a newspaper, ebullient and ready to talk. Fernando saw he was a man who, because he had tortured a prisoner, felt they had established an intimacy.

Homero held out the newspaper. "Would you like to read?"

Warily, Fernando held out his hand. This was strictly against the rules. "All right."

"There's nothing new or important in it," Homero said apologetically, "but this whole experience is incredibly boring for me. I never have anything to discuss with these other torturers. God!" he exclaimed, leaning against the bars. "What I'd really like to do is get away for a weekend in Santos."

Sometimes the middle-level officers, the ones entrusted

with the torture, boasted to Fernando that they had been trained in the United States. One army officer had once reminisced in front of Fernando about going on a raid against a group of Brazilian rural guerrillas. Much to his disgust, the other men in his party had gone stomping loudly across the fields. "It was obvious," he said, "that they had not been trained in the United States."

The torturers found one sardonic way to honor their North American patrons. They would cut open a sardine can and force a prisoner to stand with the sharp edge of each half cutting into the soles of his bare feet. They would then put something heavy in his hand and make him raise it aloft. He had to hold that pose until he collapsed. The police called that torture the Statue of Liberty.

In most cases those men who had graduated from a U. S. military or police school were the analysts and intelligence specialists, and they were chary about appearing inside a torture cell. They were also the men Fernando feared most. They read transcripts of the interrogations and picked out contradictions, either within his own answers or among the responses of other prisoners from MR-8. They gave lists of trick questions to the torturers and outlines of what they wished to know before the day's torture could end.

Within the jail, prisoners compared notes, and some told of seeing U. S. markings on the field telephones and the electric generators used for electric shocks. But all of them attributed the new Brazilian efficiency to United States training. Before the U. S. advisers helped to centralize information, it had taken days to discover whether a new prisoner was a leader in the rebel movement. Now it took hours.

The subject of retribution came up often among the prisoners. Some took an impotent pleasure in describing the tortures they would inflict on their guards after the revolution, when the electrical generators would be in their hands.

On the Isle of Flowers, cell mates tried to convince Jean Marc Von der Weid that torture, however repugnant, might be required at that future day when they were running the country—but only in extreme cases.

"Maybe I am a purist," Jean Marc answered them, "but from the moment you accept one exception to the rule, you accept all. And, speaking practically, torture is a weapon that always backfires against those who use it."

The others said, "The Brazilian government has managed to keep the scope and cruelty of its torture muffled for several years. We will keep it secret, too."

"All things secret are wrong," replied Jean Marc.

At DOPS in Rio, at least one investigator agreed with the revolutionaries who tried to convince Jean Marc that torture was a neutral tool, useful to either side. "I'm here," the officer, whose name was Massini, told a prisoner, who passed along the offer to Fernando Gabeira. "I'm a serious professional. After the revolution, I will be at your disposal to torture whom you like."

With their religious sentiments never far beneath the surface of their politics, most revolutionaries believed that they could never do to others what had been done to them. One navy captain who tortured Fernando also saw it as a difference in character: "I'm a torturer," he taunted Fernando, "but you are not. If the socialists ever come to power, I'll be in a good position, because you're a coward, and you won't torture me."

After two months in São Paulo, Fernando was shipped to Rio and taken by motor launch to the Isle of Flowers. He had never recovered from the shooting and torture. Now he was having trouble urinating. He was too weak to protest himself, but as he lay on his cot, he was touched to hear the other prisoners risk more beatings by pounding on the bars and shouting, "Do something! This man is going to die!"

He was sent to another hospital, then back to an isolation cell on the island, where he stayed for two months, cut off from all contact. But he did hear occasional stirrings in the next cell. For fifteen days, Fernando tapped on the wall. His sound had to be loud enough for the prisoner to hear, yet low enough not to alert a guard.

At last he persuaded the other man to put his mouth close to a crack in the wall and speak to him. "I'm alive," the man whispered. It was the only thing Fernando understood. The man was mad.

Once out of isolation, Fernando came in contact with common prisoners besides the revolutionaries. Homosexuals were usually forced to clean the corridors. At night, as relief from the prevailing drabness, they staged fashion shows, modeling filthy uniforms with a high-fashion commentary on their elegance and taste. It was no carnival ball, but the other prisoners whistled and stamped their feet.

The poor and out-of-work were often run into prison, as were the deranged and incompetent. To Fernando, it seemed that the police had arbitrary arrest quotas to meet. Not every lunatic was as reticent as the insane man in isolation. Schizophrenics tended to scream through the night.

One evening the police hauled in a young man with an obsession. When he could hold a job, he had assisted a truck driver. The duty that must have weighed most on his mind was parking the truck, because during his first night in jail, he became convinced that his cell was a potato truck. He was crying with frustration as he tried to maneuver it into place.

Across the cellblock, the others all began to help him park. "No! Attention! That's it! To the right! No, not yet! Wait! Slowly!" When they finished, the man's truck was safely at the curb.

The main question for Fernando, for Jean Marc, for

every political prisoner, was whether or not to answer the interrogator's questions. Saying nothing—not a word— was called Turkish behavior. Most men freely admitted that such stoicism was beyond them. A woman, Angela Camargo Seixas, was one of those who adhered to it.

Much had happened in Angela's life since the day she helped to carry Edson Luis's corpse to the parliament building. The experience had made a public speaker of her. And she stopped smiling quite so easily. Her less political friends considered that a pity, for her smile had been wide, a little daft, and very endearing.

Angela spoke before the Communists and Popular Action, but she joined PCBR, the dissidents who in 1967 had followed Carlos Marighela out of the Brazilian Communist party. For a year or two, the group had been undecided about armed struggle; but by the time Angela became a member, PCBR was as far left as any other student movement in Brazil. Its hero was Ché Guevara.

PCBR had both a military arm and a political one. The decision was not Angela's to make: she was assigned to the political side. The military members took the risks—stealing weapons, commandeering automobiles, robbing banks.

Then, in December 1969, the armed group of PCBR staged a bank robbery. One revolutionary was captured. A policeman had been shot during the raid, and the torture of that prisoner was unrelenting.

For the intelligence units, the man had been the best sort of catch. As chief of logistics, he knew the entire chain of command and every house where members took shelter. However, he did not know Angela, and her photograph had never appeared in the newspapers. Thus, it fell to her to arrange new rooms for the fugitive PCBR members, as well as quarters for an allied group called MR-26.

Angela heard of a flat in Copacabana, Rio's celebrated three-mile strand of white beach. Many years and songs ago, Copacabana had been fashionable. Now, although its

shops and apartment houses were a bit shabby, it remained
the most vital part of the city.

The police had received a tip about the apartment Angela was coming to inspect, and at 10 P.M. they were hiding
behind the door when she came up the stairs with an immense black comrade named Marco Antonio. Even for
Rio, a city proud of its indifference to race, the two formed
a notable contrast, Angela being so slight, her skin so very
pale.

As they reached the landing, there was another of those
power failures that the *cariocas*, the residents of Rio, had
been laughing about since the invention of the electric
light. Throughout the district, everything went dark. The
police may have suspected a ruse, for they burst from the
apartment and began shooting. Marco Antonio returned
their fire and wounded two policemen before he was shot
in the head. Angela was struck low in her back. She passed
out.

When she came to—it could have been only a few sec-
onds later—the hall was still dark. The police were gone,
perhaps to treat their wounds. Angela was alone on the
stairs with Marco Antonio's unconscious body.

Then began a sequence of terror that most people know
only in their nightmares. Marco Antonio was breathing,
but when Angela tried to lift him, he was far too heavy and
slipped from her arms. Instinct told her to hide. Along the
landing she ran from door to door, knocking softly, knocking louder. Everyone had heard the gunshots. No one
would open a door. She ran up a flight of stairs. Just as she
reached the top, power was restored and the lights went
on.

She thought, Maybe I can just walk away. From its hum,
the elevator was running again. She pushed the down button and waited for it to reach her floor. The door opened.
Two policemen got out. Angela pressed a handkerchief
deep into her wound to stanch the bleeding.

Blithely she asked, "What was all that noise?"

"Go home," one officer told her. "Go back to your apartment."

"No," she said, "I must go to the street to use the telephone."

It was a plausible excuse even in an expensive apartment building. Customers in Brazil bought their telephones, often paying $1,000 or more, and even at that price, there were still long waiting lists.

Downstairs, one policeman was standing guard at the entrance. Angela slipped past him. She was on the street. She started walking faster. She was nearly out of danger when a voice called, "Stop her! No one can leave the building!"

Policemen on the street grabbed her and brought her back to the building. Marco Antonio's body was surrounded by police. "Who is this man?" they asked her.

"I don't know."

They hit her with hard, random blows and asked again.

A police car took her to the headquarters of the Operational Center of Internal Defense (CODI). When the officers stripped off her clothes, they saw the wound and said, "If you don't give us your name, you will die."

Angela's mind told her that she must say nothing at all. For the past week she had known the names of almost every member of her party. The very next day she had been scheduled to meet fifteen of its leaders. If they could frighten her into giving her own name, whose name would she give next?

Her wound sent Angela to the hospital for ten days, frustrating the interrogators. When she was moved it was to PIC, the small building within the downtown police headquarters where Flavio Tavares had been tortured.

She was held there naked to be beaten and shocked with wires. One of the torturers was Costa Lima Magalhães, a distinguished name in Brazil. This Magalhães was a very small man with a large head and an appetite for torture. Some prisoners attributed his zeal to the wound he had received in the spine during a shoot-out with revolutionaries.

But his torture in this case proved self-defeating. Angela's wound opened and blood poured out until she had to be returned to the hospital. From that time on, she regarded the wound as her ultimate protection. If the torture became unendurable, she could force open the wound and they would have to send her back to the infirmary.

The torture room was being painted a bilious and unsettling lavender. The lights were hot. Noises were piped in from the ceiling, screams and gunshots to add to the sense of impending disaster. Angela told herself that the sounds were a composition by Stockhausen, a composer she admired, and after that the noises stopped bothering her.

The interrogation technique followed the lesson plan from Panama and the IPA by presenting one officer as friendly, one as hostile, the classic method of "good guy, bad guy." They brought in the man who had been picked up during the bank holdup. The torture had shattered him, but he said, "I hope you can hold out. I couldn't."

She also heard news about Mario Alves, a founder of the PCBR. The police had stuck a broomstick so far up his rectum that it ruptured his spleen. Trying to make him talk, they had pulled out his teeth, a technique that both revolutionaries and police could recognize from *The Battle of Algiers*. The police also injected Alves with sodium pentothal.

One day, after Angela had been beaten terribly with rubber truncheons and bare fists, a doctor who saw her asked, "What happened to you?"

She told him about the lavender room. His surprise and indignation did not seem feigned. He had never seen a woman tortured, and he was vulnerable to her being a college student and only nineteen years old.

"Do you know who tortured you?" this doctor persisted. "Give me his name. I'm going to report him."

Angela was able to tell him. When the police were torturing, they usually pasted masking tape or a bandage over their nameplates and called each other by an alias. At other times, around a prisoner but not torturing him, they were often slipshod and their nameplates were exposed. She said, "Costa Lima Magalhães."

The doctor reported that Angela had been whipped and sexually abused, that electric wires had been inserted into her vagina. His charges were impossible to ignore, and Magalhães was reprimanded for the record. During the next six weeks Angela stayed unmolested in the infirmary. Except for one lapse when she admitted to being a member of PCBR, she revealed nothing.

Two events, however, sent her back to the lavender room: now that he was aware of the continuous torture going on around him, the doctor was so sickened that he applied for a transfer; and two more prisoners from PCBR were brought in. After severe torture, they outlined the important duties Angela had assumed before her capture.

The next day at 3 P.M., the hour that her torture had usually begun, the police brought Angela back for another session. This time they warned her that if she refused to talk, they would turn her over to the Death Squad.

They told her about uncovering a cache of explosives and kept demanding to hear what she knew about it. Staying silent that day was easy. She knew nothing. But she heard stories about other prisoners: a union organizer, Manuel de Conceição, was being tortured at the same center. As a fellow prisoner with Fernando Gabeira, Manuel had once had his testicles nailed to a table. Now, because his new wounds were not treated, the military doctors amputated a leg.

Throughout her hours in the torture cell, two voices fought a steady battle in Angela's head. One said, "They'll kill you if you don't talk." The other voice said, "They'll kill you if you do." Although the pain was always intense, Angela discovered that the torture never reached through to her subconscious. Every word she spoke to the police was rehearsed and rational. The spasms of pain never caused her to blurt out an answer.

The torture brought with it another reaction, mystical in its way. Angela would faint and awake to find her mind clearer than ever before. She seemed to be floating above her body, and she could look down and watch herself being tortured. The sensation of being outside her body, the distance between her mind and the pain, helped to stop her from talking.

In the lavender room, Angela realized how simplistic her own attitude and that of her comrades had been about torture. They had all agreed that none of them would ever speak, whatever the provocation. If you don't keep your mouth shut, they said, you deserve to die.

Now, after a two-hour beating, she understood why the man arrested in the bank robbery had spoken. She could forgive him. But she would never forgive the United States for its role in training and equipping the Brazilian police.

Since the 1964 coup, Marcos Arruda, the geology student who had protested foreign control over Brazil's mineral wealth, had lived a scrambling sort of life. For the two weeks after Goulart fled to Uruguay, Marcos left Rio for the country and waited there until friends assured him that he did not seem to be on one of General Golbery's lists.

In Brazil, employers had no use for an outspoken student leader. To stay alive, Marcos tutored students and translated technical papers. After a few years, this life was not satisfying his reformer's urge, and in 1968 he applied under his own name for a permit to do manual work in a factory.

Marcos's one deception was listing his highest education as elementary school. Had he been exposed as a university graduate, his motive would have been suspect. Neither the factory owners nor the government would have risked his contaminating fellow workmen with his discontent.

The company that hired Marcos was a foundry and smelting group owned by Mercedes-Benz. The three thousand workers there manufactured parts for wagons and tractors. Marcos was a machine operator, and each day he turned out a thousand molds. Despite the labor laws passed by the democratic regimes, a worker was required to work twelve hours a day. The overtime accounted for $3 or $4 of a $15 monthly wage.

Since college, Marcos had been married and separated. As a single man once again, he could pay rent, eat, and even ride a bus to work on his meager salary. Married men, however, ran through their pay before the month ended. For the last week or ten days, they had to get up in the middle of the night to walk to work and plead to put in fourteen or fifteen hours a day for the extra bit of overtime pay.

The job itself was arduous. The building was open at each end, and in the winter the workers stood burning before the ovens while their backs froze from the São Paulo cold. Iron dust filled the air so densely that even on sunny days a man who took a few steps away from his machine was gone from sight, swallowed up in the gray murk. Marcos discovered that company doctors recommended that men contracting tuberculosis be laid off before they became a burden to the company.

It was little different from conditions forty and fifty years earlier in the United States, except that every Brazilian John L. Lewis and Eugene Debs had been killed, jailed, or hounded underground.

Marcos met with his fellow workers each day for coffee. They needed no lectures about injustices in the system. They felt those in their muscles and in their lungs. Their question was what they could do about them.

Certainly a man acting alone had no recourse. One worker who fell sick with lung disease was told by his doctor to recuperate in the cleaner air of the south. The factory owed him back pay; and before he left for Rio

Grande do Sul, he went to collect it. A guard stopped him at the gate.

The man said, "I need the money the company owes me."

"Wait here." The guard went to the personnel office and came back. "You're not a worker here any longer. I can't let you in."

Frustrated beyond his endurance, the man drew a knife, stabbed the guard, and ran from the scene. No one heard of him again.

Such were the minor grievances, the disputes a union might have settled with one telephone call. The Metal Workers Union of São Paulo, however, was controlled by men named by the military after the 1964 coup.

Marcos and his friends collected evidence that before mass meetings some union leaders met privately with agents from DOPS, the secret police. Together they arranged that if a delegate they did not control took the floor and forced a vote against the official company-union position, the DOPS men would provoke a fight, thereby giving the union president cause to suspend the assembly.

Since the union held no answers, Marcos and other workers formed a committee to meet with delegates from other factories in the area. They would discuss mutual problems and weigh possible solutions. They were seeking change; and by the prevailing definition, that made them subversives.

In May 1970, Marcos was introduced to Marlene Soccas, a woman from the resistance who was not only out of work but living in a house compromised by earlier police raids. Marcos volunteered to find her a job and a safer place to live. By now he was not working either, having developed a spot on his lung and a case of sinusitis. The doctor at the public health service told him he must give up his job in the factory.

"I cannot," said Marcos. "I must work to eat."

"Then you must work only the regular schedule, eight hours a day."

Marcos asked for a statement to that effect and presented it to his supervisor. A week later he was fired. "It's not the quality of your work," the supervisor told him. "It's that you can't work long enough. There are a hundred people out there waiting for this job."

Marcos spent the next week hunting for work, and he felt guilty about not helping Marlene. He stopped by the house of a mutual friend and left a message: "I don't know how you're getting along. Let's have lunch." He named a small restaurant in São Paulo's Lapa district.

Marcos did not know that Marlene had been arrested four days earlier and tortured continuously. Police agents now intercepted the note and brought her to the café to point Marcos out to them.

When he arrived, five policemen were waiting, their shirttails outside their trousers to conceal the pistols in their belts. Surrounded, Marcos tried to rip up a schedule he was carrying, names and places of others in the movement whom he had planned to see that day.

In front of patrons and passers-by, the police fell on him, kicking and punching to get hold of the scrap of paper. Marcos was small and slight, with hands barely larger than a child's. They got his list away from him. They then shoved him into the back of a station wagon. Marlene was sitting in the front seat. "Show him your hands," one of the agents commanded. "Show him your hands so he'll see what he's going to go through."

Marlene raised her hands. Beneath their bandages, they were swollen to twice their normal size. The tips of each finger and the heels of each hand were black. From that moment, Marcos did not blame Marlene for betraying him. He told himself, I am no judge of what she has endured.

As soon as the station wagon pulled into the courtyard of OBAN, the three policemen in the back with Marcos began to beat him. Once inside, they beat him for hours before they asked a question.

Then the interrogation started. They wanted to know who was listening to the workers at the factory and advising them on their problems. Marcos decided that although he knew very little, he would not reveal even that much. Instead, he tried a tactic that occurred to most prisoners early in their torture. He would stall, buy relief from the beatings, by giving them valueless information that would take several hours, perhaps a day, to check. It was time dearly purchased. When the police uncovered the ruse, their torture would become even more punishing; but for a day it might stop the pain, and tomorrow Marcos might be dead.

He gave them the address of his ex-wife's aunt. It would be obvious at once that the old woman was no revolutionary. All she would be able to tell them was that Marcos stayed with her for a few nights. She knew nothing of his activities.

The respite was very brief, and Marcos had not died before it came to an end. The policemen tied his knees to his elbows and ran a pole through to connect them. They lifted him into brackets that held his back suspended four feet off the ground. With the paddle full of holes, they beat his buttocks a hundred times on the same place, until the skin under his flesh was black with blood. As they flailed away at him, they called him "Bastard!" and "Son of a whore!" The way he was hanging exposed his anus, and they threatened to rape him.

Marcos heard all of this very distantly. The threats and excoriation seemed more for their own ears, to goad them on with the work of beating him raw.

They connected the wire of an electric field telephone to Marcos's small toe and the other wire to his testicles. The electricity shot up and down his legs. Marcos did not know he was screaming until a guard shoved a cloth into his mouth. The guards themselves laughed at his shouts, but neighbors around OBAN had been complaining of the noise. Later they put on a record by Roberto Carlos, a leading Brazilian pop singer. "Jesus Christ," the song went, "here I am."

Marcos thought, I have no regrets. My friends and I were struggling for something good, humanly good. I am playing a little part in bringing about a new society. In the Gospels, Jesus had lived among thieves and prostitutes. In the factory, I was living a life as Christian as Christ's life.

Sweat was pouring off Marcos's body. Under the gag in his mouth, his tongue felt crooked. Even without a gag, his voice was gone. His eyes were swollen shut. He heard a voice say, "Let's have some fun."

The policemen washed his body with water. To make the circuit longer and send the shock farther along his body, they moved the wire up to his belly. Then to his throat. To his mouth. Into his ear. When they lowered him at last to the floor, Marcos went into convulsions, which did not stop. For the next month and a half, Marcos could not stop shaking. The police sent him to a military hospital and called in a priest to administer the last rites.

Sometimes, even as the convulsions went on, Marcos fell into a sleep. The police appeared at his bedside and woke him. "You are not a worker," one said. "You are a geologist. That means that you were in the factory to spread subversion. When you get better here, you'll go back to that place again."

But Marcos got no better, and the army doctors had no remedy to stop his convulsions. Two nuns came to his bedside. Marcos was grateful to see them. They were women. The idea of women soothed his spirit.

"How horrible," he heard one murmur. "How can they do that? It is so sad."

Marcos thought, They understand nothing.

The police came again to his bed and called him a Communist. "What is your organization?" "Who are your comrades?" "Why do you work in a factory when you could get a job that pays better? It must be to subvert the others, to make them strike for higher wages."

"Don't you want higher wages?" Marcos asked, but mildly. He did not wish to provoke them to more torture.

"Don't try to sell us your Communist arguments," a policeman said, and Marcos stopped trying to explain.

When his shaking subsided, the police brought him back to OBAN headquarters and told him he had three days to prepare a full confession. They said Marlene had told them he was a member of a subversive group.

Marcos took the three days but gave them nothing. "This is worthless!" they said when they saw the little he had written.

They took him to see Marlene. Marcos heard a policeman tell her, "Get ready to see Frankenstein."

Marcos came hobbling in, a broomstick for a crutch. One leg had no feeling in it, one eye was still shut from the beatings. He asked her, "Did you say I was in a subversive organization? It's not true."

"Shut up, you two," said a guard. "Who's asking the questions here?"

They led Marlene next door and gave her more electric shocks. Marcos could hear her screaming. For himself, his feeling about torture was almost peaceful. He had survived two terrible sessions. They had no worse pain in store for him. But now it was Marlene and not him they were causing to scream.

"We're going to kill her if you don't speak," a policeman said. It was the worst anguish Marcos ever knew.

They brought her to face him in a cubicle. An army captain was there with two lieutenants. "You skunk!" the captain said. "Making her suffer this way! You stink!"

"You are beating her," Marcos said. "Not me."

"You know what we want," the captain said. "You must be stupid, working for that shit wage. You're a geologist. You could have an apartment. A car. Women. You must be out of your head. Look at her." He pointed to Marlene, bruised and sobbing. "Isn't that right?" he asked her.

"No, he is right," said Marlene, indicating Marcos. "I wish I had the courage he has."

They pulled her out of the cell and began to beat Marcos

again. One of them held the broomstick to Marcos's throat from behind and pulled so hard that Marcos thought he would strangle to death and this would all be over.

But there was a wooden door to his cell, and from behind it Marcos overheard one guard whispering to another, "What are we going to do? This guy won't talk." At that, Marcos felt his spirit soar. His enemies were powerless. They had electricity, wires, and clubs, but it was he who had the power.

A general came to see Marcos in his cell. He was also a medical doctor, an old man with white hair. He talked about plankton. Ah, said Marcos to himself, he wants to see whether I really am a geologist. The general seemed to be a cultured man. Patiently Marcos answered his questions. Finally the general asked Marcos why he was in prison.

Marcos told his story, ending with the way he had been tortured and crippled.

The old general grew furious. "That's not true!" he exclaimed. "Nothing like that happens in these army units."

"Stay one day, just one day," Marcos said. "I am not here by choice."

The general called to a captain. "This man is telling me lies! Suspend all salt from his diet. And give him no medicines."

Marcos had been receiving treatment for epilepsy. He was not an epileptic, but it was the only prescription the hospital's doctors had devised to end his shaking.

The captain was even angrier than the general: "We'll suspend his food."

The fury of each worked on the other. The general said, "See that he gets as little water as possible."

Within two days, the shaking had resumed, and Marcos was drooling uncontrollably. He returned to the hospital. In another bed was a prisoner who had been shot; then, with the bullet still in his body, he had been tortured until his flesh rotted. Down the hall, on the edge of insanity, was a sixty-year-old woman, her face deformed from beatings.

Another woman, this one twenty-one years old, had been arrested for distributing leaflets to workers outside a government steel mill. The police administered their ritual beatings. Then they learned she was pregnant. They laid her down and stomped on her abdomen, and succeeded in making her miscarry. But she continued hemorrhaging and was brought to the hospital.

Through the hospital's network of whispers, the prisoners exchanged news from other wards. That was how Marcos heard of two friends who had been tortured in the presence of men who spoke only English.

Later, in a security cell, an army corporal remarked to Marcos how odd it was that Marcos should be in jail with the corporal, an uneducated man, standing guard over him. "It's weird," the soldier said as he offered Marcos a cigarette. "Many of the prisoners are students or professional men. It's funny."

Marcos did not smoke, but he thanked the man gratefully. He had found that army-enlisted men sometimes showed human feeling. The police were worse than animals.

"Doesn't that tell you something?" Marcos said. "We've studied, we've read books. We have something in our heads. And we don't accept the situation in Brazil. Doesn't that tell you something?"

"You have strong arguments," the corporal said. "Let me go away or you'll convince me."

Murilo Pinto da Silva had been a schoolboy in Belo Horizonte when Dan Mitrione arrived to show the police how to be more effective. Nine years later, as a member of the Commandos of National Liberation (COLINA), Murilo was trapped with five comrades in their Belo hideout by a police cordon. In the exchange of gunfire, two policemen were killed. None of the rebels was hit.

Murilo was charged with four crimes: unlawful possession of a gun; being a member of an illegal association; armed actions; assassination. As a result, he also played a role in the training of Brazil's police.

In August of 1969, Murilo and his colleagues were transferred from prison in Belo to the Policia Especial of the army's Vila Militar, a jail for political prisoners in Realango, on the outskirts of Rio.

On October 8, Murilo was led from the jail with nine other prisoners and ordered to wait in an open courtyard. Seven of those nine were also political prisoners from Belo, including a fellow member of COLINA, Irany Campos, who had taken the code name Costa. Two of the others were Brazilian soldiers who had been court-martialed. One had stolen a gun. Murilo did not know the offense with which the second soldier was charged.

Being taken from the cell was always a bad sign. But the mood among the guards in the courtyard this day was jovial, and Murilo began to relax. There would be no torture today.

Then one soldier passed by carrying a heavy stick of the kind used for the parrot's perch. Another carried a metal box about eighteen inches long, which Murilo recognized as a generator for electric shocks. It was capable of greater precision than the field telephone.

Still, Murilo was not alarmed. It all looked so routine, so passionless. Then he overheard a corporal asking, "Are they the stars of the show?"

A soldier laughed and said, "I think they will be."

The joke alerted him. Something bad was going to happen after all.

The prisoners were led single file into a low building and told to stop outside a closed door. From beyond the threshold, Murilo heard the laughing and talking of many men. It was high-pitched and sounded expectant. The prisoners stood very still, a guard beside each of them.

From inside the room, Murilo heard an officer giving instructions. He recognized the voice of Lieutenant Ayl-

ton, an officer who had greatly impressed Murilo over the
weeks he had spent at Vila Militar. As Aylton oversaw the
beatings and shocks, he displayed a calm and control that
a less assured college student could only envy. Setting up
the tortures, Aylton always seemed so—odd description
but true—serene. Now Aylton was displaying that same
poise before a crowd of men, speaking with absolute self-
confidence. Who could hate a man like that?

Murilo could make out only a little of what he was
saying. "Approach them as though we are their friends. As
though we're on their side." That was followed by what
seemed to be a lengthy explanation of interrogation methods, but Aylton's voice rose and fell, and Murilo missed
most of the details.

The lieutenant then raised his voice to say, "Now we're
presenting you with a demonstration of the clandestine
activities in the country."

There was a stir at the door, and one by one six of the
prisoners were led inside. Each young man had his own
guard, an army private or a corporal. The room looked to
be an officer's mess. Six men were seated at each table.
Murilo guessed there were about eighty men in all. They
wore uniforms, some from the army, some from the air
force. They seemed young: lieutenants and noncoms, sergeants.

At the front was a stage that made the room look like a
cabaret. The impression was heightened by the skillful way
Lieutenant Aylton was using the microphone. One side of
the stage was bare except for a screen. The prisoners were
lined up on the other side. Aylton called out a name and
gestured to the man so that the audience could identify
him. From dossiers, Aylton read aloud everything the intelligence services had supplied about the prisoner: his background, details of his capture, the charges against him.

As he spoke, slides on the screen showed various tortures, drawings of men strapped to the parrot's perch or
wired for electric shocks. When Aylton finished, the

guards turned to the six prisoners on the stage and told them to take off their clothes. The men stripped to their shorts. Then, in turn, each guard forced his prisoner into position for the demonstration.

Pedro Paulo Bretas had his hands bound together. His guard put triangular pieces of metal twenty centimeters long and five centimeters high through the four spaces between his fingers. The soldier pressed down hard on the metal bars, then ground them to one side. Murilo had never experienced that torture. He noticed that when the torturer turned the sticks one way, Bretas screamed and fell to his knees. When he turned them the other way, Bretas screamed and leapt into the air.

Murilo was forced to stand barefooted on the edges of two opened cans. The edges cut into his soles, and the pain rose up along the muscles of his calves.

The next guard attached long wires to the little finger on each hand of a prisoner named Mauricio. Those were connected to the generator that Murilo had watched being carried through the courtyard.

One of the army prisoners was put into the parrot's perch. Another was beaten with the *palmatoria*, the long-handled wooden paddle with the little holes. To illustrate, he was beaten on his buttocks, his feet, and the palms of his hands. At the microphone, Aylton said, "You can beat with this for a long time and very strongly."

Nilo Sergio was forced to stand on one foot with his arms outstretched like the Christ of Corcovado. Something heavy—Murilo could not see what—was put in each hand.

A prisoner was kept on display while Aylton moved on to discuss the next method. He wanted to impress on the audience that these tortures need not be used singly, that the parrot's perch, for example, was even more effective when combined with electric shocks or beatings from the wooden paddle.

The parrot's perch seemed to be Aylton's favorite, and he explained its advantages to the crowd. "It begins to work," he said, "when the prisoner can't keep his neck strong and still. When his neck bends, it means he's suffering."

As Aylton spoke, the prisoner in the perch let his head fall backward. Aylton laughed and went to his side. "Not like that. He's only faking the condition. Look"—Aylton grabbed the prisoner's head and shook it soundly—"his neck is still firm. He's only shamming now. He's not tired, and he's not ready to talk."

There were other refinements. Use the electricity where and when you like, Aylton said, but watch the voltage. You want to extract information from the prisoner. You don't want to kill him. He then read out numbers—a voltage reading and the length of time a human body could withstand it. Murilo, his feet cut and bleeding, tried to remember the figures, but the pain was driving everything else out of his mind.

There's another method that we will not be demonstrating today, Aylton said, but it has been most effective. It's an injection of ether into the scrotum. Something about that particular pain makes a man very willing to talk.

The lieutenant also recommended, but did not show, an improvement, the *afogamento*—pouring water in the nostrils while the head is hanging backward. To prove that water on the surface of the skin intensified the shocks, one guard poured some over the prisoner in the parrot's perch and resumed the shocks so that they could all see the increased writhing of his body.

As the water strengthened the current, the prisoner in the perch began to scream. Aylton gestured to the guard, who stuffed a handkerchief into the prisoner's mouth. "Normally you shouldn't use a gag," Aylton said archly, "because how can he give you information when he cannot speak?"

The class had been in session forty minutes, and the tortures had proceeded continuously while Aylton spoke. Now it became clear that Mauricio, strung between two long wires, was suffering unendurably. The soldier assigned to him had been forcing the generator faster and faster until, as Aylton had warned, too much voltage was coursing through Mauricio's body.

Mauricio fell forward onto the nearest table. From the army men, there was a roar of outraged laughter. They pushed him off and hit him and kicked him with their boots. All the time, they kept laughing and shouting jokes at each other.

Murilo came out of his pained trance long enough to have it register with him that these men, the eighty of them, had been laughing throughout Aylton's lecture. Not so boisterously as when Mauricio fell onto the table, but steadily, loudly. Their wisecracking had formed a counterpoint to the demonstration.

I am suffering, Murilo thought, and these men are having the time of their lives.

Or perhaps not every one of them. Sargento Monte became nauseated during the torture and bolted from the room to vomit. It surprised Murilo, this show of sensitivity, because Monte had once ordered a lower-ranking sergeant to give Murilo his daily electrical shock.

The class was coming to an end. Murilo wanted to remember who else was there, joining in the tortures. He might not emerge from prison alive, but if he did, he would remember. There was Aylton and Monte, and Sargento Rangel, from Vila Militar.

Murilo particularly remembered Rangel because of the day Murilo returned from the visitors' room with cigarettes that had been palmed to him. Rangel got a tip that either Murilo or his brother, Angelo, had received the cigarettes, and he ordered each of them beaten with the paddle until he found the cigarettes and pocketed them for himself.

Aylton asked whether the class had any questions about the tortures they had seen. No one had a question.

Murilo was jostled off the sharp edges of the cans and led

away with the others. In the anteroom he saw his brother
and another prisoner, Júlio Betencourt. They were being
led in as an encore. Júlio suffered the torture called the
telephone: a guard cupped his hands like shells and beat on
Júlio's ears until he could no longer hear. Murilo found
that out later. He never did learn what use Aylton had
made of Angelo.

Back in the cells, none of the guards mentioned the class;
but the prisoners who had gone through the experience
with Murilo were consumed with hatred and disgust. On
his cot, Murilo heard one shouting to the universe, "Son of
a whore!" Another kept repeating, "Well, that's the end of
the world." Others traded back and forth a Brazilian
phrase, *"É o fim da piada!"* It meant, It's the end of the joke.
It's unbearable for me to think about.

On his bunk, Murilo considered the ordeal. His greatest
concern had been that if he did not appear to be suffering
enough, he would be taken off the sharp edges of the cans
and moved to another torture. The cans had cut and stung,
but they were bearable. The electric wires were not. So he
had grimaced with pain and hoped that his torture would
not be traded for Mauricio's.

He had no emotions left over. He felt no shame at being
put on display as a guinea pig. No rage at the men laughing
at him. No sympathy for Mauricio. Only self-protective-
ness. That he would not be taken off the open cans and
shocked insensible.

He had got through another day. His feet would heal.
He heard a man shout, *"É o fim da piada!"* Murilo felt calm,
at peace. He knew that after today, whatever his provocation or the justice of his cause, he would never hurt another
human being.

CHAPTER

8

WHEN DAN MITRIONE asked Byron Engle to give him another overseas assignment, Engle knew that the reason once again was money. A man with six of his nine children still living at home had a difficult time getting by on the pay of a five rating in the Foreign Service Reserve—the equivalent to a GS-11, which paid $12,000 to $13,000 a year. In addition, at home in the United States, Mitrione was paying his own rent on a house in Wheaton, Maryland, whereas overseas there had been living allowances and temporary duty pay.

Mitrione had been a good instructor for IPA. Not brilliant, but solid and sympathetic. He had a gift for remembering a student's name after only one introduction, and the Spanish and Portuguese surnames came especially easy to him. But he was restless. In the spring of 1969, Engle called Mitrione to his office and gratified the adviser's wish to return to Latin America.

"We've been thinking about an overseas assignment for you," Engle began.

Mitrione brightened but said, "I love the academy."

"Yes, but what about Uruguay?"

"Boss," Mitrione said, dropping all pretense, "when do you want me to leave?"

Six years after Mitrione's murder, Engle would deny that in 1969 he had even heard of the Tupamaros, the growing rebel movement in Uruguay, or that he had chosen to send Mitrione there because of his experience with the Brazilian police. Engle preferred to be seen as an ingenuous, even inept administrator than as a knowledgeable professional deploying a tough cop where he would be most effective in carrying out U. S. policies. Looking back, he claimed that he had pictured Uruguay to Mitrione not as a troubled country, but as "one of the nicest, most peaceful places" on earth.

Yet, if Engle's account were true, he would have had to blind himself to the field reports from Uruguay passing across his desk every month. Those U-127 forms marked CONFIDENTIAL and sent in by Adolph Saenz, the chief adviser whom Mitrione would be replacing, treated Uruguay's political problems in exhaustive detail—the labor strikes, the student unrest, and the revolutionaries who called themselves Tupamaros. When the Tupamaros stole 40-odd weapons or made off with 140 kilos of dynamite or distributed a stack of propaganda leaflets, Saenz immediately informed Washington. When suspected Tupamaros were arrested, their full names were passed along for U. S. intelligence files.

Despite later disclaimers, it is clear that Mitrione was heading for Uruguay entirely aware that his main assignment would be to improve the capacity of the nation's police to put down the insurgents. Certainly, Uruguay was no sinecure; in fact, the easy assignments were becoming increasingly rare. As rebellion spread around the world, criticism of the tactics U. S. advisers employed was becoming harder for the Office of Public Safety to shrug off. Ugly reports had come in from Athens, where the Greeks believed the CIA had conspired to bring a military junta to power; from Portugal, where Washington had supported a dictator for generations; and from South Vietnam, where reports of savagery were the most persistent of all.

In Portugal, officers from the intelligence agency called PIDE were boasting to their victims that a grade-school education was no longer sufficient for their work. The new interrogation methods were too complicated. The source of PIDE's improved technical expertise seemed clear enough. U. S. officials from the Lisbon embassy called in regularly at PIDE headquarters; the director of PIDE's investigative branch was the Portuguese representative of Interpol; and in the late sixties, four senior PIDE inspectors toured Brazil.

In Vietnam, although civilian victims were often nameless to the U. S. troops, there were exceptions. Ms. Nguyen Thi Nhan, a widow, was arrested several times in Saigon, the first in 1969, and charged with being a member of the National Liberation Front. At police headquarters, she was given electrical shocks, and an iron rod was forced up her vagina. Three Westerners in U. S. uniforms watched her being tortured, and the police told her that they were CIA officers. One of them ordered a Vietnamese interrogator to ram needles under Mrs. Nhan's fingernails.

Another woman, Mrs. Nguyen Thi Bo, was taken into custody that same year in Danang because she had neither an ID card nor money with which to bribe the police to release her. At the police station, Mrs. Bo had a stick poked into her vagina; then her face was held in a toilet bowl filled with shit. She was next moved to Non Muoc station, where she was questioned by five U. S. agents wearing green fatigues. After they tied her up, three of the men kicked her.

Stories like these were beginning to discredit the U. S. intelligence services, and there were worse to come. Although it was not yet public knowledge, the United States had been running torture camps, which were always passed off as schools for survival. Two such secret installations, in northwest Maine and in California, near San Diego, were run by the navy. One torture technique involved strapping the navy men face up and pouring cold water on towels placed over their faces until they gagged and retched. A navy doctor stood by to prevent them from drowning.

On the army's side, Donald Duncan, a Green Beret, went through training at Fort Bragg, where the sergeant giving a lesson in hostile interrogation described in detail a number of tortures, including the lowering of a man's testicles into a jeweler's vise. Finally a soldier in the class interrupted: "Are you suggesting that we use these methods?"

The class laughed, and the instructor raised a solemn face with mocking eyes. "We can't tell you that, Sergeant Harrison. The mothers of America wouldn't approve." The class burst into more laughter at his cynicism. "Furthermore," the sergeant said with a wink, "we will deny that any such thing is taught or intended."

Torture training was not restricted to North Americans. On the island of Niterói, across the bay from Rio, the Brazilian military had set up a camp modeled after that of the *boinas verdes*, the Green Berets. The students were kept awake, starved, and caged. They were hung on beams in mock crucifixions. As a way of breaking a man, it proved too effective. After eighteen hours, the Brazilian soldiers were confessing to crimes they had not committed.

As a result of all this, the Office of Public Safety faced serious problems in 1969. Its connections with the CIA, the war in Vietnam, and the similarities in the accounts of torture turning up around the world were rendering the advisory program politically vulnerable. Worse yet, the rebel movements, especially in Latin America, seemed to be growing. In the eyes of OPS and the U. S. military, the Tupamaros of Uruguay presented a particularly grave threat to established order throughout the hemisphere.

That Uruguay should become a breeding ground for revolutionaries seemed to be one of history's incongruous accidents, like Switzerland being the birthplace of Jean Paul Marat. Indeed, though Uruguay was more than four times the size of Switzerland with half the population, it was most often compared to that country. For one thing, it was wedged between Argentina and Brazil, very much as the Swiss Confederation separated Germany and France; for another, its very existence depended on its being a good and mild neighbor.

Of the two nations, nature had been kinder to Uruguay, giving it a gentle climate and a seacoast with ports for commerce and attractive beaches for tourism. In place of the forbidding Alps, Uruguay had a broad plain for the growing of wheat and vast, temperate grasslands for the raising of cattle and sheep.

To cultivate the Uruguayans' garden, fate sent an idealist named José Batlle y Ordóñez, a newspaper publisher who came to power in 1904, after a punishing civil war. Perhaps as a consequence of seeing Uruguay divided, Batlle was determined to treat the small nation as one family, with labor occupying an honored place at its table. The preceding fifteen years had seen waves of Spanish and Italian migration, but Uruguay's Italians did not settle meekly into communities like Goosetown. They brought to the New World their militant syndicalist ideas, and with Batlle's support they created a powerful labor movement.

Batlle resisted relying upon foreign capital to build his nation, because he believed such dependency led inevitably to foreign control. Instead, he fostered a benign statism, with utilities and industries owned by the government but incorporated as separate entities. Their goal was not to amass profits but to provide inexpensive services to the public and high salaries to their employees.

Batlle sought to temper Latin America's predilection for dictators by proposing a nine-member executive, six from the majority party, three from the minority. That idea met more resistance than his plans for universal schooling, pensions, and health care. It was not until 1951 that Uruguayans at last agreed to being governed by a nine-headed executive.

During the first half of the century, Uruguay seemed to fulfill most of Batlle's other utopian dreams. It was a one-crop country; but the crop, rather than sugar or coffee, was cattle; and since Europe had both the money and a taste for Uruguayan beef, the economy flourished. Cattle were an ever-renewable resource, which encouraged Uruguayans to take life with more than customary Latin ease. They began to joke that in their country, the only one who worked was the bull.

Occasionally, there were warning signs of trouble. Even when the price of beef dipped, pension costs kept rising. In addition, the government spent the bulk of its money on the cities; but since more than half of Uruguay's 2.7 million population lived in Montevideo, that seemed no injustice. Over the years, however, the system had neglected the farm workers, particularly those who harvested sugar cane. The cane cutters received their pay in vouchers good only at the plantation's store. They had to build their own huts at the edge of the plantations. When the harvest was in, the plantation owners would have the huts set on fire, forcing the cutters to move on. They were compelled to work as many as sixteen hours a day. Every attempt to organize or strike was broken up by the police.

The cane cutters formed a mute and helpless underside to Uruguay's model democracy, that statistically negligible 9 percent who could neither read nor write. When they found their voice, it was in the person of a young socialist, Raúl Sendic Antonaccio.

Like Jean Marc Von der Weid in Brazil, Sendic was one of those men marked for the good life. His family were small landowners in the department of Flores; but Sendic, indifferent to his surroundings, chose to live in a poor section of Montevideo. A member of Uruguay's Socialist Youth, Sendic was only one examination short of getting his law degree when he abruptly dropped out of school.

He went instead to Artigas, 450 miles north of Montevideo, and volunteered to be a legal adviser to a new union of cane cutters. Possibly he expected that once the plight of the cutters was brought to the attention of his enlightened fellow citizens, they would rally against the injustices; or he may have worked solely from a sense of mission. Men who knew him early in this crusade said that Sendic never thought his cause would prevail, but he intended to go forward just the same.

Whatever his expectation, in 1962 Sendic led a march of cane cutters to Montevideo. They asked for a law to limit their working day to eight hours, the standard shift among office and factory workers. Uruguay's press gave the march wide coverage. A legislative investigating team went to Artigas and reported that conditions were as bad as the marchers claimed.

Yet no law was passed. The middle class in the cities had its own problems: inflation, unemployment, a growing foreign debt, corruption. Especially corruption. Citizens who neglected to bribe the right official could wait up to ten years for government documents to be processed, establishing welfare eligibility. The banks, the highest levels of industry, the courts, all were believed to be bilking the people and the federal treasury.

Sendic tried another march but found that his demands sounded too radical to an urban labor movement that had comfortable ties to management. Having become an increasing embarrassment to the complacent Socialist party, he broke free from both the unions and the socialists. His goal became to blast through Uruguay's smug indifference.

In 1963, Uruguay's newspapers reported an event incomprehensible to most readers. A group of burglars broke into the Swiss Club, a hunting lodge outside Montevideo, and made off with some old and worthless weapons.

(Five men were involved. One was Sendic. Another was a medical doctor, a club member nicknamed Loco.)

That was the beginning. Then other brazen criminals held up customs officials at Uruguay's borders and took their weapons away from them. Although the police intelligence unit began to suspect these arms thefts were somehow connected, it was not until 1965 that their scraps of information fit into a pattern.

The final clue was a convention. Those Communists who wanted to stay within the law and work through elections, as Salvador Allende was doing in Chile, agreed to meet with dissident leftists who took recent events in Brazil as a portent for all Latin America. Out of that meeting came the Tupamaros, officially the Movement of National Liberation. Police spies called them "the most intelligent and clever of the group."

In time, the Tupamaros produced their share of revolutionary literature. But at the start, their approach was to put results before theory, and they took as their slogan, "Words divide us; action unites us."

That decision to forego manifestos in favor of guerrilla action was shrewdly calculated to win over Uruguay's liberals. Throughout 1965, the Tupamaros bombed a number of subsidiaries of United States corporations. They did not try to maim or kill. Their bombs were only noisy public-relations devices to introduce themselves, and at each site they left behind leaflets on which the name Tupamaro was printed. The name derived from an Inca Indian chief, Tupac Amara, who had led a rebellion against the Spanish in Peru in 1780. A noble name, a revered cause. Yet that revolt had failed, and Tupac Amara had been drawn and quartered in a public square.

At first, the new band sought to avoid confrontations with the police, a tactic that earned Byron Engle's contempt. Cowardly, he called them, because they did not stand up and fight. Half a world away, General William Westmoreland was making the same complaint about the National Liberation Front.

When the Tupamaros did appear in public, they took the guise of public benefactors. One December, ten young people stole a food truck, drove it into a run-down quarter of Montevideo, and passed out turkeys and wine to the poor. Breaking into armories, the Tupamaros stole police uniforms and wore them to hold up banks around the city. If customers were waiting in line, the Tupamaros insisted that the clerk enter each deposit so that the bank, not the customer, would be liable for the losses. On one occasion, they burst into a gambling casino and scooped up the profits. The next day, when the croupiers complained that the haul had included their tips, the Tupamaros mailed back that percentage of the money.

On August 7, 1968, the Tupamaros tried a new tack. They kidnapped the closest friend of President Jorge Pacheco Areco, Ulises Pereira Reverbel, and held him captive in what they called a people's prison. From a public-relations standpoint, the Tupamaros could hardly have chosen better. Pereira, who once killed a newsboy for selling a paper attacking him, had been denounced as the most hated man in Uruguay.

The Tupamaros held Pereira a mere four days. But it was long enough to set the Uruguayans laughing at him, at their police department, at the president. When Pereira was released, not only unharmed but apparently a few pounds heavier, the poor in Montevideo were quoted as joking, "Attention, Tupamaros! Kidnap me!"

While the Tupamaros were staging this popular guerrilla theater, the government of Uruguay was, in fact, undergoing changes very different from any the Tupamaros were promoting. Since 1950, Uruguay had been a part of the International Monetary Fund. Disregarding Batlle's admonitions, the country had been accepting foreign loans, many from the United States, to see the country through droughts and drops in the price of wool or meat.

Although the Tupamaros were dramatizing the need for reform, more Uruguayans were probably convinced of

that need by an inflation rate of 136 percent. To overhaul
the government, voters decided to do away with the nine-
member executive and return to a single president. In
March 1967, they elected as president General Oscar Gestido, whom both supporters and detractors compared to
Dwight Eisenhower. Before the year was out, Gestido
died.

Almost as soon as he took office, the vice-president,
Jorge Pacheco Areco, began to cry "Communist." An
Uruguayan joke ran that they had voted for Eisenhower
and got Nixon.

Philip Agee, seasoned by nearly six years of field
work, put in a productive term in Uruguay, helping to
achieve one of the CIA's major goals. The agency had
already installed much of its usual apparatus in Uruguay,
including an active arm of AIFLD, the labor front. In
addition, a special branch for police intelligence work, secretly underwritten by the CIA, had been set up in Montevideo.

Its chief was an ambitious young police commissioner,
Alejandro Otero. By scoring well on police aptitude tests,
Otero had advanced past many men with more seniority.
He was Agee's age, thirty or so; and although within his
department Otero was regarded as a spoiled child, the two
men got along well.

Slender, dark, nearly handsome, Otero was no less intelligent than Fleury in Brazil, but his campaign against the
revolutionaries never took on the same deadly earnestness.
For all his energy and determination, something about
Otero, perhaps his wide-eyed solemnity, usually made people smile. In addition, he was too preoccupied with the
fortunes of his fellow officers, always sure that the ones he
had outstripped in promotions were plotting against him.
So Montevideo's police headquarters roiled each day with
new tales of Otero's noisy feuds and his displays of ego.

In the spring of 1966, the CIA sent Otero to the United States for a course at its International Police Services School. He was supposed to believe that the school was run by U. S. AID. After that course, Otero was transferred for several weeks of special training directly under CIA control, and not being ignorant, he presumably saw through the IPSS cover.

By that time, Otero was himself on the CIA payroll. Phil Agee knew that his superiors in Washington trusted any foreign contact far more once he was accepting U. S. dollars. With Otero, as with other police officers contacted, the CIA followed a tested procedure. A CIA officer would first comment on the heavy expenses of a new office or process and suggest that since much of the information was useful to Washington, it was only fair that the United States pick up a portion of the bill. When he handed over a sum of money, it was more than any reasonable estimate of the added costs, and he would remark easily, "Don't worry about it. What with inflation and the costs of raising a family, a policeman is never paid enough anyway. Keep it for those expenses that aren't covered by your expense account." Guided by the reaction of the officer being bribed, the CIA officer increased the monthly payments until there could be no question in either man's mind that the local official was now accepting a salary from the United States.

Otero had succumbed to those blandishments. After his training in the United States, the CIA station hoped he would return to Uruguay ready to do battle with the new urban guerrillas who called themselves Tupamaros. But Otero was not notably political except in advancing his rank within the police. In a short time, he was mired once again in intradepartmental intrigue.

The experience with Otero ranked only as a qualified success. But with another assignment, the Montevideo station scored much better. For years, the CIA wanted to introduce U. S. Public Safety advisers into Uruguay. Now at last the Uruguayan government had agreed. But when the OPS sent as chief a man named Adolph Saenz, he proved something of a pest for Agee and his colleagues. To their dismay, he was forever dropping by the CIA office to shoot the bull.

This simply was not done. At best, the Public Safety advisers enjoyed low prestige around the CIA; and Saenz, a former cop from Los Angeles, enjoyed none at all. At each intrusion, the CIA men would try to convey the message: You worry about the police, and we'll take care of intelligence. Most police advisers responded by becoming even more deferential, but not Saenz. Whenever he left their office, John Horton, the CIA station chief, would shake his head despairingly. Then Cesar Bernal arrived, also from the Southwest and a veteran of Panama, and the CIA officers agreed that he was even less prepossessing than Saenz.

Although Saenz was not welcomed at CIA headquarters, he could turn his office at the *jefatura*, the Montevideo Police Headquarters, into a hub of sociability. He always seemed ready to drop work for a story or joke, and the local policemen enjoyed hanging around his office.

The *jefatura*, at the intersection of San Jose and Yi streets, was a large pile of stone with shallow columns to relieve its façade and windows shaped like portholes. As the threat from the Tupamaros grew, the police chief ordered small wooden guard posts installed at each door. Inside, the walls were shabby pink and green, reflecting better than the imposing exterior the policeman's status in Uruguay. A beginning policeman—an *agente segunda*— drew about $36 a month. Even given Uruguay's generous social benefits, that was poor pay.

The U. S. police advisory office was only a small room divided into four cubicles. Everyone understood that William Cantrell would not be there often. A CIA operations officer under the cover of the Office of Public Safety, Cantrell could not reach Uruguay as speedily as the station wished. He was coming from Vietnam and had to stop over in Washington for intensive Spanish lessons. His assignment in Uruguay would be primarily field work; his Uruguayan driver would be Nelson Bardesio.

It was in March or April of 1967 that Colonel Santiago Acuna, head of the police general staff, put Bardesio in touch with Cantrell. Uruguayans who knew the comic strip "Mutt and Jeff" laughed at the sight of Cantrell with his squat little driver. Around the Office of Public Safety, however, the other employees regarded Bardesio coldly. Officially he was only a police photographer; but within the *jefatura*, the Uruguayans knew he had been singled out for more important duties, and they simply could not understand how the U. S. had ever lit on Bardesio.

As it happened, the more Uruguayans got to know about the Montevideo branch of the police advisory program, the greater their questions about North American judgment. Cantrell—quiet, tensely ungiving—was widely known to be a CIA officer, and he strode around the city with the air of a man pleased with his performance. But how could he be pleased when he had teamed up with both Bardesio, a man of obvious weakness, and with Manuel the Cuban?

Manuel was supposed to be an exile from Havana. Whenever he came to the police advisers' office he said little but sat silently doodling. He was said to be separated from his wife and children, who had stayed behind in Cuba. That was why he drank heavily. He was also reputed to detest Fidel Castro.

But modest Uruguayans, clerks with no CIA training, noticed that while Manuel never defended Castro, he never spoke against him; and fishing through his scratch paper in the waste basket, one secretary discovered that Manuel's drawings most often consisted of outlines of the Cuban isle. Then one day Manuel decamped for Havana, and the

Uruguayans heard that he had been a Cuban agent all along.

Saenz had complained privately that he did not trust Manuel. But, as Bardesio had observed, although Saenz was a notorious busybody, he did not dare stick his nose into Cantrell's operation. Cantrell also had his own money, which came directly through the U. S. embassy, not through U. S. AID.

Bardesio had begun to work out of the headquarters of the Department of Intelligence Services at the corner of the Eighteenth of July and Juan Pallier avenues. Through Cantrell, Bardesio and other Uruguayans—some policemen, some merely friends of the police—obtained photographic equipment, a radio, and other supplies for an "Office of Information."

Each morning, Bardesio picked up Cantrell in an embassy jeep and took him to this new intelligence office. At noon, he took Cantrell to the embassy, then home again at five or six.

Copies of the work done by the Office of Information were sent to the U. S. embassy on a daily basis. Both the chief of police and the minister of the interior knew about the arrangement. Both also knew that under Uruguayan law it was illegal.

Cantrell often visited Inspector Antonio Pirez Castagnet, a CIA agent, at his office. Other prominent CIA agents around the *jefatura* included Colonel Ventura Rodriguez, Montevideo's chief of police; Carlos Martin, the deputy chief; Alejandro Otero, of course. And Inspector Juan José Braga, a torturer.

Torture was not a total novelty to Uruguay. Even before President Pacheco's war on communism, gangsters and petty thieves had been slapped around in jailhouses. But the use of violence against political prisoners was a barbarity that Uruguayans thought they had put behind them along with the death penalty.

Philip Agee learned otherwise when he went with his CIA station chief, John Horton, to call on Colonel Rodriguez, Montevideo's police chief. The purpose was to involve the chief in a CIA plot that would pressure Uruguay to break diplomatic relations with the Soviet Union.

The CIA plan was inventive. Dick Conolly, an operations officer, had chosen four Russians from the Soviet embassy and concocted for them a history of subversion within Uruguay's labor movement. Another CIA man, Robert H. Riefe, made up stories about leftist officials in Uruguay's unions to interlock with Conolly's fiction, thereby suggesting a conspiracy. The fabricated report was to be slipped to an Uruguayan politician who would use it to justify severing diplomatic ties with the USSR. First, though, to give it an appearance of authenticity, Horton and Agee took the CIA handiwork to police headquarters.

As Rodriguez leafed through the false report, Agee heard an odd sound, low at first but gradually growing louder. Agee listened more closely. It was a human voice crying out. Probably a vendor on the street, he thought. Rodriguez told his aide to turn up the radio. A soccer match was in progress. By then the moan had become a scream. The chief called again for the radio to be turned up, but the screaming drowned out the broadcast.

Now Agee knew that a man was being tortured in the small room above Rodriguez's office. He suspected that the victim was a leftist named Oscar Bonaudi, whom Agee had recommended to Otero for preventive detention. The screaming continued. Rodriguez finally accepted the CIA report; and with their mission accomplished, Horton and Agee walked out to their Volkswagen for the drive back to the embassy.

To most CIA officers, the Uruguayan police were an unending source of amusement—their ineptness, the hopelessness of ever making them efficient. That was what made a man like Saenz so pathetic, that he was so sincere, so straight, that he could never see the humor of the situation.

John Horton was a prototype of the sardonic CIA operator. Now on the drive back, he referred to what they had
heard from upstairs and gave his usual nervous laugh.

Shortly afterward, Otero confirmed that Bonaudi had
been the man Agee had heard screaming. Braga, the deputy
chief of investigation, had ordered the torture when
Bonaudi refused to talk. His beatings had gone on for three
days. Agee resolved that he would never turn over another
name to the police as long as Braga stayed with them.

This was not the first time Phil Agee found himself
troubled by his work. Secrecy no longer seemed so glamor-
ous; and the aliases, with their surnames always capitalized,
struck him as less larkish: Daniel N. GABOSKY for Ned
Holman; Claude V. KARVANAK for Bob Riefe; Jeremy
S. HODAPP for Philip Agee.

Other aspects of the job also disturbed him. In Washington, one training duty had been to run name checks for
Standard Oil to reassure the company that it was not em-
ploying leftists or subversives at its overseas plants. The
lists came in each week from Caracas, where the security
officer of a Rockefeller subsidiary, Creole Petroleum, was
an ex-FBI agent with close ties to the CIA.

The checks had been only part of the game in those days.
Now, in the field, those same security checks went on
informally for the local branches of U. S. corporations. A
club of seven or eight U. S. businessmen met weekly in
Montevideo with the U. S. ambassador and the CIA station
chief. The head of the General Electric subsidiary sat in,
and the man from Lone Star Cement. (But not the International Harvester representative; he was considered a loud
mouth.) The subversive checks were run for them out of
the CIA station's local files.

Faced by both the direct and indirect evidence of how
his various identifications were being used, Agee could
come up with no better solution than not to give the police
any more names. What if he had protested the torture?
Agee was sure that they would not have listened to him.

To have an impact, any protest would have to come from either the CIA station chief or from the U. S. ambassador. Horton's dismissive laugh suggested that he would not be the one; and safe at the embassy, the ambassador never heard the screams.

Not long before Mitrione's arrival in Uruguay, Cantrell's position within the U. S. mission began to erode. He had survived the debacle with Manuel the Cuban, but now rumors spread that money irregularities were at the root of his troubles. Substantial funds had been made available for intelligence work in Montevideo, especially for bribes to informers who could supply information about the workings of Uruguay's Communist party. Since those payoffs could hardly be subjected to close auditing, every conduit for funds came under suspicion. Was Otero pocketing more than his share? Was Cantrell slack, or worse, in his accounting?

Usually the CIA did not want to waste one of its own officers as chief police adviser. There was too much paper work to the job, too many public ceremonies to attend. But in Uruguay, Cantrell was being recalled, and it had not worked out to have an easy-going man like Saenz as chief adviser. Although Mitrione was not a CIA officer, from his first day in the office, the Uruguayan employees knew at once that their routine was going to be tightened.

U. S. businessmen who had dropped by to pass an hour with Saenz found that his successor was all business. Sparing a minute to be sociable, Mitrione might complain about his pay, how low it was compared to his responsibilities. Mostly, though, he was hard at work; and by the time Cantrell was recalled in February 1970, Mitrione was clearly in charge of police operations in a way Saenz never had been.

That change in the top spot at the Public Safety office had intrigued everyone around the *jefatura*, but no one took a keener interest in Mitrione than a young officer, Miguel Angel Benítez Segovia.

Benítez had risen to the not inconsiderable rank of sub-commissioner, only two grades below inspector. As he advanced, he had distinguished himself as one of the most vocal enemies of the Tupamaros. Around police headquarters, Uruguayans and U. S. advisers alike called them *Putamaros*, the pun being the Spanish word for whore. But Benítez seemed to take the rebel movement as a personal affront. He would snarl and say, "We really ought to get those bastards!"

Such crudity was not Otero's style. As his associates saw it, Otero was still charging out against the Tupamaros like a knight gallant going to do battle with a worthy adversary. They observed sardonically the respect with which Otero treated the outlaws, the esteem he showed for their sly and elusive tactics. It was quite all right with them if Otero wanted to play Don Quixote, but they tried to remind him that he was tilting with true enemies, not with windmills.

For their part, the Tupamaros found Otero the perfect foil. He lamented their daring; but whenever a tip came into his office, the police moved so sluggishly that the Tupamaros could almost always escape.

The Tupamaros were still stealing cash from banks. They were also "liberating" records from finance companies and publishing what they found, records that indicated tax evasion and fraud in high places. Pacheco's government was falling in public esteem, and the pressure for change continued to spread. Pacheco responded by invoking emergency security measures. Newspapers were forbidden to use the words "Tupamaro" or "Movement of National Liberation." Reporters responded by calling the group "the unmentionables."

Those were the conditions of Dan Mitrione's nice and peaceful new assignment. Once again, as in Rio, the surface of his life seemed agreeable. The Mitriones moved into a two-story house on Pilcomayo, a quiet residential street. As wife of the chief adviser, Hank took Spanish lessons and involved herself in community affairs, particularly a thrift shop run by the women of the U. S. community.

Yet, the Tupamaros allowed the new chief adviser no time at all for settling in before they made another dramatic strike. It had been more than a year since Pereira Reverbel had been released. Now the Tupamaros carried off another wealthy victim, Gaetano Pellegrini Jiampietro, and extorted about $60,000 for his return. Mitrione reported to Washington that they had probably been inspired by the recent kidnapping of Burke Elbrick in Brazil.

The police themselves were vulnerable. When the police chief decided that the children of Jorge Batlle, grandnephew of the great Batlle, should be protected, he sent around two policemen armed with .38 Colt revolvers. Batlle spoke with the men and learned that they had never fired their guns. Policemen had to pay for their own ammunition, and these two could not afford the cost. Batlle bought each of them six bullets.

Mitrione also had to deal with another Uruguayan custom. Confronting a criminal, the policeman was trained to fire in the air. He was justified in returning gunfire but never in initiating it. That restriction had to be removed.

With Mitrione in charge, Montevideo, like Belo Horizonte and Rio de Janeiro, experienced a marked increase in U. S. equipment, especially tear gas, gas masks, and police batons for crowd control. More important, however, was the change in attitude.

When a police commissioner named Juan María Lucas had studied at the IPA, Mitrione had been one of his teachers. Upon hearing of Mitrione's appointment to Montevideo, he called together his assistants, including Benítez, and told them, "Now we have someone who will support us in our activities."

As it had in Brazil, Mitrione's assignment also led to an

increase in the number of Uruguayans sent to the United States for training. But these days all students did not spend their time entirely at the IPA or the CIA's IPSS in Washington. In their fifth week, some were sent to Los Fresnos, Texas, where they were taught to build bombs.

The instruction at Los Fresnos became particularly embarrassing to the Office of Public Safety later on, when the press learned that the CIA had been running those courses. OPS said that it had asked the U. S. Army to give the training but the Pentagon had refused. "Maybe they didn't have room for it at any of their bases" was one OPS official's best explanation.

The obvious answer was more accurate. Intelligence agents at the Pentagon had picked up traces of what the CIA was doing, and they wanted to keep the army uninvolved. The instructors at the Texas school, however, were Green Berets.

Except for one detail, OPS could have had an unassailable explanation for sending students to Los Fresnos. By now the world had entered upon a time of bombs and bomb threats. Public opinion might have readily accepted the argument that any nation's policemen needed training in the defusing and demolition of bombs. The problem for OPS was that the CIA's course at Los Fresnos did not teach men how to destroy bombs, only how to build them.

The instruction was called T.A.I.; in English, Investigation of Terrorist Activities. The students were required to sign oaths of secrecy, and to live at the camp, under permanent guard, in tents on the isolated Texas plain. Their course began with a review of various explosives, including C-3 and C-4 plastic bombs, and a scientific analysis of TNT. The students were instructed in fuses—how to light them, how to time them. To overcome their fears, they were made to put dynamite under their shirts and walk toward the camp with the detonator set.

Next the students had to race the clock, setting a charge against a gas tank or a telephone pole in a specified number of minutes. They learned to catapult bombs. Practicing on the camp fence, they were shown how to cut through steel. In the clear Texas air, they blew up jeeps carrying cans of gasoline.

The students were called guerrillas, and they were told, This is what guerrillas do. Given that instruction, it was not surprising that Byron Engle later denied that IPA students had been shown *The Battle of Algiers*, with its scenes of policemen excusing themselves from a dinner party to go off to bomb a rebel's house.

Then grenades: ten or so for each student to lob at gasoline cans or old cars. Next: the Claymore anti-personnel mines, a staple of the Vietnam war. Filled with long nails, one mine could wound a dozen men at five hundred yards. Finally, the thirty students of the course, all from Central and South America, were given a major assignment: blow up a convoy of trucks; hit a gas depot surrounded by booby traps; interrupt enemy communications by slipping past sentinels and knocking over telephone poles. The director of the IPA and a cadre of Green Berets sometimes oversaw these commencement exercises.

At the end of the course, one student who asked his hosts why the training had been given was told: "The United States thinks that the moment will come when in each of the friendly countries, they could use a student of confidence—who has become a specialist in explosives; that is why the different governments have chosen their favorite persons."

Mitrione sent at least seven men to take the CIA's course in Los Fresnos. Among them was Inspector Lucas, who had hailed Mitrione's arrival in Montevideo. Another was Subcommissioner Benítez, who hated the Tupamaros from the bottom of his heart and at the top of his lungs.

During this period, the CIA stations of Latin America's Southern Cone entered into a period of even greater cooperation. The Western Hemisphere Division had always been an active liaison office. In 1964, when the CIA's Office of Finance in Washington could not secure enough Chilean escudos for its election campaign against Salvador Allende, it set up regional purchasing offices in Buenos Aires, Rio, Lima, and Montevideo.

Helping out in that emergency, Philip Agee had contacted the assistant manager of the Montevideo branch of the First National City Bank of New York, who was also a CIA agent, and he sent men to Santiago to buy $100,000 in escudos. Those bills were then sent back into Chile via the U. S. embassy's diplomatic pouch.

In the late 1960s, that CIA network began handling matters more sensitive than illegal money. The agency was putting Brazilian, Argentinian, and Uruguayan military and police officers in touch with each other for training in wire tapping and other intelligence procedures, and for supplies of explosives and untraceable guns. Those contacts also led to the surveillance, the harassment, and finally the assassination of political exiles. Between the time Allende was elected president of Chile and his overthrow in 1973, the CIA arranged similar meetings between the Brazilian right wing and Chilean army and police officials opposed to Allende.

Members of Brazil's Death Squads were introduced to the police in Montevideo and Buenos Aires. After he shot Carlos Marighela in November 1969, Sergio Fleury of São Paulo became celebrated among Uruguayan police. He met with groups of them, on at least two occasions through CIA contacts.

One Uruguayan police official, proudly nationalistic, resented the way in which U. S. intelligence operators seemed to be melding the intelligence services of the Southern Cone into one interlocking apparatus. He was convinced that given Uruguay's small size and its position between Argentina and Brazil, this surrendering of autonomy would one day prove harmful to his country. If this work was so valuable in stopping communism, he wondered, why did the CIA officers take such care that their role be secret? For example, a high-ranking official from Argentina's Ministry of Justice arrived in Montevideo to discuss ways of monitoring the two countries' political exiles. A CIA man had arranged that particular meeting, then found an excuse for not attending it.

The Uruguayan, who understood the concept of "deniability," wondered why a U. S. intelligence officer should feel his country's reputation was more valuable than Uruguay's. Another point gnawed at him as well. The turning over of Uruguayan intelligence to the CIA was treason. Despite the motive, despite its expressed goal of allowing the CIA to help protect Uruguay against subversion, it was still treason.

But the official, until he retired, never spoke out. When he did, many years later, it was nervously and after exacting repeated promises of anonymity. Had he complained earlier, he could never have been sure whether a colleague agreed with him or pretended to agree and immediately picked up the phone to call his CIA contact.

William Cantrell's former driver, Nelson Bardesio, seemed to have no doubts about the virtue of the CIA's anti-subversive methods. After Cantrell's departure, Bardesio readily accepted an assignment to a secret team under the control of the Ministry of the Interior. Of his five fellow team members, three came from the traffic police and two from the police institute.

The director of the effort was President Pacheco's personal secretary, Carlos Piran, who later sent the Uruguayans to Buenos Aires for training with the Argentinian Information Service (SIDE). While in Buenos Aires, Bardesio called on a SIDE captain who gave him three charges of gelignite to deliver to Piran.

Bardesio and his associates then formed an Escadron de

la Mort, which bombed the houses of lawyers and teachers considered sympathetic to the Tupamaros. On at least one occasion, they killed a suspect they had kidnapped. Bardesio's crew rode to and from their bombings in police cars. After the bomb was exploded, Bardesio would tell the central radio operator at police headquarters where he was leaving the getaway car.

The importance of his illicit life turned Bardesio's head. In fact, once when he decided the car issued to him was not adequate, he refused the mission. The minister of the interior ordered the Montevideo police chief from that time forward to give Bardesio whatever he wanted.

During his first year in Uruguay, Mitrione's duties became increasingly arduous, but he took time to enjoy himself on the golf course and to keep in touch with his family in Richmond. Early in 1970, he wrote to Ray, asking him to send a set of irons and numbered cloth wood covers; he enclosed a check for $158. The condition of his present set had brought out Mitrione's jocular humor: ". . . the war-clubs that Daniel Boone used to hunt bears with that I bought second-handed back in 1948 are not doing much for my game."

The clubs and covers were missent. When he inquired about their whereabouts, Mitrione also supplied Ray with innocuous observations about his life: "I came back yesterday from a two-day trip of about 700 miles. Sure is pretty country."

The jaunt had actually been part of Mitrione's effort to improve the efficiency of Uruguay's interior police departments and to scout the countryside for potential IPA recruits. The Tupamaros were an urban group with their foco in Montevideo. If the battleground later shifted to the country, Mitrione wanted the rural police to be prepared.

"The country situation is still calm," Mitrione wrote Ray in February 1970. "However, when summer is over and everyone starts thinking about something else besides the beach, it may get a little livelier. I hope not." He added that he could now work at home. "I have an office they furnished for me all set up." At the *jefatura*, the policemen noticed that Mitrione was spending less time in the OPS office.

Benítez once visited Mitrione's embassy office, where his camera eye swept the room. Mitrione's office had thick green carpeting, a bulletin board covered with white nylon, two armchairs, a small sofa. It was air conditioned. Benítez admired three photographs of waterfalls, decorative touches supplied by U. S. AID. Mitrione, he noticed, sat at his desk with his back to the window; and although he was on an upper floor, he seemed to present a tempting target.

"Don't you worry," Mitrione explained. "Those window panes can stop a .45-caliber bullet." Mitrione, however, was now carrying a pistol, a .38-caliber Smith and Wesson. In Belo Horizonte and Rio, he had felt secure without one.

In March 1970, his family in Richmond informed him that his mother's condition was deteriorating. He replied that it would take forty-eight hours from the time he left Uruguay to make the connections and arrive in Richmond. He also reminded his brother that although he was now a chief by title, he was still only a non-com in the Office of Public Safety: "It would also be well to advise Dr. Mader that he is the one that has to convince Washington that Mom's condition warrants my being there."

He ended his next letter: "Take care and God bless, as ever," and then added a postscript: "Things could get a little 'hot' here in the next couple of months." One word had been crossed out and changed. He had first written: "Things should get a little 'hot' here . . ."

Late in March, the worsening news from home caused Mitrione to fly to Richmond alone. It was the last time he saw his mother. Still, except for the sadness underlying his return, Mitrione had a fine time. He was back with people who admired him and away, for the first time in eight months, from the tensions of his work. To his closest friends from the Richmond police, he confided something of the dangers he was facing in Montevideo. With his brothers and sisters, as with his wife and children, Mitrione was less forthcoming.

His reticence with the man who cared most about him may have troubled Mitrione, for a month after his return to Uruguay he wrote Ray: "The situation here is still pretty (you know what), and I wish I could have told you more when I was home with you. I am not trying to alarm you, because you know what it's like in most Latin American countries at this time."

On April 13, 1970, a band of Tupamaros shot Inspector Héctor Romero Moran Charquero to death with a machine gun as he was driving to work. In his monthly report to Washington, Mitrione noted that Moran was a graduate of the International Police Academy and was head of Montevideo's Special Brigade to fight terrorists. He also wrote that one Uruguayan newspaper, an "extreme leftist daily," had been carrying out a week-long press campaign vilifying Moran as one of the principal police 'torturers' of terrorist suspects." He added that Pacheco's government had closed the newspaper in a "quick-reaction to [its] smear campaign."

Near the end of the report, in the section marked EVALUATION, Mitrione wrote: "It is felt that the police will continue to be a target and that there may be other attempts to kidnap and/or kill key police officials."

For Benítez, the predictions about Mitrione from Lucas had turned out to be accurate. Mitrione brought a new spirit of dedication and expertise to police work. In the land of mañana, he never postponed today's work to tomorrow.

That much had been true of Mitrione ten years ago, but he was different in 1969, heavier, tougher than he had been in Belo Horizonte, very knowing about the ways of U. S. intelligence overseas, and totally committed to the policeman, his miseries, his poor pay, his war on subversives.

Over the years, Mitrione had raised his sights. Measuring himself against the average police adviser had given him considerable confidence, and in Brazil he had learned to cooperate with those CIA officials who he felt were the real leaders in the fight against communism. He could believe that in Rio he had earned their respect, as in Montevideo Adolph Saenz had not.

Was it far-fetched to speculate that when J. Edgar Hoover finally retired from the FBI, his successor might be a former Midwestern police chief with international experience? Mitrione's loyal family saw nothing impossible about that vision. Naturally, any such extraordinary promotion would depend on Mitrione's success in quelling the Tupamaros. He was now forty-nine. This assignment could be the best, the last, chance of his life.

Mitrione had been chief police adviser only nine months when a respected Uruguayan weekly ran an issue with one word on the cover: *Torturada*. The magazine, *Marcha*, was reporting the results of an investigation by liberal members of the Uruguayan Senate who had found that the police were systematically torturing suspected Tupamaros. The methods would not have surprised a Brazilian prisoner— electric needles under the fingernails; electric shocks along the body, particularly on the captive's sexual organs.

Mitrione filed a report of the Senate's findings to the Office of Public Safety in Washington without explanation or elaboration. But in the EVALUATION section, he wrote: "One major problem seems to be that the general public considers the fight one between the police and the extremists, and are not too concerned about it. Until they realize that the activities of the extremists threaten their pursuit of social, political, and economic betterment and assist the police by providing information and stop playing ostrich, the situation will not improve in the foreseeable future."

Under RECOMMENDATIONS, Mitrione wrote: "None."

One day a story about Mitrione's toughness passed through the ranks at the *jefatura,* and Benítez noted it. Mitrione had watched a trade-union official, the head of the bank workers, come to the *jefatura* during a strike and observed the man in his dealings with the police clerks. Then Mitrione offered his ideas on how to break a man like that.

He had always emphasized finding out as much as possible about a prisoner before the interrogation began. Learn the suspect's breaking point and reach it quickly, he told the interrogating officers. Like them, he was not a brute. He wanted the questioning over as soon as possible.

In the case of the labor leader, Mitrione said: Undress him completely and force him to stand facing the wall. Then have one of the youngest policemen goose him. Afterward, put him into a cell and hold him for three days with nothing to drink. On the third day, pass through to him a pot of water mixed with urine.

In Richmond, Indiana, it was hardly credible that Dan Mitrione would advocate that kind of behavior, particularly with its sexual overtones. But Mitrione had been out of the United States for most of ten years, and the police forces of Latin America were filled with youngsters barely out of their teens. Sexual joking was endemic, along with what sergeants in the U. S. Army called grab-assing. Standing guard duty at the *jefatura,* a young Montevideo policeman could expect his colleagues to make false passes at his genitals, to tease him about being attracted to men, to pat his buttocks mockingly. It went on all the time. So when Mitrione urged a method for breaking the control of an arrogant suspect, he was only talking to his students in the terms they knew best.

For all his curiosity about Mitrione, Benítez never saw him torture a prisoner. He knew, though, that Mitrione directed certain interrogations; and as the equipment for torture became more sophisticated, he gave credit for the change to the chief U. S. police adviser.

According to the notes Benítez was keeping, when Mitrione arrived in Montevideo, the police were torturing prisoners with a rudimentary electric needle that had come from Argentina. Mitrione arranged for the police to get newer electric needles of varying thickness. Some needles were so thin they could be slipped between the teeth. Benítez understood that this equipment came to Montevideo inside the U. S. embassy's diplomatic pouch.

Philip Agee could have informed Benítez that the CIA routinely sent its equipment through the pouch. Even a lie detector, large as a suitcase, came to a CIA station trussed up and sacrosanct from Uruguayan inspection within the pouch. Audio and bugging equipment came the same way.

The Technical Services Division made ingenious use of the abundant technological skills in the United States, giving support to every agency division and supplying experts in listening devices, lock-picking, and photography. It also supplied containers with hidden compartments, methods for secretly opening and closing letters, tools for invisible writing. It provided disguises, as the world found out when a former CIA officer named Howard Hunt wore a red wig supplied by the agency to call on an ailing female ITT executive.

Under the direction of psychologist James Keehner, TSD had devised personality tests with geometric designs to merge with other data and form psychological profiles. The CIA maintained 30,000 of those dossiers. (The one on Fidel Castro noted that he kept his pants on while having sex.) The tests could establish a good deal more about a person: whether or not he was moral; whether he would be more loyal to a person than to a cause; what sort of torture would be the most effective against him. TSD also tested hallucinogenic drugs; the news of those experiments, and the death that resulted from them, was revealed only after two decades of secrecy.

Keehner observed that most CIA employees were the type of people who could compartmentalize their work in their minds. "They can do horrible things all day," he told a reporter, but only after he had left TSD, "and then go home and forget about it."

In the Montevideo *jefatura,* it was a badly kept secret that TSD maintained a support office in Panama, which supplied emergency riot guns and tear gas to Latin American armies and police forces. Under Pacheco, Montevideo's Metropolitan Guard was shooting so much gas that its leaders were constantly badgering their U. S. contacts for more from the Panama depot. The weaponry was secretly stowed aboard the military aircraft that flew to Montevideo, flights that often also carried groceries—eggs and bread—for U. S. officials who refused to eat the local products.

It was less well known that the Technical Services Division operated another office in Buenos Aires. Only a few Uruguayan police officers learned that the improved torture equipment, the wires and the generators, as well as such explosives as Bardesio's gelignite, passed through that TSD office in Argentina.

When it came to the interrogation of Tupamaros, Mitrione conveyed his instructions through a few such high-ranking Uruguayans as Lucas. But if Benítez never saw Mitrione actually inside the torture room at the *jefatura,* others did. After Mitrione's murder, male and female prisoners at Uruguay's jails traded stories about his participation in the torture. Usually those were secondhand accounts repeated to convince a doubter that the Tupamaros had been justified in killing Mitrione.

The more reliable information about his activities came from Uruguayan policemen themselves. One officer later recalled Mitrione coming into the third-floor room, probably inadvertently, while the police were administering electric shocks to a Tupamaro suspect. Mitrione had come in only for a minute, to ask for other information. The prisoner heard Mitrione's voice and shouted a vile insult against all Yankees.

The officer who observed the incident said that Mitrione did not seem angry. It was for that reason that his behavior was talked about, as evidence of his admirable control. He simply glanced over at the man getting the *picana* applied under his fingernails. The Uruguayan police officer took that look to mean: They can say what they like, but we have our own ways of answering them.

Another time, the Montevideo police unwittingly brought in a young woman who, while in fact a Tupamaro sympathizer, was also a friend of Alejandro Otero's. In the course of the interrogation, she was tortured severely. Upon her release, she contacted Otero and told him that Mitrione had watched and assisted in her torture. For Otero, that was the breaking point. For four years, he had known of intermittent torture; but with Mitrione's arrival, it had intensified. Otero rejected torture on pragmatic grounds: it only radicalized both the police and the Tupamaros. Some of the police supported that reasoning; others, the chief of police among them, sided with the *norte-americano*.

After all, Otero's methods had not worked. Once, as he was standing beside Secretary of State Dean Rusk on a ceremonial occasion in Montevideo, his squad had allowed a young man to dash up to Rusk and spit in his face. The Tupamaros had been spitting in the face of Uruguay's police long enough.

All the same, Otero, who was vain, who was troublesome, who could be lax and indolent, was not a torturer. Philip Agee had never heard of him torturing a prisoner, nor had anyone else. He was no hero, and sometimes he had turned his back while other policemen beat a prisoner. But torture seemed to offend Otero, and he was doubly affronted when he went to Mitrione to complain about the abuse of this woman, his *amiga*.

Mitrione heard him out impassively. He had the weight

of his own government, and Otero's, on his side. Soon after their meeting, Otero—in his words—was put on ice.

Only a few months later, Otero gambled his career on one reckless attempt at vindication. He told a man, a reporter, about the torture of his *amiga*, and that indiscretion began an unraveling that would shut down the entire U. S. police advisory program.

On July 30, 1970, Don Gould, the information officer at the U. S. embassy in Montevideo, received his first telephone call from a Tupamaro. After that, the calls came every day of the week but Sunday.

"Mr. Gould," a man's voice said, using the English salutation but delivering the rest of his message in Spanish, "get out of Uruguay or you will be killed."

No U. S. official could serve long in Latin America without receiving some threat to his life. In Gould's case, he had been in Honduras when revolutionaries shot up his hotel. This call, however, was more specific, and he went to Mitrione's office to discuss it.

Gould had lately used the facilities of the U. S. Information Service to print posters for a police campaign, so he knew Mitrione and regarded him as a good corner cop who had probably come overseas for the living allowances, being a Catholic with God only knew how many kids.

After Gould reported the threat, Mitrione explained his own philosophy: "I'm in danger and I carry a gun. But if I were approached, I'd size up the situation. If I could get away, I'd use my gun. Otherwise, I'd go along with them."

The next morning, Nathan Rosenfeld, the embassy's cultural attaché in Montevideo, called the apartment of Gordon Jones, a young member of the political section, to say that he was ready to leave for work. The two men lived in the same building, and most mornings they drove to the embassy together.

Jones said he was on his way, and Rosenfeld went ahead to the garage. He was walking toward his yellow Ford convertible when he saw a tall man in the shadows. Rosenfeld took him for Jones and called, "How the hell did you get down so fast?"

With that, two men jumped Rosenfeld from behind. They were waving .45- or .38-caliber automatics and seemed very nervous. "Don't say anything," one warned Rosenfeld. "We're Tupamaros."

Swarthy and balding, wearing tortoise-rimmed glasses, Rosenfeld was twice the age of his assailants. The most aggressive thing about him was his flashy wardrobe. He was certainly not going to try to overpower them.

"Are you Gordon Jones?" a Tupamaro demanded. Rosenfeld said he was not. Jones, twenty-seven years old, could have been his son.

They pushed Rosenfeld to the wall. "Get your hands up," a voice commanded. Rosenfeld was wearing an overcoat and scarf. During Montevideo's July winter, temperatures could fall to freezing.

When he felt metal connecting with his bald spot, Rosenfeld gave the Tupamaros what he considered his best Lee Strasberg fall. His heavy overcoat softened his impact on the cement floor.

They aren't professionals, Rosenfeld thought. No one has come over to kick me in the ribs to see whether I'm shamming.

Meantime, Gordon Jones had come into the basement and saw Rosenfeld's body on the floor. As he ran over to examine the body, the Tupamaros jumped him. While they were tying him up, Jones puffed out his chest enough so that when he exhaled, the ropes went slack. They then rolled him in a blanket and laid him on a bed of sand in the back of a small truck.

Once on the street, Jones shouted for help. At the sound, a Tupamaro clouted his head with a gun butt hard enough to rip the skin. But at a stoplight, Jones was able to throw his feet over the edge of the truck, jump down, and hop to the curb screaming, "Help! Help! Help!" The truck roared off without him.

Jones wriggled free and called the embassy from a wine shop. The first thing he said was, "Nate's dead!" "No," an embassy staff man assured him, "he's all right."

At the garage, Rosenfeld had waited until he was sure the Tupamaros were gone. Then he called the security office and reported the kidnapping attempt. "Yes," said a security guard. "They've also taken Dan Mitrione."

Mitrione's driver, a police sergeant named González, left the garage of the *jefatura* that morning in a white Opel. He drove out to the Malvin district and parked in front of Pilcomayo 5398. Mitrione never kept him waiting more than a minute or two.

With Mitrione inside the car, González turned down Alejandro Gallinal. There, on a grade, with the muddy winter Atlantic in the near distance, the Opel was cut off by a white truck with a red sun visor.

An eyewitness told the newspaper *El País* that four young men jumped from the truck and took Mitrione away at gunpoint in a second truck. It happened so quickly that the onlooker could not offer a detailed description of the kidnappers.

Sergeant González, who had been struck on the head, located a telephone and called the *jefatura*. Sometime during Mitrione's ride to a people's prison, he was shot in the shoulder.

The Brazilian vice-consul, Aloysio Mares Dias Gomide, had been abducted that same morning by four Tupamaros pretending to be telephone repairmen. His wife and six children were elsewhere in the house and were not harmed.

Had the Tupamaros' plan succeeded, they would have held three prisoners to bargain with, because for the first time in Uruguay's history, the rebels were about to emulate the tactics of Fernando Gabeira and his Brazilian colleagues by demanding that a group of political prisoners be released in exchange for their captives. They had chosen Dias Gomide much in the spirit that the MR-8 had Burke Elbrick, more for the country he represented than for anything in his background. Dias Gomide turned out to be a singularly disagreeable captive, but the Tupamaros could not know that in advance.

For the last six years, Uruguayan liberals, even those with no admiration for the Tupamaros, had apprehensively watched the developments in Brazil. Arriving in Montevideo, their Brazilian friends would step from the plane and breathe deeply. "It's wonderful," they would say, "to be in a democracy again." But with the Tupamaros as his excuse, President Pacheco had been using the police and the army to tighten his control over Uruguay, until these days the air in Montevideo was not so free. Moreover, looming above the Uruguayans was the constant threat of Brazil's powerful military apparatus. Already Brazilian agents disguised as shepherds and farmers had crossed the northern border on scouting raids. The Uruguayans knew that if one morning Brazil were to invade them, their country could be subdued before lunch.

Yet that same harsh Brazilian government had shown on four separate occasions that it was willing to trade political prisoners to save a diplomat's life. If Pacheco balked at this trade, surely Brazil could bring enough force to change his mind.

The Tupamaros also expected that when Mitrione's activities with the police were exposed, even apolitical Uruguayans would concede that he was as natural a target as Moran Charquero or Inspector Juan María Lucas, who had been badly wounded by a Tupamaro bullet.

After the exchange of prisoners, Mitrione would be sent back to the United States in disgrace, and U. S. assistance to Uruguay's police would be at an end.

The case of Gordon Jones was different. A young man of considerable self-confidence, he had stirred himself out of the embassy's closed society to meet with a range of Uruguayans. Given Montevideo's temper at the time, many of his acquaintances were either Tupamaros or their friends, who expected that Jones, so knowledgeable and opinionated, would have a great deal to tell them during his days of captivity. Also, Jones had just become the father of twins. The Tupamaro cell, which did not foresee a bloody ending any more than Elbrick's abductors had, thought that the large families of two of their victims, and this new family of Jones, would be another reason for the Uruguayan government to yield to their condition.

Left to himself, Jorge Pacheco Areco probably would not have agreed to release the 150 prisoners the Tupamaros were demanding. Even his political backers did not claim that he was a compassionate man. Consequently, he announced that his government regarded the Tupamaro prisoners as common thieves and killers. Constitutionally, he said, he could not release them. However, better lawyers than Pacheco pointed out that since the president had the power of pardon, the 150 prisoners could be on the next flight to Algiers.

But the decision was not entirely Pacheco's. At the time that Elbrick was kidnapped, Richard Nixon's administration was less than a year old, and it had not formulated a policy for dealing with this new guerrilla tactic. In urging the prisoner exchange for the ambassador's release, the U. S. embassy in Rio had acted largely on its own. Its pressures were taken as representing Washington's policy when Washington had no policy.

Now the seizing of Dan A. Mitrione set off a great deal of discussion at the State Department about establishing one standard line for these cases. At first, Secretary Rogers and his chief aides considered this criterion: If the host country had carried out normal responsibilities for protection, then Washington would discourage the payment of any ransom.

But that still left the U. S. government judging each

kidnapping separately. What Washington needed was an iron-clad rule, especially since individual victims were likely to be well known to the top echelon at State—or, rather, the ambassadors and the CIA station chiefs would be known. As Alexis Johnson said afterward, there would never have been occasion for him to meet Dan Mitrione.

The dilemma was resolved when word came down from the White House that President Nixon adamantly opposed any trade or deal with the rebels of any nation.

The United States now had a policy. Held beneath the earth in a basement prison in Montevideo, Dan Mitrione did not know that he would be the first sacrifice to Richard Nixon's show of strength.

CHAPTER

9

THE TUPAMARO who entered the cell sounded like a son worried about his sick father. Tentatively he asked, "Are you sleeping?"

"Yeah," said Dan Mitrione, "I was, yes."

"Well, I'm sorry."

"No, that's great."

"Would you like to have a meeting?"

"Huh?"

"Yes," said the Tupamaro. "Would you mind?"

"I'd be happy to."

"All right. Okay." Anyone overhearing them, catching the young man's skittishness and the older man's self-assurance, would have assumed that Mitrione was the jailer. The Tupamaro seemed to be deferring to his prisoner because of Mitrione's age or because he was an Uruguayan and Mitrione was a Yankee.

"You have—how many sons do you have?"

"I have nine."

"Nine sons and daughters?"

"Well, four sons and five daughters."

"Gee," said the Tupamaro. "I see. Are some of them here?"

"Four of them are here, yes."

The Tupamaro seemed to remember that he had come for information. "Tell me, you had some important, um, work in the States while you were there?" He spoke fluent English. The pauses were from embarrassment, not from a groping for words.

"Well," said Mitrione with a slight chuckle, "I don't think it was."

The Tupamaro laughed politely at that deprecation.

"I think it's a matter of what—what is important." Mitrione's hesitations seemed to come from finding the right, the blandest, phrase to convey his meaning with no possibility of giving offense. "It was advisory. Advisory—"

"Yes?"

"We used to advise the men who came to the States in the latest techniques. Of course, this has been going on for, oh, gosh, twenty years."

"Twenty years?" Not disbelief, simply a reflex, a verbal nodding to encourage the other man to say more.

"Yeah, at least."

"That must be around—?"

"Because I remember some people from Iran and Tunisia and every place, over twenty years ago."

The Tupamaro, who was obviously young, laughed in admiration of the idea of a program twenty years old: a lifetime. "Did they go and learn?"

"Well, they—they—they learned some of the things," Mitrione said with an anxious stutter. All the same, his manner was one of an IPA instructor spelling out the basics to an incoming class of mixed abilities. "They can't learn everything. They can't use everything they learn because every society is different."

"I agree with that." The Tupamaro's voice was thoughtful, investing Mitrione's commonplace with another level of meaning.

"But the main thing is to, ah, teach them possibly the better ways or the newer ways to do things."

"What kind of 'things'?"

This was the heart of the interrogation, and Mitrione's laugh acknowledged it. But he said nothing. The Tupamaro had not been trained in interrogation in Panama or at the IPA or anywhere else. Later, when the tape was played back, other revolutionaries groaned to hear him moving on to another subject.

"And, ah, you have been chief—of police, or something?"

"Yes. I was chief of police."

"I heard that. Where was that?"

"In Indiana."

"Indiana?" The Tupamaro turned the word over on his tongue.

"Indiana, yeah." As Mitrione said it, it sounded very far away, and very dear.

"Is it a large state?"

"No." Almost a sigh. "Well, about four million population. Four and a half million."

"Is it hard to be chief?" Reporters would recognize that kind of question as something to ask until a better question presented itself.

Mitrione took up the answer vigorously. This was safe ground to linger over. "Well, I wasn't chief of the state. I was chief of a city in that state."

"Oh, I see."

"And my city was only about fifty thousand population."

"Umh," said the Tupamaro, sounding a bit bored. "And, ah, which city was it?"

"Richmond."

"Richmond?"

"Mmm."

"And how is it? Difficult work?"

"No. No, it's pleasurable work. It's . . . to me, it's the same thing as a schoolteacher and the people who pick up the *basura.*" Mitrione used the Spanish word for garbage. "It's a little bit of everything around the city. Some people

work in a factory." That was his father. "Some people
work out in the fresh air." That was his brother, Dom,
tending the golf links. "It all depends."

"That's right."

"But police work is a little bit different. Very much
different in many instances. But in a city like that, it's not
too bad."

"Is it—it was too long ago?" The Tupamaro meant very
long ago.

Mitrione heard the mistake but understood the question.
"When I was chief?"

"Yes."

"Nineteen sixty, I left there."

"Nineteen sixty. Well, things change."

"Oh, yes." From Mitrione a comradely laugh.

"Probably now you have a different kind of work, being
a chief of police in the States."

"Altogether. Altogether different." Mitrione repeated it
again, wistfully. "Altogether different. You're right."

"There are different kinds of works for the police?"

Mitrione, tired and resigned, said, "Yeah."

"And you know things change. And how about your
work in Brazil?" The Tupamaro was sounding more sure
of himself, but he was only angling for some chance indiscretion. Mitrione had been an adviser in Brazil for seven
years. The Brazilian police had preceded Uruguay's police
in the use of electrical torture. The Tupamaro had those
two parts of the equation, and he seemed to expect Mitrione to draw for him the logical, damning conclusion.

"I was a, a, a *asesor*." Again Mitrione used a Spanish
word, this one for adviser. "I worked in the interior of
Brazil, and I worked with the—I was an adviser to the
military police. And we worked on, uh, training."

"Oh, I see."

"You know how the . . . in Brazil and in Uruguay, the
way things are, they walk, how a policeman walks when
he's on duty. Well, we try to teach a way that will be a little

better for them and a little better for everyone, to walk a little more. How to stand."

The Tupamaro picked up the word "interior," although Mitrione meant only Belo Horizonte, away from the coast. "Have you been in the jungle then?"

"No, no, not *that* kind of walking." They both knew the stories of official atrocities committed against the Indians in Brazil's remote forests, and they laughed together at Mitrione's eagerness to clear himself of that stigma. "And we also try to teach them better maintenance, better maintenance of equipment."

"Yes, well, very often, you know, we stole about seven hundred weapons." The Tupamaro laughed modestly as Mitrione said with a sigh, "Yes, I know."

"They cannot take care of them." The Tupamaro was complaining to the U. S. adviser about the habits of the Uruguayan police. "And some of them were very badly, you know—"

Mitrione sounded sympathetic to this protest against an abuse of firearms. "Bad shape, weren't they?"

"Oh, yes, all dirty." It was the guerrilla's turn to sigh. "We had to work a lot to put them in condition. You know, all those guns—"

"Yes."

"But the guns were all right, but the long arms, you know—"

"They weren't taken care of, huh?"

"We have to do it now." Again the Tupamaro laughed, and Mitrione joined in at the absurdity of the rebels being forced to clean up the policemen's weapons. "We have them pretty good now."

"I'll bet." Mitrione's tone was low-keyed but flattering.

"Fortunately," the Tupamaro concluded. "And how about your work in Uruguay, tell me."

"It's about the same. It's about the same. We have—we have an office in the *jefatura*, and we work with, ah, the Ministry of Interior and the, ah, chief of police, the head of the *jefatura*, and we work on communications in the interior. You know, for the states of the interior, a basic— a basic network. And they bring in automobiles for police cars, but Uruguay buys them. We don't buy the cars."

"Oh, I see."

"On the radios, it's fifty-fifty on some." Mitrione was giving away nothing they could not read in the transcript of any year's appropriation committee hearings. "But on others, Uruguay buys them all."

"I see. But I think that the Uruguayan police learn very fast. Do they?"

"Oh, I don't know, I think the Uruguayan, the Uruguayan young man, is a pretty smart young man. I think he is better than any place else in Latin America, because of your good education system here."

Mitrione's words were measured, analytical. Nothing in his manner suggested that he was trying to ingratiate himself and thereby pull himself out from the tightest hole of his life.

The Tupamaro took his praise for Uruguay's schools as no more than their due. "Yes," he said.

"You have schools, and the other thing, I think, is wrong is maybe the desire." Pressure caused Mitrione to garble Uruguay's assets with its liabilities. He also seemed to forget for the moment that he was not giving a pep talk to a class of rookie cops. "You know, you need a little more will and a desire to do a better job."

"Yes," said the Tupamaro to this misdirected lecture.

"And because they don't pay very much." It was the recurring complaint of Mitrione's adult life. "That would help, if they paid them more."

"And what can you say about those guys like Moran Charquero and all that?" A crucial question. Moran was the guerrilla fighter, trained at the IPA, who had acquired a reputation as a torturer and had been assassinated the previous April.

Mitrione's voice went higher as he answered. The strain

to sound offhand was becoming more apparent. Moran's work had figured favorably in Mitrione's U-127 reports to Washington, but now was not the time to recount the successes of Moran's Special Brigade. "I didn't know Moran Charquero too well. I never worked with him. I met him when he went to the States, 'cause I went to the airport to say good-bye and, ah, when he came back I saw him. But I never—never worked with Moran Charquero or with . . . what was the other fellow's name? From Canelones? That went to school at the same time?"

"Legnani?"

"Who?"

"Legnani?"

"No, Legnani's the chief up there. The other one, ah, the one who went for training with Moran Charquero at the same time."

"Oh, I see. I can't remember his name."

"I can't either." They shared a light laugh at this mutual frailty. "I never worked with any of those men." Mitrione went on, pressing his advantage. "I knew them when I saw them, you know. I never worked with any individual police because I worked in the administrative part."

"And in which department?"

"Well, I worked in my office in the embassy."

"Oh."

"I spent ninety-nine percent of my time in the embassy."

"Yes." The Tupamaro's "yes" was a Latin American "no." He wanted Mitrione to know that he was not going to be deceived. "I think my mates know that. Because they've been checking everything about you for a long time." This last was said with a laugh that was apologetic but boastful too.

"Meaning your who?" "Mates" was more Australian slang than Midwestern.

"My friends."

"Oh, yes. About me, you mean?"

"Yes."

"You'll find that I spend most of my time in the . . . well, I haven't been in the *jefatura*, to be exact. I haven't been there for . . . for two and a half weeks. Maybe three weeks."

"Though you have a place to park your car, down there in the garage, you know."

"At the *jefatura?*" A debater's question, a stalling for time.

"Yes."

"That's not for me. That's for the other *asesores.*"

The Tupamaro asked matter-of-factly, "Who are they?"

"We have three other men here."

In exactly the same tone the Tupamaro repeated, "Who are they?"

Mitrione answered with a challenge. "Well, you know their names, don't you?"

The Tupamaro laughed deprecatingly.

Then Mitrione, weary with the fencing, said, as though scolding one of his children, "Well, I think you know their names."

"Yes, I do. But"—a gentle reminder that Mitrione cannot take that fatherly dismissive tone—"you know we changed the place. Now I'm the police."

Mitrione gave an open-throated laugh. If it was not a mirthful sound, it was, given his situation, a gallant attempt.

The Tupamaro met the laugh with a new persuasiveness. "No, you should tell me the names, really."

"I should tell you the names." Mitrione was not arguing, only trying to get the rules straight.

"Yes, please."

"What advantage would they be?"

"Just to know that you are really . . . willing."

"Well, there's no need for me to lie," Mitrione said briskly, "because you have their names."

"Yes."

"One man's name is Martinez, Richard Martinez."

"Yes."

"Another man's name is Richard Biava."

"Yes."

"Another is Lee Echols."

"One of them is Cuban, isn't he?" The Tupamaro may have meant Manuel, who had disappeared by this time. The Tupamaros' network was not infallible, nor did they always distinguish between the police advisers and the CIA officers operating under police advisory cover.

"No, Mexican."

"Mexican."

"Mexican. Yes, Mexican descent. He is from the United States but Mexican descent."

"*Muy bien.*" Very good. "And how do you think the Uruguayan government will behave now? You know, what do you think they'll do?"

"About me?"

"You and the others who are in prison now. We have some of you."

The Tupamaros had set President Pacheco a deadline of midnight, Friday, August 7. He had remained obdurate; and to press him further the Tupamaros kidnapped another *norte-americano*, Dr. Claude Fly, a sixty-five-year-old agronomist from Fort Collins, Colorado.

Most guerrillas did not suspect the mild Dr. Fly, with a distinguished reputation as a soil analyst, of being a CIA officer. But one Tupamaro was well acquainted with his laboratory in the suburb of Colón, and Dr. Fly was easier prey than other U.S. staff members, who were now taking such elaborate security precautions that the embassy resembled an arsenal.

The Brazilian government was making a concerted effort to have Dias Gomide released. Washington seemed less concerned about Mitrione, and some Tupamaros were wondering whether the Nixon administration, for its own purposes, was prepared to let Mitrione die. Possibly so obvious a political innocent as Dr. Fly would improve the rebels' bargaining position.

Mitrione said, "I hope they—I hope they bargain with

you." He knew nothing of the U. S. policy against trades and deals. The State Department had polled its ambassadors world-wide on the issue, and those gentlemen had supported Nixon's hard line overwhelmingly.

The Tupamaro said, "Yes, we hope it too. We don't like it."

"Yeah."

"We don't like this mess. We're terribly sorry about your wound, you know, but we helped—"

Mitrione cut in to say, judiciously, "That was a mistake, I think."

"Yes, yes. We are making an investigation about that."

"I don't know why he shot me," Mitrione said. "I really don't. I was laying on the floor of the truck."

"Yeah, we're trying to find out, and there is already people trying to find out that." Then, playfully, "You know who is your roommate here?"

"No, I do not." He was separated by a wall from Dias Gomide. "I heard you call him 'consul.' "

"Yes, he is with you."

"No, I don't know him."

"Well. Ah, and how about your government? What will they do?"

"I, you know, I cannot answer that. I think that the government will definitely talk to the Uruguayan government and ask them to—to intercede. But I don't know just what they can do, what the pact is, I—I have no idea."

The deadline clearly weighed on the guerrilla's mind. "But you think they will do some pressuring, don't you? They should, at least."

"Well, I would hope so, definitely hope so. I would guess that they would say, yes, please, put some pressure, do something."

"Yes," said the Tupamaro, "we hope so. We've done it in our country."

"That's right." Perhaps Mitrione knew what his interrogator meant, perhaps he was merely being agreeable. He paused and asked, "How long will something like this take, you know?"

"Hmm?"

"How long would a situation like this take?"

"Well," said the Tupamaro, "that doesn't concern us, you know. We have everything prepared to have you months here, here and in different places."

The Tupamaro could not know that his mates would hold Dias Gomide for 206 days; Dr. Fly for 208; and the British ambassador, Geoffrey Jackson, for eight months, from January 8, 1971, to September 9.

"But we hope to, you know, to do it short," the Tupamaro added. "That's for the best for everybody."

"Lord, I hope so."

"We also want our friends free."

"Yes."

"You understand that?"

"I understand that, yes."

"Probably, the government will do some pressure. Some of the people who is now in prison with you is very important. We think that you are very important too. Really. So—"

"I'm glad somebody thinks so." Again they laughed together.

"Yes, you probably would. Well, now tell me something about the CIA." He said it as Latin Americans often did: cee-ah. "You know, we like James Bond. About the CIA, what can you say?"

"Well, you know you're not going to believe me—"

"Yeah."

"And no matter what, what, ah, I have to convince you that I tell the truth: I know nothing about the CIA. Absolutely nothing about the CIA."

"About the FBI?" As soon as Mitrione was captured, the Tupamaros found three identification cards in his pocket. One was from the Department of State, Agency for International Development, and signed on the back with a facsimile of David Bell's slanting signature and Mitrione's careful penmanship signing his own name. There was also a card from the Montevideo Police Department, and one identifying Mitrione as a member of the FBI National Academy, Associates, of Indiana. The Tupamaros had released copies of that card to the press as evidence in the case they were building that their prisoner was not just one more U. S. AID technician.

The Tupamaro may not have expected Mitrione's enthusiastic response. The FBI training had been the real launching of his professional career; and even here, in enemy hands ten feet under the ground, he was a proud alumnus.

"FBI? I know very much about the FBI because I went . . . I graduated from their academy."

"I see."

"I know everything about . . . well, not everything. I know lots about the FBI."

"What are the names of the FBI in other departments of —" The Tupamaro apparently meant Uruguay's other states. In fact, the FBI did maintain agents overseas in several U. S. embassies under the transparent cover of Legal Officer.

But Mitrione had an opportunity to instruct his questioner on a subject close to his heart. "Well, one of the reasons why I know a lot about the FBI is because the FBI is a—a very open—a very open information-gathering investigation department. There you have agents all over the United States, and they work right in with the police departments. However, the FBI is only allowed to work, ah, on certain cases. For example, in my city, if there was a— a burglary of two thousand dollars or three thousand dollars, the FBI couldn't work on that. The FBI, it has to be a certain amount of money, or it has to be somebody that they think ran away and ran into another state."

"I see, I see. That's federal." It was an odd word for the Tupamaro to use unless he had studied in the United States.

In the Montevideo jails, the prisoners joked about the fact that both political factions had been to the United States. The Tupamaros had gone as students on scholarships from the American Field Service or Youth for Understanding; the police had gone as guests of the IPA.

"That's right," Mitrione said. "Because they only come into the picture on federal laws. They have nothing to do with the protection of people. That's the Secret Service. They have nothing, with that. That's the Treasury Department."

"How come that you can say that you really know *nothing* about the CIA? You must know something."

"Well, let me say that I know the CIA is just like every other organization that every other country has." It was an accepted answer at IPA, where a student's questioning of the CIA was met with horror stories about the Soviet Union's KGB. "Every country has an organization like that." Mitrione did not add, if he knew, that neither Brazil nor Uruguay had had such an organization until the United States helped to establish one. "But the interior parts of the CIA, I am sorry I know nothing about it. And I'm speaking sincerely."

"Well, I believe you. I think—"

"I'm speaking sincerely because our work, the four people here, our work is strictly on top of the table, everything, on top of the table."

"Um hmm. Um hmm. Though," the Tupamaro said speculatively, "they must have some—"

"Well, I'm talking about my division," Mitrione said quickly. "I don't know anything about anything else." He added it so forcefully there could be little doubt that there were other things to know. "If there is anything else, I'm sure I don't know about it, and I—"

The Tupamaro talked over him. "We know some," he said, and missed Mitrione's conclusion, which sounded later on the tape like, "and I don't want to know about it."

"We have a pretty good CIA ourselves, you know," the Tupamaro continued, with his modest, bragging laugh.

"Well, I would think so. I would think so. But we both know . . . we are smart enough to know that every country has its own intelligence-gathering unit."

"Well, I don't blame them."

"But I am not part of ours. That's what I am trying to impress on you."

"Well, we will have the last word. You know. But we have the means to know it."

"Sure." It was noncommittal, neither an admission nor an agreement.

"Ah, well, what do you think about us?"

It was a question every traveler from North America to South America was likely to hear. What do they think in the United States about Rio? Or Lima? Or Santiago? There were as many diplomatic answers as there were travelers. But the only truthful answer was, They don't think about you at all.

Now the Tupamaro was trying to put Mitrione at his ease, another technique that an IPA graduate might have handled better. "I mean I don't want to . . . just, you know, chat."

"Tupamaros?"

"Yes, you know pretty much about us. At least, you have been here for long. How long have you been here?"

"One year."

"One year?"

"Yes."

"Long enough."

Mitrione said in a sincere voice, "You do a pretty good job." He repeated it. "You do a pretty good job. You're well organized. You must have good leaders."

"Well, that I must tell you, and I hope *you* believe me"—the Tupamaro laughed—"we don't have leaders at all. We have people who is more important than others. But we don't have anything like being chiefs, you know. We don't receive orders."

"Is that right?"

"Yes, we discuss everything. You know, we are absolutely nonimportant, at least me, you know. But there are some here who are pretty important, and, you know, they are just names."

It was as romantic a view of the rebel movement as Mitrione's assurance that the FBI was a very open agency. As it happened, on Friday, August 7, the Montevideo police had captured thirty-eight Tupamaros, including its most important member, Raúl Sendic. All of the prisoners denied knowing the whereabouts of Mitrione, Dr. Fly, or the Brazilian diplomat.

Later, in jailhouse debates, some Tupamaros argued that the capture of Sendic and others from the top leadership had doomed Dan Mitrione. Not only did their arrest persuade Pacheco that his guerrilla war might be nearing an end, but it removed from the deliberations those more experienced Tupamaros who might have vetoed killing Mitrione.

Mitrione listened to the Tupamaro deny that his group had leaders. Then he said, "Uh huh. Well, it is very evident, to me, that your organization is a good organization. I would say that you have very good discipline."

"We try to."

"Because you have been very successful."

"We probably are the first Uruguayans that don't leave for tomorrow things that can be done today."

Mitrione said, "Sure, sure."

"And what do you think about what we think . . . politics and history?"

"Well, I don't know. I find it very hard to know, to know enough about . . . you have to live with the people a long time before you know what the real—the real problems are. I would say there are problems here, and I would say in some of your—your points you are right. But I don't think, I can't agree with the way you are doing it. I think that is a very common statement that many people would make."

Then, as the guards from MR-8 in Brazil had explained

the realities of their political life to Burke Elbrick, the Tupamaro tried to reason with Mitrione: "You know, I will tell you something just for you to be informed. Today —I mean, yes, today—because we read in the newspapers this morning—two newspapers have been censored, for ten days, you know, and that makes ... I don't know how many. You see?"

Mitrione was no Elbrick. The Tupamaro found no spot of common ground. "Two papers censored today?"

"Yes," said the Tupamaro, "because—"

"Two more?"

"Besides the other yesterday and the day before yesterday. They can't tell why, really. They inform something they shouldn't inform. And you know there are many political parties who are forbidden here. You know that."

"Sure." Then, more tentatively, "I suppose. I don't know much about it, but—"

"Well, you met Zina Fernandez. Did you?"

He was speaking of the army colonel who had been named Montevideo's chief of police. Romeo Zina Fernandez's tenure as chief was an unhappy one. First, a group of female Tupamaros escaped from prison through an unlocked door. Then police officials were exposed as having spent thousands of pesos on birthday parties and other amusements at their station houses. Worst of all, despite restraints on the press, the torture by the police was gradually becoming known, and the opposition in parliament was making it an issue. After the assassination of Moran Charquero, Pacheco forced Zina Fernandez to resign.

"Yes, yes, I met Zina Fernandez, sure."

"What did you think about him?"

"Well"—a slight laugh—"I knew him as a police chief and as a colonel in the military. That is the only thing I knew. I've never been to his house."

Slyly: "Or his parties?"

"No, I know nothing about his parties. What was he?"

"What was he?"

Mitrione meant which political party. It was hardly a germane question. Perhaps he had misunderstood his captor. "Yeah, was he a *Blanco* or a *Colorado*. Or—"

"I really don't know."

One more bond of ignorance. "I don't know either."

"But you know that he wasn't so honest, really."

"According to what I read, he wasn't."

"He was a chief of police, and I bet you are far more honest." Both sides could try a bit of discreet flattery. "I mean, I feel that you are, you know, engaged in something you believe and you are paid for and you just—"

"Well, you're right," said Mitrione, passing over any implication that he was a fanatic or a mercenary. "I feel strongly that way. I feel that if city government people can't be honest, how can you expect anyone else to be honest?" It was a popular theme at the police academy, where morality sometimes seemed defined entirely as the taking or not taking of bribes.

"We are fighting that," said the Tupamaro. "We hate to be violent, you know. You noticed the way we treat you after you were injured, the way we tried to bring you doctor. You have the doctor very fast."

"You were very kind. I must say that."

"There have been many doctors here to take care of you, and we have ... everything to avoid, you know, any surprises. And we really don't like to kill people at all but"—the Tupamaro gave an apologetic snort—"we will. And we do, when it's necessary, you see. We killed Moran Charquero with a smile, you know, because we knew that we were doing something some mates will, you know, will thank. Because he really was a tortu—I don't know, how do you say—tort-too-er."

"Torturer."

"*Si*. And there are many, and we will kill everyone of them, sooner or later, you know, and, ah—"

"I hope—let me say this—I hope you get the problems solved before you have to kill any more on either side." It was Mitrione's abstract public voice again, as though he were not at all involved. "That doesn't accomplish anything really."

"Ah, we hope it too. But we don't see it very soon."

"I hope so. Miracles have happened before."

"Hmm?" asked the Tupamaro.

"Miracles have happened before. The thing I say is that the Tupamaros—the MLN—are not people from Mars. You are all Uruguayans, and you are not strangers from outer space or enemies. You are Uruguayans that want to see your government do things. What you consider better, and that is why I say you ought to be able to get together, because it isn't a case like in the United States, where we do have a very definite separation between the black and the white."

"Yeah, that's a pretty rough problem, isn't it?"

Mitrione had spent two years in the environs of Washington, D. C., and his response was emphatic. "Oh, yes, my goodness! Is it a rough problem! But here you don't have that. Everybody is an Uruguayan, but the philosophy and the ideology is different, that's all."

"Yes. Yes. And it's pretty hard to do it without violence, you know. Pretty hard. I've been trying for long before I decided to work with violence, you know. I didn't care about my life. I cared more about hunger and exploitation. So we wouldn't care to die, really. We have been chosen for that, you know, because we really give our lives for something we feel is important. You see?"

Something told the Tupamaro to drop his attempts at conversion and get back to the questioning, this time about the connection between the Policia Militar and the Department of Political and Social Order. "So when you were working with the PM there in Brazil, ah, what kind of relations do they have with the DOPS?"

"With the DOPS?"

"Yes."

"Oh, I think the DOPS back in those days—I didn't know too much—DOPS are the political police, right?"

"Yes."

(Nine months later, Senator Frank Church's subcommittee asked Ted Brown about OBAN, Operation Bandeirantes. "I have heard that expression," said the chief Public Safety adviser in Brazil, "and it slips my mind right at the moment what it is.")

Mitrione said, "Yeah. Um, I think one of the problems that they had was the political police—the DOPS—were more ... mostly political appointments, and the military police were, you know, people who came up from the ranks, came in and they were—"

"Disciplined?"

"Yeah, like army, you know. Like military. I had very little to do with DOPS. I didn't know much about them."

"Well, I understand that the training—the training to the military police now is mainly against guerrillas, because, you know, that's the main problem now."

"Well," Mitrione sounded insistent about clearing himself at least of the worst excesses of the era of OBAN and DOPS, "back in those days we didn't do that, because guerrilla problems were not the news—the thing—then. All we trained for was how to handle, ah, ah, labor strikes, you know, labor problems and, ah, maybe demonstrations of people and how to use humane methods and how not to hurt anybody if you could help it. And how to be ... how to fight if you had to, too. You know—"

"Yes." The Tupamaro sounded knowing. "We read all those documents you sent to the police department in Latin America, you know."

"Ah, yeah. Yeah, well, they're changing now. You know that."

The Tupamaro laughed again in the way that suggested he was embarrassed to know things that Mitrione wasn't admitting. "We've been reading special means on, you know, interrogation. That's very interesting." He paused. "And when are you planning to retire, I mean, if—if everything runs well and we can go out free and all that? Go back to family?"

Mitrione answered with conviction. "Well, if I go back to my family, I'd like to gather up my family and finish my days in my country."

"Yeah." The Tupamaro seemed to understand what the last week had meant. "That's pretty rough."

"As quickly as possible."

"We hope it too. We been . . . and, uh, you go to Indiana?"

"Yes, well." Mitrione seemed to mull his options at the age of fifty. "Yes, I'd have to go to Indiana. That's my home."

"What about the universitarians there in Indiana?"

"University?"

"Yes."

"They're having their problems too. They're having demonstrations, and the hippies—"

The Tupamaro snorted again. Revolutionaries of any country seldom approved of the flower children.

"And the Yippies," Mitrione continued, "and the Students for a Democratic Society, and—"

"Weathermen?"

"Weathermen. But they're not all wrong. They're not all wrong. They have some good ideas too."

"Do you think?"

"Yes, I'm sure. There are a lot of smart people there. They're not all dummies. I think some of them are lazy." Mitrione's prejudices died hard, even in a *carcel do pueblo*, a people's prison. "But I think some of them have some ideas, and I think the older people ought to listen to them a little more."

"Yes, that I understand," the Tupamaro said. "They made enough noise to be listened to, at least."

"Yeah, well. Well, just like you said a while ago. They tried to talk but you finally had to resort to violence because nobody would listen."

"Have you seen *Zabriskie Point*, the film?" The

Tupamaro referred to Michelangelo Antonioni's vision of youthful disaffection in California's Death Valley.

"No. I haven't been to a film here, a movie, in . . . I think the last one I saw was *Funny Girl* about—a long time ago."

"Pretty good movie."

"Very good film," Mitrione said heartily.

"Yes," the Tupamaro agreed with no enthusiasm.

"What's *Zabriskie Point* about?"

"Well, about violence in the States."

"Is it?"

"Yes."

"Oh, boy," said Mitrione.

"It's pretty interesting."

"Well, I stay home with the children and the family. I don't go out too much at night. Sometimes we have to go to cocktail parties, that type of thing."

The Tupamaro snorted, this time sympathetically.

"Most of the time we're—I'm home with the family."

"A lot of diplomatic work?"

"Not too much, not too much."

"Have you met the president?"

"Of what? Of—of Uruguay?"

"Yes."

"No, no I haven't."

"You should. Nice guy." The Tupamaro's deprecating laugh took in President Pacheco.

"I never had the pleasure."

"Pleasure? I would like to meet him too. Under the same circumstances I met you. Or even worse, really. I don't feel that . . . bad about him, really, but about what he's doing, you know. That's a nice talk. I mean, I think you are very smart. You chose the best way of dealing with us, you know. You know you are, really, under our power and can't do anything so—"

"I'm strictly at your mercy," Mitrione said, as though he were saying, I'm entirely at your service. "Really. And I understand that."

"Well, it's not mercy. Well, I don't know the word in English, but I'd translate it . . . I wouldn't call it mercy, you know. It depends on your government, and the pressure it can do, and ours—our government—and . . . But, uh, you know your neighbor." He meant Dias Gomide. "He makes a little more noise."

Mitrione said, "Well, the only thing I regret all about this, I—I—I don't like the thing and that is too many innocent people suffer." His voice came strong and indignant. "My wife and children at home, there's no reason for them to be suffering."

The Tupamaro now sounded halting and very young. "I—I—I have wife and children too. But you know, you do it for money and I don't. You even said it before. You choose your work, and the States choose a political way to do things, and you are engaged with your country, and so you are under your own, you know, law."

"Um," said Mitrione.

"I'm sorry about them too. I'm sorry about other families of our friends who are in prison, being tortured or killed."

"Well, that's true too," said Mitrione.

"There are many, really. Many innocent people have to suffer. But do you know that about one million boys and girls under five years die every year in Latin America?"

"Of hunger?"

"Yes, sir! And that is not a way of control, birth control, you know."

"No."

"And how do you feel about other guerrilla movements? You know, we don't work all the same way. You have seen that."

"Well, every one of them has to work according to his surroundings. Whatever he can work best. From what I have read, I think the Tupamaros are . . . a little smarter than some of the others because the Tupamaros don't kill unless they have to. I think they shoot and then ask questions later."

"Well, you know"—with a laugh—"what happens probably, ah, I feel a little the way you feel. But it's the conditions there are different than here. You know the
Uruguayans—and Uruguay—has a different history than
other countries."

"Oh, I'm sure that's true."

"Violence in Brazil is harder than in Uruguay. Or in
Bolivia or in Guatemala. You know."

"It's accepted, isn't it?"

(Not much later, José Yglesias, the novelist, was in Rio
to interview Brazilians for a magazine article. One histori-
cally minded Brazilian told him, "I wonder if you know
that all this—these tortures, the death penalty for subversive acts, the terrorism of the underground groups—is new
to our country? We have had coups and coups but they
have never involved this.")

"Yes," said the Tupamaro, "I feel human life is cheaper
than here. So—"

"Yeah, yeah."

"So—"

"In other words," Mitrione yawned. "Excuse me.
Uruguayans, I am sure, are different."

"But they torture here too. Brazil is horrible, you know.
I would kill—I would *like* to kill Monsieur Fleury, you
know. Fleury, chief of—"

"Of the police there? Chief of police?" They were fencing once again. The Tupamaro's question could not have
been so careless as he tried to make it, and though Fleury
operated out of São Paulo, his exploits were well known to
men far less involved than Mitrione in Latin America's
police campaign against guerrillas.

"No, you know they have this special—"

There had been a third person, perhaps a guard, in the
cell as Mitrione was being interrogated. Now he prompted
in a whisper that the Tupamaro and Mitrione both ignored. "Death Squad."

"What is his name?" Mitrione asked.

"Flowry. Floo-ree. I don't know how they pronounce it."

"I don't know either. In Brazil? In Rio? In Brasília?"

"All I know is Brazil. He has been here, teaching, too. About four or five months ago."

"Oh, yeah?"

"Yes. You know, the Death Squad or something."

"Oh, yeah."

"He's been here. In Punta del Este. We couldn't meet him." He laughed.

Mitrione, who had chuckled, said, "But you met me, huh?"

"Yes. All—we've been doing everything to meet you. Not myself, I didn't know who you were until you told me and the mates told me. Yesterday morning we met you really." It may be that Mitrione was transferred for safe-keeping to a different cell. "Because we don't have any information we don't need to have, so we can't talk too much. But that's the way it works. But you should talk more than me."

"Can I have another glass of water, please?"

"Yes." When the water was fetched, Mitrione took a deep swallow and sighed.

The Tupamaro asked, "What do you think is going to happen with all Latin America?"

"Well," said Mitrione, "Latin America is going to be all right. I don't care. I don't know how long it is going to take. But there are people here that love life, there are people in every country that love life. Governments have problems, but some day it's going to be solved. You mark my words."

"It is." From the Tupamaro, it was a vow.

"It's going to be solved. It's going to be solved. All these buildings and all these stores and all these schools and football fields are not accidents. They were built by intelligent people. They're not going to be destroyed overnight."

"No. We hope not."

"No, I *know* they're not. It's just going to be a case of how long it is going to take. Some countries will take longer than others."

"You know, there are some people who love very much the things they have, and they have very much, and they have too many things, though. Then it's very difficult to take them out, you know."

"This is true. This is true. That's one of the problems in Latin America."

"You know, there are a few people who are holding so many interests, you know: The Bank of America, the First National City Bank, and the Manhattan—the Chase Manhattan Bank. You know they are very strong."

The guard had filled Mitrione's cup again. He said, "Thank you," and took another swallow.

"They are really very strong," the Tupamaro repeated.

"This is something that's been going on for hundreds of years. It isn't just—"

"Yes. But we have to finish it."

"What I mean is, something that's been old. It isn't something that's just started."

"Will you excuse me a minute?" The Tupamaro stepped away. When he came back, he said, "Well, I have to do some other work now, so we'll keep talking later." They had been speaking together for half an hour. "All right?"

Mitrione said, "All right. Fine."

These were the last words his family heard from him, and they heard them many days after his death.

CHAPTER

10

AT 4:25 A.M. on Monday, August 10, 1970, Dan Mitrione's body was found on the back seat of a stolen 1948 Buick convertible. He had been bound and gagged and shot twice in the head.

At 9:00 A.M., President Pacheco decreed a period of national mourning for Mitrione.

At 11:30 A.M., the Uruguayan General Assembly ended a discussion of individual rights and reconvened ninety minutes later to approve extensions of Pacheco's executive power.

At 5:15 P.M., seventy-six of the 106 members of the General Assembly voted to waive temporarily the rights guaranteed under Article 31 of Uruguay's Constitution. Declaring a state of emergency, the assembly suspended for twenty days the rights of property, assembly, personal liberty, and free expression.

The killing of Mitrione had allowed Pacheco and his security forces to assume dictatorial powers over Uruguay. The government now had 14,000 troops and policemen on the streets searching for Dr. Fly and Dias Gomide.

The extinction of Uruguay's democracy had been threatening for two years. One man who understood that his country would never be the same was Alejandro Otero.

He was no longer the leading specialist in combating the Tupamaros, having been replaced months before, when the CIA and the U. S. police advisers had turned to harsher measures and sterner men. Otero still rankled from the indignity of being replaced.

Artur Aymoré, a Brazilian journalist, had come to Montevideo to report on Dias Gomide's kidnapping for the *Jornal do Brasil*. From informants, Aymoré also had been gathering material about the Uruguayan police and their handling of the Tupamaros. He had learned that Dan Mitrione had bestowed technical equipment on the security police; that the United States had introduced a system of nationwide identification cards, like those in Brazil; that torture had become routine at the Montevideo *jefatura*.

But none of that was why Aymoré had been sent to Uruguay. His assignment was to report on the prolonged holding of Dias Gomides, for the Brazilian people were incensed at the heartlessness of the Pacheco government in not agreeing to the terms that would free their consul. (The consul's wife ultimately raised a quarter of a million dollars; and after six and a half months in captivity, Dias Gomide was released, on February 21, 1971.)

But the kidnapping story began to slow down after Mitrione's body was found; and Aymoré asked one of his contacts to put him in touch with a mutual friend, Alejandro Otero, so he could learn more about the U. S. police advisory program. Otero had been teaching at Montevideo's police academy, and a meeting was arranged in his office. To this foreign reporter from a distant newspaper, Otero confided all of his resentments.

Otero began by granting that in conducting an interrogation, the police were justified in many deceptions. It was a duel of wits, and the policeman's weapons included lies and tricks; but the U. S. advisers, especially Mitrione, had introduced scientific methods of torture that violated Otero's philosophy of life. The advisers advocated psychological torture, Otero told Aymoré, to create despair. In the next room, they would play tapes of women and children screaming and tell the prisoner that it was his family being tortured. They used electrical shocks under the fingernails, on the genitals. He told Aymoré about his friend, the woman who had been tortured, and about the way Mitrione ignored his protests. Mitrione had been very hard in his methods, Otero said.

Aymoré stood up, ready to go off to file his story. "One last thing," Otero said. "I must not appear in your story." Aymoré agreed. He sent out a story quoting "police sources," but he added a memorandum to let his editors know where the accusations against Mitrione had come from. When Aymoré made his next routine call to the newspaper, his editor got on the line: "We can't publish this without Otero's name."

Aymoré called Otero and explained the problem. "If anything happens," Otero said, "you have to tell them that I didn't talk with you. I could lose my job."

How Otero thought his name might be used without compromising him was hard to understand. The *Journal do Brasil* played the story conservatively on an inside page, but such damning accusations could not be buried.

The day after Aymoré's story appeared in Rio, two Uruguayan intelligence officers and an agent from Interpol came to his hotel with written authority to question him. Aymoré was not in his room at the time; when he learned of the visit, he spoke with the Brazilian ambassador, who promised him diplomatic protection but advised him to go willingly to the police.

Aymoré and a colleague, Alberto Kolecza, presented themselves at the prison. They were locked in a small cell with no seats, where they remained for four hours. Kolecza was the first to be led away for questioning. Then Aymoré was called in.

"Why am I here?" he asked.

The chief of the three-man unit replied, "We are conducting an investigation to determine whether Otero said what your newspaper reported. Kolecza has told us every-thing."

Aymoré knew that much was a bluff; he had not told Kolecza anything.

They put a piece of paper in front of Aymoré and told him to sign it unread. He refused. "I want to read it. I might sign it if I can read it."

The chief tore up the statement.

Aymoré, small but bearlike, had his country's embassy behind him, as well as one of the continent's major newspapers. Still, he was worried. It appeared that Otero was not denying having talked with him, only that he had criticized Mitrione.

"Where and when did you speak with Otero?" the chief asked.

Aymoré answered that although he had talked with him, he could not say where or who had arranged the interview.

The chief asked Aymoré about his own political philosophy and how he regarded the Tupamaros. Aymoré responded in monosyllables. The chief grew angry and warned Aymoré that he would suffer the repercussions of his silence. For two hours, the police repeated the same questions.

At 4 P.M., Aymoré was released. At 7 P.M., the Brazilian ambassador informed him that Uruguay had declared him *persona non grata*. He suggested that Aymoré stay at the embassy until a flight could be arranged. Aymoré slept on a couch and flew to Rio at 6 A.M.

Being home did not end his difficulties. His editor at *Jornal do Brasil*, Alberto Dines, called him in to say that the U. S. embassy was bringing immense pressure on the newspaper to fire him.

Dines asked, "Aymoré, do you promise me that what you wrote is true?"

"It's true."

The *Jornal do Brasil* resisted the embassy's demand, and Aymoré kept his job.

In Washington, Byron Engle may have reasonably expected to see Dan Mitrione transformed into a martyr. The case met all the classic requirements: there was a victim; Engle's men got possession of the corpse; other policemen paraded Mitrione's coffin through the streets of Indiana; there had been a public burial; commemorative services were scheduled; even *The New York Times* had joined the cause with an editorial calling Mitrione's killing "absurd" and accusing the Tupamaros of using the techniques of Hitler. Consequently, Engle was taken aback by Aymoré's news story and the treatment of the entire affair in the *Jornal do Brasil*. Engle offered a tale of conspiracy to explain the situation: "The three Brazilian reporters in Montevideo all denied filing that story. We found out later that it was slipped into the paper by someone in the composing room at the *Jornal do Brasil*."

In Uruguay, the war with the Tupamaros intensified after Mitrione's murder. The rebels blew up the Carrasco bowling alley patronized by the U. S. community. On one night-club wall they scrawled their most pungent slogan: *O Bailan Todos O No Baila Nadie*—Everyone dances or no one dances.

On January 8, 1971, Tupamaros snatched the British ambassador, Geoffrey Jackson, who had been disdainful of his personal security. He paid for his hauteur with eight months in an underground cell. At the U. S. embassy, the political staff watched with fascination when an agent from the British secret service arrived and set to work to free Jackson. Then, early in September of 1971, more than one hundred Tupamaros made use of an old fifty-yard tunnel, broke out of Punta Carretas prison, and escaped through a neighboring house.

At first, journalists treated the incident as one more example of the incompetence of Uruguay's police. When the Tupamaros released Jackson, however, it began to look as though the kind of trade that Pacheco had refused for Dan Mitrione had been accomplished covertly on behalf of the British ambassador. Certainly it was evident that the career of the colonel responsible for prison security had not suffered from the jailbreak. He was promoted to the job of chief aide to General Gregorio Alvarez, one of the four leaders of Uruguay's powerful emerging junta.

In Richmond, Ray Mitrione read of the jailbreak and noticed that one of the occupants of the house through which the Tupamaros escaped was named Billy Rial.

Since Ray first received a tape of the interrogation between his brother and the English-speaking Tupamaro, he had been playing it over and over, listening for clues. This obsession went on so long that his family urged him, for his own sake, to give it up.

To Ray, the voice on the tape sounded like that of the young Uruguayan who had called on him at Kessler's Sporting Goods. Now he saw Billy Rial's name in print, connected with the Tupamaros in that suspicious way, and he called Washington to tell them the whole story.

In Montevideo, Billy Rial, a convert to the Church of Latter Day Saints, was arrested and jailed. The Montevideo police granted that although Mormons were almost never revolutionaries, possibly Rial was an exception. But Ray had been mistaken about the voice he heard interrogating his brother. Most likely, the voice belonged to a Tupamaro named Blanco Katras, who had studied in the United States and was killed in a Uruguayan police raid in April 1972.

In March of 1971, Dr. Claude Fly suffered a heart attack in his underground hiding place. The Tupamaros first took him to one of their sympathizers, a heart surgeon, who examined him and insisted that he be sent immediately to a hospital.

Dr. Fly was left outside an emergency room at the British Hospital with a sheaf of electrocardiograms and a prescription for suggested treatment. Those instructions were clearly expert, and the hospital staff followed them. Dr. Fly survived and returned home to Colorado.

By tracing the machine that matched the EKG graph paper, U. S. investigators were able to track down Dr. Jorge Dubra, the Uruguayan heart specialist who had examined Dr. Fly. Dr. Dubra was arrested and imprisoned.

Morris Zimmelman, an elderly U. S. businessman in Montevideo, was shocked by the news, because that same Dr. Dubra had pulled him through his own heart episode. You never could tell, Zimmelman and his wife agreed, just who those Tupamaros were. But like most of the U. S. community, they were impressed by the skill of the intelligence officers from Washington. If they had not been able to save Mitrione's life, at least they had caught the man who had saved Dr. Fly's.

In Brazil, the kidnapping of Burke Elbrick had gone so successfully that the rebels employed the same tactic on three more occasions. In June 1970, while Fernando Gabeira was in prison on Rio's Ilha Grande, a broadcast was interrupted by a news bulletin announcing that Germany's ambassador to Brazil had been seized by rebels who were demanding the release of forty prisoners.

Within five minutes, prison guards stormed through the cells and stripped away all radios. One prisoner managed to hide his under a pillow, and he lay awake all night waiting for the next bulletin.

In that prison alone were 120 political prisoners. They debated until dawn about which of them would be on the list. Fernando expected to be one of the names. Most of the other prisoners were serving shorter sentences and could look forward to being released. Without a prisoner exchange, Fernando had no hope at all.

292]   HIDDEN TERRORS

No one slept. At the first light, the prisoner with the radio shouted out four names, and after each name he yelled, "Good-bye!"

Then he cried, "Fernando Gabeira! Good-bye!"

Even the sound of his name could not make Fernando rejoice. He knew how many obstacles stood between him and freedom. For example, the police could find the house where the ambassador was being held. It had happened to him.

Within half an hour, the police rounded up the forty prisoners. While they were having their hair cut, the police confiscated their wrist watches and any other personal property. With only the clothes they wore, they were taken to a cell at CODI.

When Fernando's turn came for a final interrogation, he was questioned about a suspected escape plan from Ilha Grande. There was no plan. However, because the guards decided to give him a few last electrical shocks, Fernando made up a story that would satisfy them.

It was nearly over. The police blindfolded the prisoners and placed them in a circle around an outside courtyard. As one man called out a prisoner's name, several policemen fired into the air. Another policeman moaned and gasped as though in the agonies of death. The supposed victim spoke up loudly enough for the others to know that this was only a mock execution, one final harassment. They were then herded back inside into a tank of water, where they were forced to shave with razors that gave them electrical shocks. With that, the police ran out of things to do.

At 9 A.M. on June 16, 1970, Fernando and the others were taken to the airport in police cars. They waited on an air-force base for six hours while the authorities took their pictures and fingerprints. At 3 P.M., on a jet from Varig, Brazil's national airline, they left for Algiers.

Colonel Fontenel, a particularly vicious torturer, made the flight with them. On the journey, he told jokes and recalled episodes from their life in prison together. Fernando thought, It is all very Brazilian.

The plane arrived in Algiers at 5 P.M. Journalists were waiting, along with a crowd sympathetic to the rebels. The Brazilian guards had expected to go shopping with the U. S. dollars they had been issued for the flight, but the crowd's hostility kept them aboard the plane until it made the return flight to Rio. This hostility they could not understand. After all, one policeman told the prisoners, nothing we ever did to you was personal.

When revolutionaries seized the Swiss ambassador on December 3, 1970, it seemed fitting that one of the hostages they should demand for his release was the son of a Swiss father, Jean Marc Von der Weid. It was Christmas Eve before word of the trade reached Jean Marc, and then the news came from a prison official who was suddenly solicitous of Jean Marc's well-being.

"We don't want anyone to be forced to go," the guard said. "If you want to stay, you can stay."

In prison, Jean Marc had been judged a hopeless agitator, and after eleven terms in solitary confinement, he had been transferred from the Isle of Flowers to an air-force base at Rio's Galeão Airport. Now João Paulo Moreira Burnier, the base commander, called for him. This was some months before Burnier was exposed for his role in the killings of the 1968 riots.

"If it were my choice," Burnier said, "you'd all be shot. I don't give a damn about the Swiss ambassador. But let me tell you, if he's killed, I guarantee you that you'll be killed." By then it was a more menacing threat than it would have been when Fernando Gabeira was awaiting word of his exchange. In the interval, Dan Mitrione had been executed.

Negotiations limped forward into the new year. The Brazilian government was haggling over some of the seventy names on the list, and the Swiss were not pressing as hard for their ambassador as the Germans had done. Throughout his days of waiting, Jean Marc was visited regularly by military men trying to persuade him to refuse to leave Brazil. They played on his patriotism. An air-force major named Silva, one of the worst torturers, now came to say that, after all, he and Jean Marc were both national- ists first.

Finally, on the eve of the exchange, a colonel arrived claiming to represent President Emílio Médici, an intracta- ble army general who had replaced Costa e Silva.

"I can't convince you that the government is good," the colonel said. "But if you refuse to leave, you'll be released in one year and back in school and free to resume your protests."

"The students would see it as a vote of confidence in the government," Jean Marc said.

The colonel had an answer for that: "You can write a short letter giving your reasons, which we'll release later."

"No, no matter what I said, it would appear that I trusted this government."

"All negotiations are ended," the colonel said. On his departure, an air-force torturer came into Jean Marc's cell and made a few desultory threats. Jean Marc then com- posed a statement, as the military had requested. He wrote: "Freedom is the most important thing for a person or a society. I am leaving Brazil for my freedom, but I will continue to fight for the freedom of my nation."

     Amnesty International, an organization formed in London to protest the torture of political prisoners, launched a campaign to free Marcos Arruda from prison. This was accomplished in February 1971, when he was abruptly released, pending his trial. On his attorney's ad- vice, Marcos left the country. He was tried in absentia, and found innocent of subversion.

Later that year, sponsored by Catholics in the United

States, Marcos applied to the Vatican for an audience with the Pope. Marcos regarded himself the spokesman for the thousands of other Brazilian victims who had not been as fortunate as he. Pope Paul sent Marcos a note assuring him that through his sufferings, he was becoming more like Christ. Bear your sufferings gladly, the Pope added.

In Brasília, President Médici contacted a distant relative of Marcos's, to whom he complained that Marcos was damaging the image of Brazil. Tell that young man, the president said, that if he ever—ever—tries to come back to Brazil, he won't get out of the airport alive.

Throughout the early seventies, liberals in the Uruguayan Senate had tried to form a united front. When this attempt failed and the dictatorship became ever more oppressive, they were forced to flee, usually to Buenos Aires. There the leaders were murdered by Death Squads operating unhindered by Argentina's police.

Before the Tupamaros were exterminated and Uruguay's democracy snuffed out, Nelson Bardesio was kidnapped by the rebels and compelled to tell his story. He disappeared on February 24, 1972; and in a series of interviews held underground, he confessed to police bombings and described the link between the police and military in Uruguay and Argentina. *Marcha*, before it was finally suppressed, printed a transcript of his statements.

The Tupamaros had deleted names of Bardesio's colleagues, intending to conduct their own investigation and mete out their own justice. Even with the substitutions of *X* for the names of police and military officers, Bardesio's confession confirmed that Uruguayan Death Squads had been bombing and strafing the houses of lawyers and journalists suspected of being sympathetic to the Tupamaros. He also cleared up the mystery surrounding the disappearance of Héctor Castagnetto, a student whose two brothers were Tupamaros.

"I arrived at the house just in time," Bardesio's statement read. "I saw them put Castagnetto, who was blindfolded, in X's auto [Bardesio provided a description, which the Tupamaros deleted] that had a broken windshield and belonged to the Ministry of the Interior. Castagnetto and the two functionaries of Department 4 sat in the back, X drove with José [an official of the Interior Ministry] beside him. . . . X got into my auto. . . . The three autos then went to the harbor, to the entrance beside the central railway station. I believe this is the entrance for the Rowing Club. X's auto turned in and we turned back. I took X to Department 5 and went to the house of a friendly couple on Canelones Street, where I then lived. One hour later, around 2 A.M., X phoned me to tell me the house on Araucana Street was to be 'cleaned out' because it would be searched by the police because of a neighbor's complaint, and also if I might keep some parcels that they didn't have any place to keep. X came to take me with his auto, and we went to the corner of Rambla and Araucana streets, where we met a small lorry normally used by the two functionaries trained in Brazil. In the lorry there were two people I didn't know and who were part of José's team. X told me to keep absolutely secret about them. They took me in the lorry to my studio, where I put the two parcels and box taken from the house on Araucana Street. . . . I later opened the two parcels and found machine guns, .45 caliber, without brands or numbers [they were filed clean] and some explosives. These were colored cubes with a place for a detonator in one of the extremities. They were enclosed with sheets of paper on which was written CCT [Command to Chase the Tupamaros]. . . . I understand that Castagnetto was interrogated and tortured in the house on Araucana Street and later murdered and thrown into the river. This final part of the operation was carried out by the two functionaries who went with him into the harbor."

Later, Bardesio disappeared entirely. He was first reported in Canada; but when questions were raised about the propriety of giving him sanctuary, he was sent elsewhere, apparently to Panama.

The Tupamaros were even more interested in the whereabouts of Héctor Amodio Perez. Amodio had ranked high in the rebel movement; but when his prominence as a leader was challenged, he had seemed to act from spite, providing the police with the locations of thirty Tupamaro hideouts. Raúl Sendic had escaped once from Montevideo's sievelike prison. Now he was captured again and shot through both cheeks. Sendic lived, but his jaw was destroyed.

In the spring of 1972, a young Uruguayan returned from studying law in Buenos Aires and found life in Montevideo hellish. Families were reduced to whispering to each other in their own homes. Everyone was taken for being a spy. The student himself knew two Tupamaros, reason enough for his being arrested and confined to an army jail.

There, like prisoners in Brazil, he was appalled to find doctors—young doctors, doctors his own age—cooperating in the torture. They asked him whether he was asthmatic, to know whether to use electricity on him or near-drownings in water. They measured his blood pressure to see whether he could bear more pain. They gave him stimulants to permit the torture to go forward. It was as though the police, the soldiers, and the doctors were all crazed. "I torture you," one army officer shouted at him. "Someday you will kill me! But I don't care!"

The doctors miscalculated, and the student had to be sent to Montevideo's central military hospital to recuperate. The sheets were stamped U. S. NAVY. His robe, the nicest robe he had ever worn, was dark-blue terry cloth and marked U.S. MEDICAL DOCTOR.

Back in prison, the young man was roused one day by a great din in the passageway. Guards were rushing by, excited and jubilant. One stopped long enough to tell him:

"Hey! We got one of you, and he was in our own ranks!"
The traitor was Subcommissioner Benítez.

At the *jefatura*, the other Uruguayan officers suddenly recalled peculiar episodes with Benítez. For all his cursing and threats, he had never managed to shoot a Tupamaro; in fact, on one raid, he had claimed that his weapon jammed.

During that same period, Benítez had been supplying the Tupamaros with information about the police. In the course of a police raid, copies of Benítez's notes were found. Knowing everything could be traced to him, Benítez sought out a judge and threw himself on the court's mercy. He was jailed and beaten nearly to death.

Exiled in Switzerland, Marcos Arruda kept alert for news of his former jailers. One officer who had tortured him was a captain named Dalmo Cirillo. Late in 1975, Marcos read in the newspapers that a metal worker had been killed in the torture rooms on Rua Totoya. One of the men implicated in the death was Cirillo, who had recently been promoted to the rank of lieutenant colonel.

Two of Jean Marc Von der Weid's chief torturers had also met with rewards and professional recognition. Clemente Monteiro, the graduate of U. S. training in Panama who had overseen torture on the Isle of Flowers, was named commander of the National Police Academy in Brasília. Under Monteiro's leadership, that academy, which had been subsidized by U. S. funds, was enlarged to train police cadets from other Latin American nations.

Alfredo Poeck, the navy officer who found his vocation during his training at Fort Bragg, left the Isle of Flowers to accept a promotion with SNI, the national intelligence service established by General Golbery after the 1964 coup. Poeck's new work gratified him, and he hoped to help SNI achieve the high standards of its U. S. counter-part, which he still felt had no peer throughout the world.

Poeck told SNI recruits that the most important quality in a good intelligence officer was natural curiosity; one should never be satisfied. As an instructor in propaganda analysis, Poeck now had access to the dossiers on Brazil's guerrillas, and he informed his students that a high percent-age of the rebels came from parents who were legally separated, Brazil's compromise with divorce. Fully 85 per-cent of the revolutionaries, according to Poeck, suffered from serious psychological problems.

When outsiders asked about his earlier career, Poeck said at first that it was shameful the way honest military men could be besmirched for simply doing their duty. Worse yet, he added, he himself was sometimes confused with a Commander Alfredo who had worked at CENIMAR some years ago and called himself Mike.

If his questioner did not seem to believe this story of mistaken identity or asked where this other Alfredo was living, Poeck grew solemn. It would be a great unkindness to track him down, Poeck said. He had been a top-notch pilot in his day, a real daredevil, but now he was very sick. They say it's cancer—a tumor—and to ask him to speak about the past would only be to remind him that he was not the man he once was.

In the spring of 1973, a member of Brazil's tame opposition party sought out U. S. Senator James G. Abou-rezk of South Dakota in his Washington office. Under a pledge of secrecy, the Brazilian poured out grisly stories of torture and laid out fragmentary but persuasive evidence that the United States was implicated in it.

Since his election to the Senate, Abourezk had been seek-ing an issue, a crusade, and he now began looking into the Office of Public Safety. He was not its first critic, only its most determined one. As early as 1966, Senator J. William

Fulbright had expressed doubts about the program, but he had caused no particular alarm at OPS. Fulbright was emerging as a critic of the Vietnam war; and among the police advisers who supported the U. S. intervention, that position alone was enough to discredit him.

During his years as president, Lyndon Johnson had not taken a stand on OPS. Officers at the police academy attributed this to his two preoccupations, the Vietnam war and his Great Society, and to the absence of much attack against the police program. It was not crucial that he show support at that time.

During Nixon's first term in office, the president told Byron Engle that the advisory program was a good one, and in good hands. In 1971, while Brazil's third military president, General Médici, was visiting Washington, Nixon had summed up his Latin American policy by praising Brazil as a model for the continent. By the time the drumroll of accusations began against OPS, however, Nixon was expending his energies on a burglary at the Watergate apartments.

John Hannah, the U. S. AID director, supported OPS in a letter to Congressman Otto Passman. But Hannah had been president of Michigan State University at the time the university took on secret CIA contracts for advisory work in South Vietnam, and that connection undercut his authority with the Senate's liberals.

Overseas, the U. S. police advisers waited for a high-ranking government official to stand up for them. None ever did. The CIA, adroit at lobbying for itself, let OPS go down without a struggle. When Senator Abourezk publicized the Texas bomb school, the agency cut its losses rather than wage a campaign that might have led to Congressional hearings.

In 1974, the CIA was still months away from the forthcoming barrage of leaks and charges and investigations that would devastate its reputation. "You must believe that we are honorable men," CIA director Richard Helms once told the Washington press corps, and in the main they believed him.

When OPS was abolished, its funds cut off, and the Car Barn doors locked, some advisers retired entirely from government service. Some entered into private security work. Jack Goin, for example, opened a Washington office called Public Safety Services, Inc. Other, better-connected men made an easy transition to the Drug Enforcement Agency, which put them back in touch with police overseas.

Many advisers had never served in a country where torture was the accepted means of extracting information. Others, although stationed in Brazil or Uruguay, had never taken part in a torture session. Some knew what went on; others claimed ignorance. But whatever their background, in the years following Mitrione's murder, they found themselves publicly soiled, disavowed by their government, and usually out of a job.

An early omen that three decades of preferential treatment were ending for the CIA was the word out of Paris that Philip Agee was writing a book. While at his last post in Mexico City, Agee had swung far to the political Left. He divorced his wife, a serious step for a Catholic; he left the CIA, equally serious for a man nearing forty with no training except in dirty tricks; and he began his memoirs, most serious of all for a man who valued his life.

Exercising the prudence he had been taught in Langley, Agee was able to finish an immensely detailed reconstruction of his years with the CIA. The very documentation— or the prospect of long legal battles with the agency— discouraged most U. S. publishers. But Agee's story had two happy endings. The book was published with great success in London and then New York. And in Paris he met Angela Camargo Seixas, who came to live with him.

. . .

In July 1970, Angela's guard had told her that if she would sign a confession they had prepared, she would be brought before a three-man military court. Although Angela had not told them anything, she signed the paper just the same. Tell about the torture, the guards warned her, and you will be back here with us.

The judge she faced was sympathetic. One of Angela's school friends was close to his son. Even after she had told the judge about the torture, when she returned to prison to await the next step she was not molested.

The trial itself came a full year later at the Vila Militar. Angela was found guilty of violating one article of an institutional act and was sentenced to two years and one month. Both prosecution and defense filed appeals. By the time the Military Supreme Court set her sentence at twelve months, she had already served thirty.

Upon her release, she tried to live in Brazil and exercise the freedom that had been promised Jean Marc Von der Weid if he refused to go abroad. Instead, the police followed her everywhere, and she saw that she was only compromising anyone she met.

Angela went to Paris to study economics at the Sorbonne. Early in September 1972, she attended a party of mostly Frenchmen and Brazilians. One of the guests was Philip Agee, then at the emotional and financial nadirs of his life.

When Agee's book was finally published, his dedication read: To Angela Camargo Seixas and her comrades in Latin America struggling for social justice, national dignity and peace.

Burke Elbrick, in retirement, attended the funeral of Cleo A. Noel, Jr., an ambassador killed in the Sudan with his counsellor and another diplomat. After Richard Nixon had made a statement that the United States would not succumb to blackmail, the terrorists had shot the three men to death with machine guns.

Watching Noel's coffin being carried out of Washington's National Presbyterian Church, Elbrick thought, There, but for the grace of God . . .

Upon the election of Richard Nixon as president, Lincoln Gordon left his post at the State Department and served for a time as president of Johns Hopkins University, where he sometimes was badgered by the students about his role in burdening Brazil with a military dictatorship. Gordon countered by pointing to an economic boom that Brazil enjoyed for several years. The students rebutted with statistics proving that the prosperity had come at the expense of the nation's poor: during the first ten years of the dictatorship, real wages declined by 55 percent. Gordon then argued that since the military had held power only since 1964, it was too early to assess its rule. The dictatorship tortured political dissidents, true, but at least it was not a Communist regime.

Throughout the seventies, tales of torture coming out of Brazil's prisons had not changed greatly; and the relevance of Lincoln Gordon's last defense was considerably diminished during the first two months of President Jimmy Carter's administration, when the police in São Paulo arrested 28,304 persons "on suspicion."

Occasionally, a commander whose excesses were too flagrant was asked to retire. That happened in the aftermath of the death in prison of a journalist, Vladimir Herzog. The outcome was different, however, for the commander responsible for troops who tortured a U. S. clergyman named Fred Morris. Eighteen months after Morris was released, the commander was promoted to Brazil's highest military post, despite publicity about the torture.

In Uruguay, a politician named Juan María Bordaberry had replaced Pacheco Areco as president. Before
Bordaberry's term had run out, Uruguay's generals had
stripped him of his power; then, in 1976, they put him out
of office altogether. In hardly more than a decade, the
Tupamaros had made good on their threat: in Uruguay,
the former model of democracy, there was now no dancing for anyone.

In the spring of 1977, a military court finally sentenced
a suspected Tupamaro for the killing of Dan Mitrione. For
the shooting, and his alleged part in the kidnapping of
Geoffrey Jackson, Antonio Mas Mas received thirty years
in prison.

Around the police barracks in Rio de Janeiro, Brazilian officers trained at the International Police Academy
remembered Dan Mitrione fondly as a symbol of the era
before Washington lost its will to fight the Communists.
The United States was decadent, the officers said; it
suffered from too much freedom. The torch had been
passed to the military and police of Brazil. It was now their
task to defend the hemisphere, and they would not falter.

In the police garages of Rio stood black, impregnable,
rolling fortresses, built at a cost of $100,000 each, designed
to carry troops with machine guns into the densest crowds.
They were bulletproof and so squat that they could not be
tipped over. They could withstand Molotov cocktails.
They were air conditioned against the fumes of their own
tear gas.

If Brazil's students ever dared to throw another stone,
the police would not be sitting on the curb of downtown
Rio crying.

The *coup de grace* in the campaign against the Office
of Public Safety was delivered by a motion picture. Costa-

Gavras, the Greek film director, hired an Italian, Franco
Solinas, as his script writer, and together they set off for
Latin America to make a film about the death of Dan
Mitrione. Solinas, a member of the Italian Communist
party, had written the script for Gillo Pontecorvo's *The
Battle of Algiers.*

When Costa-Gavras visited Montevideo in 1972, he side-
stepped questions from the local reporters about the kind
of film he intended to make. Privately, though, he was
collecting documents. Through Alain Labrousse, a French
writer, Costa-Gavras obtained blurred photocopies of the
material from Benítez.

Solinas traveled to the Dominican Republic, where he
tried to meet secretly with the head of the country's Communist party. Although that attempt failed, a party func-
tionary briefed Solinas on the police terror in the
Dominican Republic and assured him that Dan Mitrione
had set up the apparatus in Santo Domingo after the U. S.
invasion of 1965.

From that time on, Mitrione acquired a reputation as his
country's foremost expert in torture. *The New Scientist,* a
British publication, described a device called the Mitrione
vest. Designed for interrogations, it slowly inflated until it
crushed the ribs of its victims. The vest itself was no more
horrifying than other well-documented methods of torture
used in Brazil and Uruguay and later in Chile. Yet, no
prisoners, at least none who lived to testify at the Bertrand
Russell Tribunal in Rome or at hearings of Amnesty International, had ever heard of such a vest, and Mitrione's
friends never claimed for him the ingenuity of an inventor.

Hank Mitrione and her children could only meet the
accusations with equal hyperbole about the Dan Mitrione
they had known. "A perfect man," his widow said. "A
great humanitarian," said his daughter, Linda.

Mrs. Mitrione withdrew to a suburb of Washington to

finish the job of raising her children. She kept a large
portrait of her husband on the wall, and a photograph of
Frank Sinatra on the piano. She did not keep much in touch
with her husband's former colleagues. They had been very
kind to her, but she found it hard to respond to their notes
and Christmas cards.

      Costa-Gavras included in *State of Siege* every un-
documented rumor about Dan Mitrione from Santo
Domingo or Belo Horizonte because his aim was a compos-
ite indictment of U. S. policy throughout Latin America.
He and Solinas named their central character Philip E.
Santore, and Costa-Gavras cast Yves Montand in the role.
Montand was slim and continental; he smoked cigarettes.
Mitrione had been corpulent and Midwestern; he had
puffed, sometimes, on big cigars.

      In the film, the interrogation sequences omitted the
Tupamaro's incessant use of "you know" and Mitrione's
sententious repeating of his remarks. "You are subversives,
Communists," Santore tells his captors in the movie. "You
want to destroy the foundations of society, the fundamen-
tal values of our Christian civilization, the very existence
of the free world. You are an enemy who must be fought
in every way possible."

      With speeches of that sort, the film explained lucidly
Santore's motivation; and in public statements Costa-Gavras extended the same analysis to Mitrione, who was, he
said, "as sincere as the judges of the Catholic Church during the Inquisition. . . . He is convinced that one must cut
down everything that is liberal or Communistic and by any
means possible. He thinks that ordinary liberalism can
plunge society into chaos."

      But very few police advisers, least of all Mitrione, shared
such certainties. Their mission in Latin America was not
only secret but vague. Dan Mitrione went there to stop the

Communists. As did Philip Agee. As did Lincoln Gordon. In the years after Castro came to power in Cuba, no administration, Republican or Democrat, felt that it could afford another Cuba in the Western Hemisphere. And no one resisted the Communists more fervently than the local military and police officers, especially those who returned from Panama, Washington, or Fort Bragg persuaded that they were the Free World's first line of defense.

Philip Agee, college-educated, of the middle class, a divorced father of two, came to see the result of his official lying and cut free, a decision that took courage and perhaps a degree of fanaticism. Had Dan Mitrione been the inquisitor that Costa-Gavras painted him, his character might have equipped him for the same sort of dramatic conversion. Instead, Mitrione was self-educated, of the working class, a devoted father of nine, and dedicated to his work. In the White House and the U. S. embassies, there were brilliant men to set his nation's policy; in the CIA, there were arrogant men to interpret it.

With the overthrow of Goulart on April 1, 1964, Mitrione's job in Brazil had changed drastically. He had been working for democracy; henceforth, he would be working for a dictatorship. If no one in Washington or Brazil saw the difference, why should Mitrione?

In Uruguay, young men and women who considered themselves idealists began to shoot policemen who were often Mitrione's good friends. The U. S. government had developed harsh methods in South Vietnam for combating that kind of subversion, and some of those techniques and devices had found their way to Latin America. Mitrione merely made use of them.

In the twelve years of the Office of Public Safety, a total of seven police advisers were killed, six of them in Vietnam. Around the International Police Academy, at Fort Bragg, in Panama, the professionals agreed that Latin America would be the next Vietnam. Dan Mitrione, they felt, was a premature casualty of that Vietnam.

. . .

At Test Junior High School in Richmond, Indiana, in the mid-1930s, Dan Mitrione's advisers had filed the usual reports about his character. Their evaluations were uniformly favorable: "Honest." "Modest." "Tries to do what others would like." "Has a serious attitude toward work."

By the time he reached high school, Dan was majoring in English and Vocational Machine Shop, and he reported that he expected to work in a factory. One questionnaire called on him to list the abilities and knowledge he would need for that vocation.

"Know math," Dan wrote. "Know something of machines. Must not loaf. Have to be alert. Must take precautions. Know all the safety rules."

Then the form, designed to establish a student's talents and interests, asked, "What likes or dislikes have you developed in High School?"

And Dan Mitrione from Goosetown, who wanted to do what others would like and knew that he faced a life where he must not loaf and must know all the rules, answered, "I like all my subjects."

A Cuban Footnote

When I ended this book with brief accounts of what had happened to many of its people in the years after Dan Mitrione's death, one man about whom I expected no further information was the double agent called Manuel the Cuban. I knew only that he had soundly deceived his CIA contacts and that he had returned to Cuba. I had neither his last name nor any way of tracing him, and Cuba was not an easy country to enter. Manuel seemed fated to remain a tantalizing minor figure in Uruguay's sad story.

Then, in August 1978, I was in London when a reporter called from the *Washington Post*. At a press conference in Havana, he said, a Cuban named Manuel Hevia Cosculluela was making serious charges against the U.S. police program, in which he claimed to have served in Uruguay. I told my caller that the description fit the double agent I had mentioned in my book and that, if it was the same man, his credentials were impressive, although I could not answer for his likely political bias. The call raised my hopes that one day I would meet Manuel Hevia and hear his story for myself.

Early in 1979, I was invited to tour Cuba with a group of broadcasters and journalists, many of them affiliated with San Francisco State College. We arrived in Havana at dinner time on April 6, and the next morning, a Saturday, I set off to find Hevia.

At the fifth office I visited, the National Union of Cuban Writers and Artists, a pleasant-faced official dug through a pile of papers and produced the paperbound book Manuel had written, *Pasaporte 11333, Eight Years with the CIA*. In exchange, I handed the official, Joaquin Santana, a copy of *Hidden Terrors* turned to the page about Manuel the Cuban.

"This is a big surprise to me," Santana said. "I was the editor for Manuel's book, and I wrote the introduction to it."

It turned out that Hevia, now employed by the Ministry of Transportation, was traveling outside Cuba and would not be back before I returned to the United States. Santana spoke with me at length on two occasions, however, and he introduced me to one of Manuel's good friends. From those conversations, but primarily from Manuel's book, comes this footnote:

As a youth, Manuel had studied at the Taft School in Watertown, Connecticut, and had graduated from law school in Havana. When the CIA made overtures to him in the early 1960s, he informed officials in Cuban intelligence, who advised him to accept the CIA assignment.

Much of his story concerns the tension of a double agent's life: clandestine meetings, eluding pursuit, bluffing one's way past the CIA's lie detector. Manuel's chief CIA contact, William Cantrell, was an orderly, pipe-smoking man devoted to his family. Cantrell was posing as an adviser in the U.S. AID program to train Uruguayan police.

By the late 1960s, the Tupamaro rebels were alarming both Washington and the government in Montevideo; and as Cantrell prepared to return to the United States, he spoke to Manuel about his successors. One was named Richard Martínez; the other was not a CIA man himself but was a trusted supporter of "our program." That was Dan Mitrione. Cantrell had heard very encouraging reports about Mitrione's efficiency in Brazil.

In a meeting with Manuel, Mitrione explained that the rules were changing and that the U.S. advisers would not be spending much time at the Montevideo police headquarters. Instead, Mitrione had secured a house in the city's Malvín section with a cellar and a door to the inside from the garage.

Mitrione personally oversaw the soundproofing of the cellar. He put a record of Hawaiian music on a phonograph at full volume and went upstairs to be sure it could not be heard in the living quarters. He also insisted that his team fire a pistol downstairs while he listened above for any trace of sound.

"'Good, very good,'" Manuel quotes Mitrione as saying. "'This time I could hear absolutely nothing. Now you stay here while I go down.'" That testing went on over and over again.

The first course to be held in the cellar drew largely from graduates of the International Police Academy in Washington. The early sessions dealt in insinuation: descriptions of the human anatomy and the central nervous system. "Very soon," Manuel wrote later, "things turned bad. As subjects for the first testing, they took beggars, known in Uruguay as *bichicones*, from the outskirts of Montevideo, along with a woman from the border with Brazil. There was no interrogation, only a demonstration of the different voltages on the different parts of the human body, together with the uses of a drug to induce vomiting—I don't know why or for what—and another chemical substance.

"The four of them died."

Reading Manuel's book, I particularly regretted at this point not being able to question him. Was Mitrione present while the instruction was being given? Did he witness the deaths? The wording is vague. In Brazil, so far as the victims knew, no U.S. adviser attended the torture class. They were too prudent to compromise themselves so directly.

In Uruguay, I had heard many accusations about Mitrione's role in the torture and I had sifted through them trying to be accurate and fair to his memory. Some Tupamaros acknowledged to me that their colleagues had reason to paint Mitrione in the darkest colors in order to justify killing him. And I held to a view Manuel Hevia later put forward at his press conference in Havana: that Mitrione was not unique, not a monster; that it was too comfortable to suggest that every nation and every occupation had its brutes.

Handling the material for this book had left me cautious, aware that after all the evidence had been weighed, some conclusions would have to remain tentative. Yet at every point that Hevia and I treated the same incident, our information gathered independently dovetailed into one expanded narrative. His final pages with their unguarded monologue from Mitrione ring true to me.

And since I am persuaded of the accuracy of that proud boasting, I think now that in looking within Mitrione for traits we all share, I underestimated the effect of his ten years at a repellent trade. Certainly I didn't anticipate his awful candor and cruelty as he unburdened himself to Manuel, one professional, one realist, to another.

It was the winter of 1970, six or seven months before Mitrione was kidnapped. Arriving in Montevideo later than he had expected, Manuel called Mitrione at home instead of at the U.S. embassy. "Mitrione asked me to come to see him, and we sat together in a small room in his house. I don't know why he invited me. We had a few drinks and talked about our philosophy of life."

Mitrione considered interrogation an art, he told Manuel. First, there is a time of softening up the prisoner. The object is to humiliate him, to make him understand that he is completely helpless and to isolate him from the reality outside this cell. No questions, just blows and insults. Then blows in total silence.

After all that, the interrogation begins. Now the only pain should come from the instrument you've chosen to use. Mitrione said, "The precise pain, in the precise place, in the precise amount to achieve the effect."

During the session, you must avoid letting a person lose all hope of life. If you push too far, they become resigned to die. "Always leave them some hope, a distant light."

Manuel quotes Mitrione as continuing: "When you get what you want, and I always get it, it might be good to keep the session going a little longer with more hitting and humiliation. Not to get information now but as a political instrument, to scare him away from any further rebel activity."

The talk grew more confidential. "After that, he told me, 'When you receive a subject, the first thing to do is to determine his physical state, his degree of resistance, through a medical examination.

"'A premature death,' he emphasized, 'means a failure by the technician.'

"'Another important thing to know is exactly how far you can go, given the political situation and the personality of the prisoner.' Dan was really excited. He needed the kind of audience he had found in me. He continued, 'It is very important to know beforehand whether we have the luxury of letting the subject die.' It was the only time in all those months that his plastic eyes sparkled.

"Finally he concluded:

"'Before all else, you must be efficient. You must cause only the damage that is strictly necessary, not a bit more. We must control our tempers in any case. You have to act with the efficiency and cleanness of a surgeon and with the perfection of an artist. This is a war to the death. Those people are my enemy. This is a hard job, and someone has to do it. It's necessary. Since it's my turn, I'm going to do it to perfection.

"'If I were a boxer, I would try to be the world champion. But I'm not. But though I'm not, in this profession, my profession, I'm the best.'"

—May 1979

Acknowledgments

TO NAME many of those men and women who contributed to this book would be to jeopardize their jobs, their pensions, or their status as exiles. It could also mean prison, torture, perhaps death. Zelmar Michelini, an Uruguayan senator in exile in Argentina, was murdered by a death squad three days before I arrived in Buenos Aires for our interview. Scores of people helped me in Europe and South America, and to them I want to express my thanks and admiration.

In a different category are those men accused of torture who demanded anonymity as a condition for talking with me. As a result, I have been required to withhold from the reference notes the identities of these informants. In some instances, the reader may be able to deduce my sources; the persons involved understood that likelihood and asked only that they not be conclusively identified.

There are other contributions that I can acknowledge freely and gratefully. Not all of the people on this list will agree with my conclusions. But in every case, they were generous with their time and assistance:

Philip Agee, Rennie Airth, Eva Ållander, Captain Ray Alvardo, Miguel Arraes, Marcos Arruda, Leilo Basso, Jorge Batlle, Cid de Queiroz Benjamin, Jan Knippers

Black, William Brown, Tim Butz, Mauro Calamandrei,
Irany Campos, Luis Felipe Carrer, Carlos Castelo Branco,
Andrew Cecere, Al Chvotkin, Calvin Clegg, Orville Con-
yers, Senator Alan Cranston, Roland Cutter.

Arnold Dadian, Tom Daschle, Kader Dehbi, Glycon de
Paiva, Aristoteles Drummond, Maruja Echegoyen, Fred
Ekton, C. Burke Elbrick, Byron Engle, Charles Fleming,
Myles Freschette, Albert Friedman.

Fernando Gabeira, Eduardo Galeano, Colonel Raúl
Garibay, Louis Gibbs, Fred Goff, Lauren J. Goin, Lincoln
Gordon, Donald Gould, David Halberstam, Bruce Han-
dler, Joseph Hanlon, Maria Hennequin, Robert Her-
nandez, General Heitor Herrera, Rinard Hitchcock, Linda
Hoff, Claudia Hutchins, Paul Ingels.

U. Alexis Johnson, Edy Kaufman, Michael Klare, Alain
Labrousse, Doris Langguth, Jerome Levinson, John Lind-
quist, John Marks, John Metelsky, Father Robert Minton,
Henrietta Mitrione, Ray Mitrione, Fred Morris, Ethel Nar-
vid, Lucy Neill-Kendall, Ricard Pedro Neubert, Joanne
Omang, Dick Oosting.

Richard and Rosemary Parker, Susan Pierres, José
Magalhaes Pinto, Murilo Pinto, Louise Popkin, Michel
Puéchavy, Thomas Quigley, José María Rabello, Robert
Rockweiler, Christopher Roper, Nathan Rosenfeld, An-
thony Ruiz.

Ginetta Sagan, Harrison Salisbury, John Salzberg, Rob-
ert Sandin, Jay Scott, Angela Camargo Seixas, James Shea,
Enio Silveira, Franco Solinas, Thomas Stephens, Dan
Taher, Gary and Linda Tarter, Flavio Tavares, Richard
Tiernan, William Tuohy, Brady Tyson, Jean Marc Von
der Weid, Stephen and Susan Watkins, William Wipfler,
Louis Wiznitzer, Morris and Edna Zimmelman.

At Pantheon Books, I would like to thank André Schiff-
rin, Tom Engelhardt, Donna Grusky Bass, and Wendy
Wolf; at International Creative Management, my agent,
Lynn Nesbit.

I also received valuable assistance from Amnesty International, the Bertrand Russell Foundation, the Catholic Conference, the U. S. Department of State, the Institute of Cultural Action, the National Conference of Churches of Christ, the North American Congress on Latin America, the Office on Latin America, and the U. S. Senate.

Finally, I wish to acknowledge gratefully a grant from the John Simon Guggenheim Memorial Foundation.

References

CHAPTER ONE

Details of Dan A. Mitrione's funeral service and burial: *Palladium-Item* and Sunday *Telegraph*, 12–14 August 1970. Uruguay providing an antique casket, Ray Mitrione's response to the kidnapping, meeting with Billy Rial, Mitrione family background: interviews, Ray Mitrione, Richmond, Indiana, March 1976. Lincoln poem: Ross Franklin Lockridge, *The Story of Indiana* (Oklahoma City: Harlow Publishing Corp., 1953), p. 231. Famous men and women from Indiana: Irving Leibowitz, *My Indiana* (Englewood Cliffs, N. J.: Prentice Hall, 1964). Cobb on the Ku Klux Klan: Irvin S. Cobb, *Indiana* (New York: George H. Doran Co., 1924), p. 51. Tarkington quotation: Leibowitz, *My Indiana*, p. 246. "A box": Ross Lockridge, Jr., *Raintree County* (Boston: Houghton Mifflin Co., 1948), p. 17. Pyle writing about Clayton: Howard H. Peckham and Shirley A. Snyder, eds., *Letters from Famous Hoosiers* (Bloomington, Ind.: War History Commission, 1948), pp. 123–25. Dan Mitrione's navy service: interview, Henrietta Mitrione, March 1976. Dan Mitrione's police application: personnel files, police headquarters, Richmond, Indiana. Dan Mitrione's early police work: interview, Orville Conyers, Richmond, Indiana, March 1976. Developments in the Mitrione kidnapping: *Palladium-Item*, 2–9 August 1970. Democratic party's 1955 campaign: interview, Andrew Cecere, Richmond, Indiana, March 1976. "Smashing" victory: headline, *Palladium-Item*, 9 November 1955. Dan Mitrione's note: *Palladi-*

um-Item, 3 August 1970, p. 1. Calls from UPI and Representative David Dennis: Ray Mitrione interviews. Selection of Dan Mitrione as police chief: interview, Roland Cutter, Richmond, Indiana, March 1976. White House reaction to the killing: *Palladium-Item*, 10 August 1970, p. 1. Other official responses: *Ibid.* 13 August 1970, p. 6. Dan Mitrione as police chief: interviews, including Louis Gibbs interview, Richmond, Indiana, March 1976. Richmond's teenage crime wave: *Palladium-Item*, 6–7 July 1956; and Cutter interview. Father Minton's background and reactions: interview, Father Robert Minton, Richmond, Indiana, March 1976. John Kennedy's Indiana campaigning: *Palladium-Item*, 21 April 1960, p. 1. Sinatra call: Ray Mitrione interviews. Sinatra's preparations and concert: *Palladium-Item*, 21, 30 August1970. Sinatra's statement: *Palladium-Item*, 30 August 1970, p. 3.

CHAPTER TWO

John Quincy Adams on Cuba: Teresa Casuso, *Cuba and Castro* (New York: Random House, 1961), p. 31. Castro on the ninety-mile distance: Herbert L. Matthews, *Fidel Castro* (New York: Simon and Schuster, 1969), p. 198. Nixon memorandum, Hoover's agreement: Richard M. Nixon, *Six Crises* (Garden City, New York: Doubleday & Co., 1962), p. 352. Eisenhower ordered invasion: Matthews, *Fidel Castro*, p. 162. John Kennedy comparing Castro to Bolívar: John F. Kennedy, *The Strategy of Peace* (New York: Harper & Row, 1960), quoted by Nixon, *Six Crises*, p. 351. U. S. holdings, Castro's land policies: Samuel Shapiro, *Invisible Latin America* (Boston: Beacon Press, 1963). Sugar quota suspended: *Facts on File*, July 5, 1960. Kennedy charges: Nixon, *Six Crises*, p. 351. Eisenhower breaks diplomatic relations: Matthews, *Fidel Castro*, p. 163. Schlesinger's "perversion of the Cuban revolution": Arthur M. Schlesinger, Jr., *A Thousand Days* (London: André Deutsch, 1965), p. 201. Two hundred advisers in Brazil: *United States Policies and Programs in Brazil*, Hearings Before the Subcommittee on Western Hemisphere Affairs of the Committee on Foreign Relations, 92nd Congress, 1st session, Table VI, at 10 (May 4, 5, and 11, 1971). Mitrione refereeing softball games: Brazil *Herald*, 1 March 1964, p. 5. Mitrione denied a pay raise: Henrietta Mitrione interview. Engle's background and beginnings of police advisory program: interview, Byron Engle, Washington, D. C., March 1976. Mitrione's talk to family, the daughters' response to Brazil: interview, Linda Mitrione Tarter, Richmond, Indiana, March 1976. "A certain softness": Stefan Zweig, *Brazil: Land of the Future*, translated by Andrew St. James (New York: Viking Press, 1941), p. 9. "Remissa": *Ibid.*, p. 141. "They will never go home": Rebecca West, *The Thinking Reed* (New York: Viking Press, 1961), p. 140. "More troublesome than Argentina": Burton Bernstein, *Thurber* (New York: Ballantine Books, 1976), p. 549. Bundy on "second-rate minds" (Mr. Bundy denies making this statement): John Mander, *The Unrevolutionary Society* (New York: Alfred A. Knopf, 1969). Henry Kissinger: Later, as Secretary of State, Kissinger acknowledged that U.S. holdings in Latin America shaped his policies; not only did U. S. subsidiaries remit profits, but they were major customers for U. S. exports: Richard Armstrong, "Suddenly It's *Mañana* in Latin America," *Fortune*, August 1974, p. 216. Edmund Wilson bored by Hispanic culture: Brendan Gill, *Here at The New Yorker* (New York: Random House, 1975), p. 254. *Literary Digest* on annexing Cuba: *Literary Digest* April 1899, pp. 363—64, cited in Ernest S. May, *American Imperialism* (New York: Atheneum Publishers, 1968), p. 208. Franklin Roosevelt on Haiti's constitution: Ernest Gruening, *Many Battles* (New York: Liveright, 1973), p. 160. Mexico "dipped into the sea": *Ibid.*, p. 109. "Work is sacred": John F. Santos, "A Psychologist Reflects on Brazil," *New Perspectives of Brazil*, edited by Eric N. Baklanoff (Nashville: Vanderbilt Press, 1966), p. 249. "Not fanatically so": *Ibid.*, pp. 244-45. Zweig's suicide: J. C. Thorne, ed., *Chambers's Biographical Dictionary* (New York: St. Martin's Press, 1962), p. 1396. José Enrique Rodó, *Ariel*, translated by F. J. Stimson (Boston: Houghton Mifflin Co., 1922). Responses to Rodó: Jean Franco, *The Modern Culture of Latin America* (New York: Frederick A. Praeger, 1967). Eisenhower on constabulary, Robert Kennedy's support for police program: Engle interview. Background on C-I Group: Engle interview; interview, U. Alexis Johnson, Washington, D. C., March 1976. Latin Americans offended by Panama courses: interviews. Forrestal touring Car Barn: Engle interview. Agee's background: interview, Philip Agee, Cambridge, England, May 1976; Philip Agee, *Inside the Company: CIA Diary* (Harmondsworth, England: Penguin Books,

1975). Lincoln Gordon as "boy genius": *The New York Times*, 12 April 1967, p. 16. Gordon's background, named to Berle task force, Richard Goodwin and Alliance speech, appointment as ambassador to Brazil: interviews, Lincoln Gordon, Washington, D. C., March 1976. U. S. aircraft bases on Brazilian coast: Gerhard Masur, *Nationalism in Latin America* (New York: The Macmillan Co., 1966). Vargas's personal life: Tad Szulc, *Twilight of the Tyrants* (New York: Henry Holt, 1959). Roosevelt's joke about de Gaulle: Robert E. Sherwood, *Roosevelt and Hopkins* (New York: Harper & Brothers, 1948), p. 970. Roosevelt not accepting foreign control of utilities: John Gunther, *Inside South America* (New York: Harper & Row, 1966), p. 21. Dreiser on U. S. holdings abroad: Theodore Dreiser, *Tragic America* (New York: Liveright, Inc., 1931). Vargas on nationalism: Masur, *Nationalism in Latin America*, p. 128. Threats to the Vargas regime: Herbert Wendt, *Red, White and Black Continent* (Garden City, New York: Doubleday, 1966). Post-Vargas political parties: James Kohl and John Litt, *Urban Guerrilla Warfare in Latin America* (Cambridge, Mass.: MIT Press, 1974), p. 33. Carlos Lacerda: John Dos Passos, *Brazil on the Move* (Garden City, New York: Doubleday & Co., 1963), p. 142. Vargas suicide note: Wendt, *Red, White and Black Continent*, p. 443. Kubitschek's policy on foreign investment: Steven J. Rosen, "Rightest Regimes and Americn Interests," *Society*, September/October 1974. Eugenio Gudin's statistic: Eduardo Galeano, "The Nationalization of Brazilian Industry," *Monthly Review*, December 1969, p. 19. Gudin on "a decent life": Gary MacEoin, *Revolution Next Door* (New York: Holt, Rinehart and Winston, 1971), p. 47. Five times the amount of foreign aid leaving Brazil: Galeano, "The Nationalization of Brazilian Industry," p. 23. Goulart susceptible to Communist influence: Peter D. Bell, "Brazilian-American Relations," *Brazil in the Sixties*, edited by Riordan Roett (Nashville: Vanderbilt University Press, 1972). Quadros vulnerable to Communists: Lieutenant Colonel Edward King, quoted in Jan Knippers Black, *United States Penetration of Brazil* (Philadelphia: University of Pennsylvania, 1977), p. 40. Quadros campaigning: Wendt, *Red, White and Black Continent*. Brazilian poll on neutrality: Keith Larry Storrs, "Brazil's Independent Foreign Policy, 1961-64," Cornell University's Latin American Studies Program Dissertation Series No. 44 (January 1973), pp. 248-49.

Quadros's term: Irving Louis Horowitz, *Masses in Latin America* (New York: Oxford University Press, 1970); Donald E. Worcester, *Brazil from Colony to World Power* (New York: Charles Scribner's Sons, 1973) "Grown-up, vaccinated, and old enough to vote": *Ibid.*, p. 219. Richard Goodwin's meeting with Ernesto Guevara: Richard Goodwin, "Annals of Politics: A Footnote," *The New Yorker*, 25 May 1968. Lacerda's attack on Goulart: Dos Passos, *Brazil on the Move*, p.167. Quadros's resignation: Worcester, *Brazil from Colony to World Power*, pp. 221-23. Goin's background: interview, Lauren Jackson Goin, Washington, D. C., March 1976. CIA's attitude toward police advisers: Agee interview. Calfee resignation: correspondence, Maurice E. Calfee and Senator James Abourezk, U. S. Senate files. Belo Horizonte attitude toward the police: interviews. Mitrione's service in Belo Horizonte: interviews, including Ricard Neubert interview, Belo Horizonte, August 1976. "Mafia chief": Tarter interview. Belo Horizonte police "like Richmond's finest": *Palladium-Item*, 12 March 1962, p. 12. Mitriones had no cook: Tarter interview. Niemeyer building: Neubert interview. Assault on *Binomio* by Punaro Bley: interviews, José María Rabello, Paris, May 1976. Gabeira's background: interviews, Fernando Nagle Gabeira, Stockholm, May 1976. Arruda's background: interviews, Marcos Arruda, Geneva, April 1976.

CHAPTER THREE

Ambassador Gordon in Brazil: Gordon interviews. IPES: interview, Glycon de Paiva, Rio de Janeiro, July 1976. GAP: interview, Aristoteles Drummond, Rio de Janeiro, July 1976. IBAD background: Eloy Dutra, *IBAD: Sigla da Corrupcao* (Rio de Janeiro: Editora Civilização Brasileira, S. A., 1963). IBAD underwrote Pernambuco campaign: letter, Miguel Arraes, May 1976. Edward Kennedy in northeast Brazil: Joseph A. Page, *The Revolution that Never Was* (New York: Grossman Publishers, 1972), pp. 120-21. Background of Francisco Julião: *Ibid.*, pp. 38–43. Paulo Freyre's method: *Ibid.*, p. 173. CIA in northeast: interviews, Washington and Rio de Janeiro, March–August 1976. AIFLD: Black, *United States Penetration of Brazil*, chapter 8, pp. 111-24. Background of General Herrera: interview, Heitor Herrera, Rio de Janeiro, July 1976. Escola Superior de Guerra:

"Resistance to populism had been a mainstay of the military's Superior War College [ESG] since its inception as focus and fountainhead for the nation's military elite in 1949": Kohl and Litt, *Urban Guerrilla Warfare in Latin America*, p. 39. JBUSMC: Black, *United States Penetration of Brazil*, pp. 162–66. For a detailed discussion of U. S. training in Panama: Michael T. Klare, *War Without End* (New York: Alfred A. Knopf, 1972). Brazilian desire to be loved by U. S. counterparts: interview, Rio de Janeiro, June 1976. Poeck background: interviews, Brasília, August 1976. Gordon's relations with Goulart, Cuban Missile crisis: Gordon interviews. Pery Bevilacqua: interviews, Rio de Janeiro, July 1976. Robert Kennedy's visit to Brazil, Goulart's envy of Perón, Goulart's land reform: Gordon interviews. Walters soliciting Kruel's support: interviews, Rio de Janeiro, June–July 1976. Agee's experience: Agee, *Inside the Company;* and Agee interview. IBAD: Black, *United States Penetration of Brazil*, pp. 72–77; and Agee and Gordon interviews. Galbraith on undercutting Diem: William Bundy, "Dictatorship and Foreign Policy," *Foreign Affairs*, October 1975. "Going out to the rabble": interview, 1976. Gabeira in Brizola's Group of Eleven: Gabeira interviews. "Don't go to the Communist meeting": Brazil *Herald*, 4 March 1964, p. 3. David Rockefeller's business group: Brazil *Herald*, 3 March 1964, p. 4. Brazil's minimum wage, comparison to feeding a chimpanzee: Brazil *Herald*, 7 March 1964, p. 4. Lacerda on choosing colors: Brazil *Herald*, 13 March 1964, p. 4; three days earlier the newspaper (p. 2) had quoted Lacerda as saying that one of his first acts as president would be to repeal Goulart's agrarian reform law. March 13 rally: Brazil *Herald*, 14 March 1964, p. 1. Gordon's reaction: Gordon interviews. Darcy Ribeiro on legalizing the Communist party: Brazil *Herald*, 4 March 1964, p. 3. "Clube dos contemplados": Brazil *Herald*, 1 March 1964, p. 3. Robert McNamara briefing: interview. O'Meara's alleged offer: Robinson Rojas, *Estados Unidos en Brasil* (Santiago, Chile: Presa Latinoamericana, S. A., 1965) pp. 72–73, quoted in Black, *United States Penetration of Brazil.* Jittery mood among generals: interviews. U. S. would recognize military in São Paulo: Jerome Levinson and Juan de Onis, *The Alliance that Lost Its Way* (Chicago: Quadrangle Books, 1970), p. 89. March of the Family: Brazil *Herald*, 20 March 1964, p. 1. Archbishop forbade marching: Rojas, *Estados Unidos en Brasil*, p. 198. Labor party asked Goulart to close Congress: Brazil *Herald*, 19 March 1964, p. 2. Goulart's pledge not to be a dictator: Brazil *Herald*, 20 March 1964, p. 3. De Paiva's charges about communism: Brazil *Herald*, 22 March 1964, p. 4. Walters' telegram: Gayle Hudgens Watson, "Our Monster in Brazil," *The Nation*, 15 January 1977, pp. 51–54. Goulart's March 30 speech: Brazil *Herald*, 31 March 1964, p. 1. U. S. embassy on day of coup: Gordon interviews. Soldiers told they were fighting for Goulart: interview. Telcons from Washington to U. S. embassy: Watson, "Our Monster in Brazil," pp. 51–54; fuller documentation from the Lyndon B. Johnson Memorial Library in Austin, Texas, appeared in *Jornal do Brasil*, 19, 20 December 1976. Gordon's call on Kubitscheck: Gordon interviews. Ché Guevara's "There is only one face": Ricardo Rojo, *My Friend Che*, translated by Julian Casart (New York: Dial Press, 1968). U. S. embassy on April 1: Gordon interviews. Teixeira's hesitation: interviews. Khrushchev to Prestes: Brazil *Herald*, 6 March 1964, p. 4. Goulart not wishing to be responsible for bloodshed: Gordon interviews. Lacerda on day of coup: interviews. "Turn on the air conditioner": Gordon interviews. Doherty's testimony on AIFLD training: Black, *United States Penetration of Brazil*, p. 117. Wayne Hayes, General Andrew O'Meara, and Representative Gross comment on the coup: Foreign Assistance Act of 1965, Hearings Before the Committee on Foreign Affairs, House of Representatives, 89th Congress, 1st session, pp. 345–57.

CHAPTER FOUR

Unless otherwise credited, the information in Chapter Four came from interviews with U. S. police advisers, Brazilian police and military officers, journalists, diplomats, and others who requested that they not be identified.

No change in U. S. police advisory role after the 1964 coup: U. Alexis Johnson, Byron Engle, and other interviews. Brazilian policemen stealing flowers, plainclothesman having pocket picked: Brazil *Herald*, 3 March 1964, p. 4. Esquadrão da Morte: Jeff Radford, "The Brazilian Death Squads," *The Nation*, 30 July 1973; Edwin McDowell, "The Murderous Policemen of Brazil," *The Wall Street Journal*, 1 November 1974. Sergio Fleury: *Visao* (Brazilian magazine), 12 November 1973. Boilesen background:

Jornal do Brasil, 22 April 1971, pp. 23–24. OPS advisers in Dominican Republic were CIA agents: interview with David Fairchild, assistant program officer, U. S. AID, "U. S. AID in the Dominican Republic," *North American Congress on Latin America* [NACLA] *Newsletter,* November 1970, p. 8. Dominican Republic: Norman Gall, "Santo Domingo: The Politics of Terror," *The New York Review of Books,* 22 July 1971; Juan Bosch, the former president of the Dominican Republic, summed up the 1965 U. S. invasion: "This was a democratic revolution smashed by the leading democracy of the world, the United States": quoted by Seymour Martin Lipset and Aldo Solari, *Elites in Latin America* (New York: Oxford University Press, 1967), p. 181. CIA's International Police Services, Inc: John Marks and Taylor Branch, "Tracking the CIA," *Harper's Weekly,* March 1975. Los Angeles police officers sent to Venezuela: Engle interview. Robert Kennedy's speech to the IPA: press release, Agency for International Development, 9 July 1965. IPA exercises with mythical Rio Bravos: interviews; and Peter T. Chew, "America's Global Peace Officers," *The Kiwanis Magazine,* April 1969, pp. 22–24; David Sanford, "Agitators in a Fertilizer Factory," *The New Republic,* 11 February 1967, pp. 16–19. "First Line of Defense": *Ibid.* IPA students' essays on torture: U. S. Senate files. Le Van An, redacteur of the South Vietnam police wrote in his IPA paper: "Despite the fact that brutal interrogation is strongly criticized by moralists, its importance must not be denied if we want to have order and security in daily life": U. S. Senate files. Dan Mitrione listed as CIA agent: Julius Mader, *Who's Who in CIA* (Berlin: Mader, 1066 Berlin W66 Mauerstrasse 69, 1968), p. 364. Training of 100,000 Brazilian police officers: "Through December, 1970, the Public Safety project in Brazil has assisted in training locally over 100,000 federal and state police personnel. Additionally, approximately 600 persons received training in the U. S.": Project data for 1971 budget hearings, Table III, Brazil, Public Safety, U. S. AID.

CHAPTER FIVE

Except for the following references, material in this chapter was drawn from interviews with Jean Marc Von der Weid, Paris, May 1976.

Ambassador Gordon's protests after the 1964 coup: Gordon interviews. Angela Camargo Seixas in protest demonstration:

interview, Angela Seixas, Cambridge, England, May 1976. Lacerda's "The Front": Kohl and Litt, *Urban Guerrilla Warfare in
Latin America*, pp. 44–45. Lacerda's criticism of the "military
dictatorship": *Facts on File*, 17 July 1968, p. 279. Student protests: João Quartim, *Dictatorship and Armed Struggle in Brazil*,
translated by David Fernbach (New York: Monthly Review
Press, 1971), pp. 139–42. Policeman sitting on curb: interview.
Aristoteles Drummond summoned to Costa e Silva: Drummond
interview. For further discussion of Governor Abreu Sodre's
conflict with local army commanders: Ronald M. Schneider, *The
Political System of Brazil* (New York: Columbia University Press,
1971) pp. 291–92. Mitrione's "I had to come back": interview.
Theodore Brown before Senator Frank Church's subcommittee:
United States Policies and Programs in Brazil (Washington, D. C.:
U. S. Government Printing Office, 1971), p. 36. Earlier in the
testimony, Senator Church asked Brown, "In light of the many
reports that we hear of torture in Brazil, do you think you have
been successful in inculcating humane methods in restraint?" Mr.
Brown: "Yes, sir; I do, Senator." *Ibid.*, p. 18. Nelson Rockefeller's
tour, report: Nelson Rockefeller, "Quality of Life in the Americas: Report of a U. S. Presidential Mission for the Western
Hemisphere" (Washington, D. C.: U. S. Government Printing
Office, 1969). Rockefeller holdings: Gary MacEoin, *Revolution
Next Door*, pp. 146–53. OBAN: interviews; also, Riordan Roett,
Brazil in the Sixties, pp. 43–45. CENIMAR and U. S. Naval
Mission, Rear Admiral C. Thor Hanson overhearing screams:
interviews. Buckley column: "Torture in Brazil," from syn-
dicated column "On the Right." After Buckley attempted to
explain away the allegations, he added, "If Brazil were Uruguay,
or Bolivia, where the political Mau Maus roam, one might understand the use of torture as an instrument of war." But since
Brazil's dictatorship was secure, the economy booming, and the
political opposition perfunctory, Buckley protested the "humiliation and disgrace" of torture. Clemente Monteiro's U. S. training in Panama: personnel records, Brazil's federal police
academy, Brasília, August 1976.

CHAPTER SIX
Much of this chapter came from interviews with Charles
Burke Elbrick, Washington, D. C., March 1976; and Fernando
Nagle Gabeira, Stockholm, May 1976.

"An old fart": interview. Elbrick's background: "A Sturdy Ambassador," *The New York Times*, 8 September 1969, p. 2. Tut-hill antagonized Brazil's dictators: interview. Mrs. Elbrick saying her house was not a public place: interview. The Haitian ambassador would have to be kidnapped twice: José Yglesias, "Report from Brazil: What the Left Is Saying," *The New York Times Magazine*, 7 December 1969, p. 165. Belton called intelligence offices: interviews. MR-8 manifesto: *The New York Times*, 6 September 1969, p. 1. "Crapping in our pants": interview. U. S. embassy negotiations with Brazil's junta for Elbrick's release: interviews. Marighela's Minimanual: Carlos Marighela, in *Tricontinental Bulletin* (Havana, Cuba), no. 56 (November 1970), pp. 1–56, and quoted by Kohl and Litt, *Urban Guerrilla Warfare in Latin America*, pp. 86–135. Taxi driver admiring Neil Armstrong and kidnappers: interview, Cid de Queiroz Benjamin, Stockholm, May 1976. Army and CENIMAR rivalry: interviews. Moura checking on exchange: interview. "Dear Elfie": *The New York Times*, 6 September 1969, p. 1. Mrs. Elbrick commented, "Even the bad guys are good. They are letting my husband write me a letter." *Ibid.* Two hundred navy men tried to block the airplane: dispatch, Joseph Novitski, *The New York Times*, 7 September 1969, p. 1. U. S. embassy staff dismay at Elbrick's remarks: interviews; "Elbrick has been having a bad time of it with the [Brazilian] Foreign Office ever since Brazil had to give up 15 political prisoners in ransom for him. Many officials of the military-dominated regime have felt Elbrick presented his captors in far too good a light after his release, and they resented it": Jeremiah O'Leary, "Elbrick's Return to Post in Brazil Is Doubtful," *The Evening Star* (Washington, D. C.), 12 June 1970. Prisoners' arrival in Mexico City: interview, Flavio Tavares Freitas, Buenos Aires, Argentina, June 1976. "They don't even know I've been arrested": *Miami Herald*, 9 September 1969. Elbrick's "I don't have time": interview.

CHAPTER SEVEN

As indicated in the text, the material in this chapter came from interviews with Fernando Gabeira, Stockholm; Jean Marc Von der Weid, Paris; Angela Seixas, Cambridge, England; Marcos Arruda, Geneva; Murilo Pinto and Irany Campos, Paris.

CHAPTER EIGHT

Engle's interview with Mitrione: Engle interview. U-127 field reports: responding to a request made under the Freedom of Information Act, the U. S. State Department supplied reports, formerly classified CONFIDENTIAL, from January 1969 through December 1970. Greek and Portuguese tortures: files, Amnesty International, London. Vietnamese torture: files, U. S. Senate. U. S. Navy torture camps: *Newsweek*, 22 March 1976. Donald Duncan's training at Fort Bragg: Donald Duncan, *The New Legions* (New York: Random House, 1967), p. 159. Brazilian camp on Niterói: "O Limite de Resistência," *Jornal do Brasil*, 6 August 1969, Section II, p. 1. Tupamaros presented a grave challenge: interviews. Batlle's benign statism: a fuller description in Martin Weinstein, *Uruguay: The Politics of Failure* (Westport, Conn.: Greenwood Press, 1975). Raúl Sendic's background: interviews. Bribery in Uruguay: Gunther, *Inside South America*, p. 233. Raid on Swiss club: interview. "The most intelligent and clever": police intelligence reports, Montevideo, Uruguay. Tupamaros: Alain Labrousse, *Los Tupamaros*, translated by Rodolfo Walsh (Buenos Aires: Editorial Tiempo Contemporáneo, 1971); Kohl and Litt, *Urban Guerrilla Warfare in Latin America*, pp. 173–95; Arturo C. Porzecanski, *Uruguay's Tupamaros* (New York: Praeger Publishers, 1973). "Words divide us": Carlos López Matteo, introduction, *Generals and Tupamaros* (London: Latin America Review of Books Ltd., 1974), p. ii. Tupamaro bombings: interviews. Tupa Amara: Captain Bactasardo Ocampo, *The Execution of the Inca Tupac Amaru* (Cambridge: Hakluyt Society, 1907), p. 230. Engle calling Tupamaros cowardly: Engle interview. Westmoreland on NLF: briefing by General William Westmoreland, Saigon, 1965. Tupamaro Christmas raid: Major Carlos Wilson, *The Tupamaros* (Boston: Branden Press, 1974), p. 30. Pereira killed a newsboy: interview. "Attention, Tupamaros! Kidnap me!": Wilson, *The Tupamaros*, p. 32. President Gestido: Porzecanski, *Uruguay's Tupamaros*, pp. 56–57. Voted Eisenhower, got Nixon: interview. Agee's relations with Otero, CIA's bribing techniques, reaction to Saenz: Agee interview. Uruguayan response to Saenz: interviews. Bardesio put in touch with Cantrell: *Marcha* (Montevideo), 28 April 1972, translated into English and quoted by Wilson, *The Tupamaros*, p. 106. Uruguayan employees' reaction to Bardesio, Manuel the Cuban: interviews. Bardesio's routine: Wilson, *The Tupamaros*, p. 107. Uruguayan CIA agents: Agee, *Inside the Company*, Appendix I, pp. 599–624; before Agee overheard the torture of Bonaudi, he had received reports (p. 443) of Braga torturing a young waterworks engineer, Julio Arizaga, suspected of belonging to the Movement of the Revolutionary Left. Gangsters and thieves beaten by police: interviews. Agee and Horton overhear torture: Agee interview; and Agee, *Inside the Company*, pp. 455–59. CIA aliases: Agee interview. CIA running checks for Creole Oil: Agee, *Inside the Company*, p. 103. CIA checks for businessmen in Montevideo, weekly meetings with them, International Harvester representative excluded: Agee interview. Cantrell and CIA funds: Bardesio's testimony described Cantrell receiving money apart from the U. S. embassy and Cantrell giving Bardesio 11,000 pesos to cover shortages from the intelligence office's petty cash; quoted in Wilson, *The Tupamaros*, pp. 106–08. Subcommissioner Benítez wrote: "Although an attempt was made to hide the reason, people heard about certain 'financial' matters [a good part of the money poured out by the CIA and FBI had disappeared without any justified cause]": cited, in English translation by Raymond Rosenthal, by Costa-Gavras and Franco Solinas, *State of Siege, Documents* (London: Plexus Publishing, 1973), p. 169. Mitrione's complaints about pay: interviews, including Morris Zimmelman interview, Montevideo, June 1976. Miguel Angel Benítez Segovia: interviews and Benítez documents. "Putamaros": interviews. Otero as Quixote: interview. Pacheco's government falling in esteem: *Generals and Tupamaros*, p. 1. Newspapers forbidden to use "Tupamaros": interviews. Hank Mitrione's life in Montevideo: interviews, including Henrietta Mitrione interview. Pellegrini kidnapping: *Generals and Tupamaros*, pp. 6, 9. $60,000 ransom: interview. Police protection of Jorge Batlle's children: interview, Jorge Batlle, Montevideo, June 1976. Mitrione's effect on police, comment of Juan María Lucas: Benítez documents. Los Fresnos bomb school: interviews, Benítez documents. Engle denying *The Battle of Algiers* shown at IPA: Engle interview. Agee's financial transactions with First National City Bank: Agee, *Inside the Company*, p. 382. CIA Southern Cone network, Fleury in Uruguay: interviews. Bardesio's Death Squad: interviews; Wilson, *The Tupamaros*, pp. 92–113. Mitrione's letters: correspondence with Ray Mitrione. Mitrione's office: Benítez documents. Mitrione carrying pistol: interviews, including interview, Don Gould, U. S. consulate, Rio de Janeiro, June 1976. Attempting to refute the contentions of the film *State of Siege,* Ernest W. Lefever, then a senior fellow at the Brookings Institution, stated erroneously (p. 5) in a paper, "The Unmaking of a 'Documentary'—Film vs. Fact," that Mitrione never carried a gun overseas. Lefever reversed Mitrione's Brazil service, writing (p. 13) that he spent five years in Belo Horizonte, two years in Rio de Janeiro. Lefever calls "the torture school scene" in Costa-Gavras's film "highly implausible and appears to be a figment of his [Costa-Gavras's] imagination." Mitrione confided dangers: interview. Moran Charquero's killing: U-127, Public Safety Report, April 1970, p. 2. Mitrione never postponed work: interviews. *Marcha*'s "Torture" cover: *Marcha* (Montevideo), 10 April 1970. "One major problem": U-127 Public Safety Report, June 1970, p. 6. Mitrione on breaking a man: Benítez documents, quoted in *State of Siege*, p. 180. Sexual joking at *jefatura:* interviews. Electric needles: Benítez documents. Agee on diplomatic pouch: Agee interview. Technical Services Division: Agee, *Inside the Company*, p. 85. James Keehner, TSD psychologist: Maureen Orth, "Memoirs of a CIA Psychologist," *New Times*, June 1976, pp. 19–24. TSD branch offices in Panama and Buenos Aires: interviews, including Philip Agee interview. Mitrione tortures: interviews. Otero turned his back on beatings: Maria Esther Gilio, *The Tupamaro Guerrillas*, translated by Anne Edmondson (New York: Ballantine Books, 1973), pp. 198–99. Threat to Don Gould: Gould interview. Attempt to kidnap Jones and Rosenfeld: interview, Nathan Rosenfeld, Brasília, August 1976. Mitrione kidnapping: *El Dia*, 1 August 1970, p. 1; *El Pais* (Montevideo), 1 August 1970. Dias Gomide a disagreeable captive: interview. "Wonderful to be in a democracy": interviews. Brazilian agents disguised as shepherds: interviews. Jones background: interview. Nixon's guidelines on kidnapping and prisoner exchange: interviews, including U. Alexis Johnson interview.

CHAPTER NINE

After the killing of Dan Mitrione, the Tupamaros released a recording of his interrogation during his ten days of captivity. U. S. government officials supplied a copy of the tape to Ray Mitrione in Richmond, Indiana.

CHAPTER TEN

Chronology of August 10, 1970: *El País* (Montevideo) 11 August 1970, p. 3. Otero's interview with Aymoré: interviews. Dias Gomide release: interview. Aymoré and Montevideo police: interview. U. S. embassy pressure on *Jornal do Brasil:* interview. Editorial calling Mitrione killing "absurd": *The New York Times,* 11 August 1970, p. 32. Byron Engle's explanation: Engle interview. Tupamaros blowing up Carrasco bowling alley: *Generals and Tupamaros,* p. 18. Geoffrey Jackson kidnapping: *Ibid.,* p. 19. Government trade for Jackson, promotion of police colonel: interviews. Ray Mitrione informing Washington about Billy Rial: Ray Mitrione interviews. Rial's arrest: interview. Tupamaro interrogator probably Blanco Katras: interview. Dr. Fly's heart attack: interviews, including Morris and Edna Zimmelman interview. Gabeira's release: Gabeira interviews. Von der Weid's release: Von der Weid interviews. Arruda's release: Arruda interviews. Bardesio's confessions: *Marcha* (Montevideo), 28 April 1972. Bardesio excerpt in English: Wilson, *The Tupamaros,* pp. 116–17. Whereabouts of Bardesio, Héctor Amodio Pérez, and Raúl Sendic: interviews. Montevideo prisoner, Benítez's arrest: interview. Benítez on police force: interviews. Cirillo implicated in death: Arruda interview. Clemente Monteiro, Alfredo Poeck: interviews. Senator Abourezk's concern over OPS: interview, Tom Daschle, Washington, D. C., March 1976. Nixon's praise for Brazil: *The New York Times,* 7–10 December 1971. Richard Helms's "honorable men": *The New York Times,* 22 January 1971, p. 8. Dispersal of police advisers: interviews. Agee's resignation from the CIA: Agee interview. Angela Seixas released: Seixas interview. Agee dedication: Agee, *Inside the Company,* p. 5. Burke Elbrick at funeral: Elbrick interview. Gordon's reflections on dictatorship: interviews, including Gordon interview. São Paulo arrests: *Latin America Political Report* (London), 22 April 1977, p. 3. Torture of U. S. clergyman: interview, Fred Morris, Washington, D. C., March 1976. Brazilian police attitude toward the United States; anti-riot equipment: interviews. Benítez documents: interview, Alain Labrousse, Paris, May 1976. Communist official tells Solinas about Mitrione in Dominican Republic: interview, Franco Solinas, Rome, April 1976. "Mitrione vest": "Building a Better Thumbscrew," *New Scientist* (London), 19 July 1973, pp. 139–41, quoted in *Science Digest* (New

York), December 1973. "A perfect man": Henrietta Mitrione interview. "A great humanitarian": Linda Tarter interview. Film treatment of Santore: *State of Siege* script (London: Plexus Publishing, 1973). Dan Mitrione's school questionnaire: school records, Richmond, Indiana.

Index

About the Author

A. J. Langguth was born in Minneapolis in 1933, graduated from Harvard College in 1955, and spent two years in the U. S. Army. He has worked for several publications; and in 1965, he served as Saigon Bureau Chief for *The New York Times*. Since 1967 he has traveled often to Brazil. He is the author of three novels and one nonfiction book, *Macumba: White and Black Magic in Brazil*.